Presented to E. & H. College
by L. S. Campbell, Etowah,
Tennessee, July 1930.

SELECTED LITERARY
AND POLITICAL PAPERS
AND ADDRESSES OF
WOODROW WILSON

VOLUME THREE

SELECTED
LITERARY AND
POLITICAL PAPERS
AND ADDRESSES
OF
WOODROW WILSON

IN THREE VOLUMES

VOLUME III

PUBLISHED BY ARRANGEMENT WITH
HARPER & BROTHERS AND
HOUGHTON MIFFLIN COMPANY

GROSSET & DUNLAP
PUBLISHERS   NEW YORK

CONTENTS

AN OLD MASTER

AND

OTHER POLITICAL ESSAYS

AN OLD MASTER

WHY has no one ever written on the art of academic lecturing and its many notable triumphs? In some quarters new educational canons have spoken an emphatic condemnation of the college lecture, and it would seem to be high time to consider its value, as illustrative of an art about to be lost, if not as exemplary of forces to be retained, even if modified. Are not our college class-rooms, in being robbed of the old-time lecture, and getting instead a science-brief of *data* and bibliography, being deprived also of that literary atmosphere which once pervaded them? We are unquestionably gaining in thoroughness; but are we gaining in thoughtfulness? We are giving to many youths an insight, it may be profound, into specialties; but are we giving any of them a broad outlook?

There was too often a paralysis of dulness in the old lecture, or, rather, in the old lecturer; and written lectures, like history and fashion in dress, have an inveterate tendency to repeat

3

themselves; but on the contrary, there was often a wealth of power also in the studied discourse of strong men. Masters bent upon instructing and inspiring—and there were many such—had to penetrate that central secret of literature and spoken utterance—the secret of style. Their only instrument of conquest was the sword of penetrating speech. Some of the subtlest and most lasting effects of genuine oratory have gone forth from secluded lecture desks into the hearts of quiet groups of students; and it would seem to be good policy to endure much indifferent lecturing—watchful trustees might reduce it to a minimum—for the sake of leaving places open for the men who have in them the inestimable force of chastened eloquence. For one man who can impart an undying impulse there are several score, presupposing the requisite training, who can impart a method; and here is the well understood ground for the cumulating disfavor of college lecturing and the rapid substitution of "laboratory drill." But will not higher education be cut off from communion with the highest of all forces, the force of personal inspiration in the field of great themes of thought, if you interdict the literary method in the class-room?

I am not inclined to consume very many words in insisting on this point, for I believe that educators are now dealing more frankly

4

with themselves than ever before, and that so
obvious a point will by no means escape full
recognition before reformed methods of college
and university instruction take their final shape.
But it is very well to be thinking explicitly about
the matter meanwhile, in order that the lecture
may be got ready to come fully militant into
the final battle for territory. The best way to
compass this end would seem to be, to study
the art of the old masters of learned discourse.
With Lanfranc one could get the infinite charm
of the old monastic school life; with Abelard,
the undying excitement of philosophical and
religious controversy; with Colet, the fire of
reforming zeal; with Blackstone, the satisfac-
tions of clarified learning. But Bec and Paris
and Oxford have by no means monopolized the
masters of this art, and I should prefer, for the
nonce at least, to choose an exemplar from Scotland, and speak of Adam Smith. It will, no
doubt, be possible to speak of him without going
over again the well worn ground of the topics
usually associated with his great fame.

There is much, besides the contents of his
published works, to draw to Adam Smith the
attention of those who are attracted by individual power. Scotchmen have long been re-
puted strong in philosophic doctrine, and he
was a Scot of the Scots. But, though Scotland
is now renowned for her philosophy, that re-

nown is not of immemorial origin; it was not till the last century was well advanced that she began to add great speculative thinkers to her great preachers. Adam Smith, consequently, stands nearly at the opening of the greatest of the intellectual eras of Scotland. Yet by none of the great Scotch names which men have learned since his day has his name been eclipsed. The charm about the man consists, for those who do not regard him with the special interest of the political economist, in his literary method, which exhibits his personality so attractively and makes his works so thoroughly his own, rather than in any facts about his eminency among Scotchmen. You bring away from your reading of Adam Smith a distinct and attractive impression of the man himself, such as you can get from the writings of no other author in the same field, and such as makes you wish to know still more of him. What was he like? What was his daily life?

Unhappily, we know very little that is detailed of Adam Smith as a man; and it may be deplored, without injustice to a respected name, that we owe that little to Dugald Stewart, who was too self-conscious and too stately to serve another efficiently as biographer. There was no suitable place amid the formal spaces of his palatial style for small illuminating details. Even from Dugald Stewart, however, we get a picture of Adam Smith which must please every one who loves simplicity and genuineness. He was not, perhaps, a companionable man; he was much too absent-minded to be companionable; but he was, in the highest sense, interesting. His absent-mindedness was of that sort which indicates fulness of mind, which marks a mind content, much of the time, to live within itself, indulging in those delights of quiet contemplation which the riches of a full store of thought can always command. Often he would open to his companions his mind's fullest confidences, and, with a rare versatility, lavish a wealth of information and illustration upon topics the most varied and diverse, always to the wondering delight of those who heard him.

All who met Adam Smith in intimate intercourse are said to have been struck chiefly by the gentleness and benignity of his manner—traits which would naturally strike one in a Scotchman; for men of that unbending race are not often distinguished by easiness of temper or suavity of manner, but are generally both *fortiter in re et fortiter in modo*. His gentleness was, possibly, only one phase of that timidity which is natural to absent-minded men, and which was always conspicuous in him. That timidity made it rare with him to talk much. When he did talk, as I have said, his hearers marvelled at the ingenuity of his reasoning, at the constructive power of his imagination, at the comprehensiveness of his memory, at the fertility of all his resources; but his inclination was always to remain silent. He was not, however, disinclined to public discourse, and it is chiefly to his unusual gifts as a lecturer that he seems to have owed his advancement in the literary, or, rather, in the university, world.

Acting upon the advice of Lord Kames, an eminent barrister and a man of some standing in the history of philosophy, he volunteered a course of lectures in Edinburgh almost immediately upon his return from Oxford; and the success of this course was hardly assured before he was elected to the chair of Logic in the University of Glasgow. In the following year he had the honor of succeeding to the chair of Moral Philosophy, once occupied by the learned and ingenious Hutcheson. He seems to have been at once successful in raising his new chair to a position of the very highest consideration. His immediate predecessor had been one Thomas Craigie, who has left behind him so shadowy a reputation that it is doubtless safe to conclude that his department was, at his death, much in need of a fresh infusion of life. This it received from Adam Smith. The breadth and variety of the topics upon which

he chose to lecture, and the felicity, strength,
and vitality of the exposition he gave them (we
are told by one who had sat under him), soon
drew to Glasgow "a multitude of students from
a great distance" to hear him. His mastery
of the art of academic lecturing was presently
an established fact. It appears clear that his
success was due to two things: the broad outlook of his treatment and the fine art of his
style. His chair was Moral Philosophy; and
'moral philosophy' seems to have been the
most inclusive of general terms in the university
usage of Scotland at that day, and, indeed, for
many years afterwards. Apparently it em-
braced all philosophy that did not directly concern the phenomena of the physical world, and,
accordingly, allowed its doctors to give very
free play to their tastes in the choice of subjects. Adam Smith, in Glasgow, could draw
within the big family of this large-hearted
philosophy not only the science of mental
phenomena, but also the whole of the history
and organization of society; just as, years
afterwards, John Wilson, in Edinburgh, could
insist upon the adoption of something very like
belles-lettres into the same generous and uncon-
ventional family circle.

Adam Smith sought to cover the field he had
chosen with a fourfold course of lectures. First,
he unfolded the principles of natural theology;

second, he illustrated the principles of ethics, in a series of lectures which were afterwards embodied in his published work on the "Theory of Moral Sentiments;" third, he discoursed on that branch of morality which relates to the administration of justice; and, last, coming out upon the field with which his name is now identified, he examined those political regulations which are founded, not upon principles of justice, but upon considerations of expediency, and which are calculated to increase the riches, the power, and the prosperity of the State. His notes of his lectures he himself destroyed when he felt death approaching, and we are left to conjecture what the main features of his treatment were, from the recorded recollections of his pupils and from those published works which remain as fragments of the great plan. These fragments consist of the "Theory of Moral Sentiments," the "Wealth of Nations," and "Considerations Concerning the First Formation of Languages;" besides which there are, to quote another's enumeration, "a very curious history of astronomy, left imperfect, and another fragment on the history of ancient physics, which is a kind of sequel to that part of the history of astronomy which relates to ancient astronomy; then a similar essay on the ancient logic and metaphysics; then another on the nature and development of the fine, or, as he calls them, the imitative, arts, painting, poetry, and music, in which was meant to have been included a history of the theatre—all forming part, his executors tell us, 'of a plan he had once formed for giving a connected history of the liberal and elegant arts;'" part, that is (to continue the quotation from Mr. Bagehot), of the "immense design of showing the origin and development of cultivation and law, or . . . of saying how, from being a savage, man rose to be a Scotchman."

The wideness of view and amazing variety of illustration that characterized his treatment, in developing the several parts of this vast plan, can easily be inferred from an examination of the "Wealth of Nations."

"The 'Wealth of Nations,'" declares Mr. Buckle, from whom, for obvious reasons, I prefer to quote, "displays a breadth of treatment which those who cannot sympathize with, are very likely to ridicule. The phenomena, not only of wealth, but also of society in general, classified and arranged under their various forms; the origin of the division of labor, and the consequences which that division has produced; the circumstances which gave rise to the invention of money, and to the subsequent changes in its value; the history of those changes traced in different ages, and the history of the relations which the precious metals bear to each other; an examination of the connection between wages and profits, and of the laws which govern the rise and fall of both; another examination of the way in which these are concerned, on the one hand with the rent of land, and, on the other hand, with the price of commodities; an inquiry into the reason why profits vary in different trades, and at different times; a succinct but comprehensive view of the progress of towns in Europe since the fall of the Roman Empire; the fluctuations, during several centuries, in the prices of the food of the people, and a statement of how it is, that, in different stages of society, the relative cost of meat and of land varies; the history of corporation laws and of municipal enactments, and their bearing on the four great classes of apprentices, manufacturers, merchants, and landlords; an account of the immense power and riches formerly enjoyed by the clergy, and of the manner in which, as society advances, they gradually lose their exclusive privileges; the nature of religious dissent, and the reason why the clergy of the Established Church can never contend with it on terms of equality, and, therefore, call on the State to help them, and wish to persecute when they cannot persuade; why some sects profess more ascetic principles, and others more luxurious ones; how it was, that, during the feudal times, the nobles ac-

quired their power, and how that power has,
ever since, been gradually diminishing; how
the rights of territorial jurisdiction originated,
and how they died away; how the sovereigns of
Europe obtained their revenue, what the sources
of it are, and what classes are most heavily
taxed in order to supply it; the cause of certain
virtues, such as hospitality, flourishing in barbarous ages, and decaying in civilized ones;
the influence of inventions and discoveries in
altering the distribution of power among the
various classes of society; a bold and masterly
sketch of the peculiar sort of advantages which
Europe derived from the discovery of America
and of the passage round the Cape; the origin of universities, their degeneracy from the
original plan, the corruption which has gradually crept over them, and the reason why they
are so unwilling to adopt improvements, and
to keep pace with the wants of the age; a comparison between public and private education,
and an estimate of their relative advantages;
these, and a vast number of other subjects,
respecting the structure and development of
society, such as the feudal system, slavery,
emancipation of serfs, origin of standing armies
and of mercenary troops, effects produced by
tithes, laws of primogeniture, sumptuary laws,
international treaties concerning trade, rise of
European banks, national debts, influence of

dramatic representations over opinions, colonies, poor-laws—all topics of a miscellaneous character, and many of them diverging from each other—all are fused into one great system, and irradiated by the splendor of one great genius. Into that dense and disorderly mass, did Adam Smith introduce symmetry, method, and law."

In fact, it is a book of digressions—digressions characterized by more order and method, but by little more compunction, than the wondrous digressions of Tristram Shandy.

It is interesting to note that even this vast miscellany of thought, the "Wealth of Nations," systematized though it be, was not meant to stand alone as the exposition of a complete system; it was only a supplement to the "Theory of Moral Sentiments;" and the two together constituted only chapters in that vast book of thought which their author would have written. Adam Smith would have grouped all things that concern either the individual or the social life of man under the several greater principles of motive and action observable in human conduct. His method throughout is, therefore, necessarily abstract and deductive. In the "Wealth of Nations," he ignores the operation of love, of benevolence, of sympathy, and of charity in filling life with kindly influences, and concentrates his attention exclu-

sively upon the operation of self-interest and
expediency; because he had reckoned with the
altruistic motives in the "Theory of Moral
Sentiments," and he would not confuse his view
of the economic life of man by again forcing
these in where selfishness was unquestionably
the predominant force. "The philosopher,"
he held, "is the man of speculation, whose trade
is not to do anything, but to observe everything;" and certainly he satisfied his own
definition. He does observe everything; and
he stores his volumes full with the sagest practical maxims, fit to have fallen from the lips of
the shrewdest of those Glasgow merchants in
whose society he learned so much that might
test the uses of his theories. But it is noticeable
that none of the carefully noted facts of experience which play so prominent a part on the
stage of his arguments speaks of any other
principle than the simple and single one which
is the pivot of that part of his philosophy with
which he is at the moment dealing. In the
"Wealth of Nations" every apparent induc-
tion leads to self-interest, and to self-interest
alone. In Mr. Buckle's phrase, his facts are
subsequent to his argument; they are not
used for demonstration, but for illustration.
His historical cases, his fine generalizations,
everywhere broadening and strengthening his
matter, are only instances of the operation of

the single abstract principle meant to be set
forth.

When he was considering that topic in his
course which has not come down to us in any
of the remaining fragments of his lectures—the
principles of justice, namely—although still
always mindful of its relative position in the
general scheme of his abstract philosophy of
society, his subject led him, we are told, to
speak very much in the modern historical spirit.
He followed upon this subject, says the pupil
already quoted, "the plan which seemed to
have been suggested by Montesquieu; endeavoring to trace the gradual progress of jurisprudence, both public and private, from the
rudest to the most refined ages, and to point
out the effects of those arts which contribute
to subsistence, and to the accumulation of
property, in producing corresponding improvements or alterations in law and government."
In following Montesquieu, he was, of course,
following one of the forerunners of that great
school of philosophical students of history which
has done so much in our own time to clear away
the fogs that surround the earliest ages of mankind, and to establish something like the rudi-
ments of a true philosophy of history. And
this same spirit was hardly less discernible in
those later lectures on the "political institutions relating to commerce, to finances, and to

the ecclesiastical and military establishments,"
which formed the basis of the "Wealth of Nations." Everywhere throughout his writing
there is a pervasive sense of the realities of fact
and circumstance; a luminous, bracing, work-a-
day atmosphere. But the conclusions are, first
of all, philosophical; only secondarily practical.

It has been necessary to go over this somewhat familiar ground with reference to the
philosophical method of Adam Smith, in order
to come at the proper point of view from which
to consider his place among the old masters of
academic lecturing. It has revealed the extent
of his outlook. There yet remains something
to be said of his literary method, so that we may
discern the qualities of that style which, after
proving so effectual in imparting power to his
spoken discourses, has since, transferred to the
printed page, preserved his fame so far beyond
the lifetime of those who heard him.

Adam Smith took strong hold upon his
hearers, as he still takes strong hold upon his
readers, by force, partly, of his native sagacity,
but by virtue, principally, of his consummate
style. The success of his lectures was not
altogether a triumph of natural gifts; it was,
in great part, a triumph of sedulously cultivated
art. With the true instinct of the orator and
teacher, Adam Smith saw—what every one
must see who speaks not for the patient ear of

the closeted student only, but also to the often shallow ear of the pupil in the class-room, and to the always callous ear of the great world outside, which must be tickled in order to be made attentive—that clearness, force, and beauty of style are absolutely necessary to one who would draw men to his way of thinking; nay, to any one who would induce the great mass of mankind to give so much as passing heed to what he has to say. He knew that wit was of no avail, without wit's proper words; sagacity mean, without sagacity's mellow measures of phrase. He bestowed the most painstaking care, therefore, not only upon what he was to say, but also upon the way in which he was to say it. Dugald Stewart speaks of "that flowing and apparently artless style, which he had studiously cultivated, but which, after all his experience in composition, he adjusted, with extreme difficulty, to his own taste." The results were such as to offset entirely his rugged utterance and his awkward, angular action, and to enable the timid talker to exercise the spells of an orator. The charm of his discourses consisted in the power of statement which gave them life, in the clear and facile processes of proof which gave them speed, and in the vigorous, but chastened, imagination which lent them illumination. He constantly refreshed and rewarded his hearers, as he still

18

constantly refreshes and rewards his readers, by
bringing them to those clear streams of practical
wisdom and happy illustration which everywhere irrigate his expositions. His counsel,
even on the highest themes, was always undarkened. There were no clouds about his
thoughts; the least of these could be seen
without glasses through the transparent atmosphere of expression which surrounded them.
He was a great thinker,—and that was much;
but he also made men recognize him as a great
thinker, because he was a great master of style—
which was more. He did not put his candle
under a bushel, but in a candlestick.

In Doctor Barnard's verses, addressed to
Sir Joshua Reynolds and his literary friends,
Adam Smith is introduced as a peer amidst
that brilliant company:

> "If I have thoughts and can't express 'em,
> Gibbon shall teach me how to dress 'em
>   In words select and terse;
> Jones teach me modesty and Greek,
> *Smith how to think*, Burke how to speak,
>   And Beauclerc to converse."

It is this power of teaching other men how to
think that has given to the works of Adam
Smith an immortality of influence. In his first
university chair, the chair of Logic, he had
given scant time to the investigation of the

formal laws of reasoning, and had insisted, by
preference, upon the practical uses of discourse,
as the living application of logic, treating of
style and of the arts of persuasion and exposition; and here in his other chair, of Moral
Philosophy, he was practically illustrating the
vivifying power of the art he had formerly
sought to expound to his pupils. "When the
subject of his work," says Dugald Stewart,
speaking of the "Theory of Moral Sentiments,"
"when the subject of his work leads him to
address the imagination and the heart, the
variety and felicity of his illustrations, the richness and fluency of his eloquence, and the skill
with which he wins the attention and commands
the passions of his hearers, leave him, among
our English moralists, without a rival."

Such, then, were the matters which this
great lecturer handled, and such was the form
he gave them. Two personal characteristics
stand out in apparent contrast with what he
accomplished: he is said to have been extremely
unpractical in the management of his own
affairs, and yet he fathered that science which
tells how other people's affairs, how the world's
affairs, are managed; he is known to have been
shy and silent, and yet he was the most acceptable lecturer of his university. But it is not
uncommon for the man who is both profound
and accurate in his observation of the universal

and permanent forces operative in the life
about him, to be almost altogether wanting in
that sagacity concerning the local and temporary practical details upon which the hourly
facilitation and comfort of his own life depend;
nor need it surprise any one to find the man who
sits shy and taciturn in private, stand out
dominant and eloquent in public. "Commonly,
indeed," as Mr. Bagehot has said, "the silent
man, whose brain is loaded with unexpressed
ideas, is more likely to be a successful public
speaker than the brilliant talker who daily
exhausts himself in sharp sayings." There are
two distinct kinds of observation: that which
makes a man alert and shrewd, cognizant of
every trifle and quick with every trick of
speech; and that which makes a man a philosopher, conscious of the steady set of affairs and
ready in the use of all the substantial resources
of wise thought. Commend me to the former
for a chat; commend me to the latter for a
book. The first will sparkle; the other burns
a steady flame.

Here, then, is the picture of this Old Master:
a quiet, awkward, forceful Scotchman, whose
philosophy has entered everywhere into the life
of politics and become a world force in thought;
an impracticable Commissioner of Customs,
who has left for the instruction of statesmen a
theory of taxation: an unbusiness-like pro-

fessor, who established the science of business; a man of books, who is universally honored by men of action; plain, eccentric, learned, inspired. The things that strike us most about him are, his boldness of conception and wideness of outlook, his breadth and comprehensiveness of treatment, and his carefully clarified and beautified style. He was no specialist, except *in the relations of things.*

Of course, spreading his topics far and wide in the domain of history and philosophy, he was at many points superficial. He took most of his materials at second hand; and it has been said that he borrowed many of his ideas from the French. But no matter who mined the gold, he coined it; the image and superscription are his. Certain separate, isolated truths which served under him may have been doing individual, guerilla warfare elsewhere for the advancement of science; but it was he who marshalled them into drilled hosts for the conquering of the nations. Adam Smith was doubtless indebted to the Physiocrats, but all the world is indebted to Adam Smith. Education and the world of thought need men who, like this man, will dare to know a multitude of things. Without them and their bold synthetic methods, all knowledge and all thought would fall apart into a weak analysis. Their minds do not lack in thoroughness; their thoroughness simply lacks in minute-

ness. It is only in their utterances that the
mind finds the exhilaration and exaltation that
come with the free air that blows over broad
uplands. They excite you with views of the
large aspects of thought; conduct you through
the noblest scenery of the mind's domain;
delight you with majesty of outline and sweep
of prospect. In this day of narrow specialties,
our thinking needs such men to fuse its parts,
correlate its forces, and centre its results; and
our thinking needs them in its college stage, in
order that we may command horizons from our
study windows in after days.

The breadth and comprehensiveness of treatment characteristic of the utterances of such a
teacher are inseparable attributes of his manner
of thought. He has the artist's eye. For him
things stand in picturesque relations; their
great outlines fit into each other; the touch of
his treatment is necessarily broad and strong.
The same informing influence of artistic conception and combination gives to his style its luminous and yet transparent qualities. His sentences cannot retain the stiff joints of logic;
it would be death to them to wear the chains
of formal statement; they must take leave to
deck themselves with eloquence. In a word,
such men must write *literature*, or nothing.
Their minds quiver with those broad sympathies which constitute the life of written

23

speech. Their native catholicity makes all
minds receive them as kinsmen. By reason
of the very strength of their humanity, they
are enabled to say things long waiting to be
said, in such a way that all men may receive
them. They hold commissions from the King
of Speech. Such men will not, I am persuaded,
always seek in vain invitations to those academic platforms which are their best coignes of
vantage. But this is not just the time when
they are most appreciated, or most freely en-
couraged to discover themselves; and it cannot be amiss to turn back to another order
of things, and remind ourselves how a master
of academic inspiration, possessing, in a great
power to impart intellectual impulse, something
higher than a trained capacity to communicate
method, may sometimes be found even in a
philosophical Scotchman.

1
THE STUDY OF POLITICS

25
26

THE STUDY OF POLITICS

IT has long been an open secret that there is war among the political economists. John Stuart Mill no longer receives universal homage, but has to bear much irreverent criticism; even Adam Smith might be seriously cavilled at were not the habit of praise grown too old in his case. He is still 'the father of political economy;' but, like other fathers of his day, he seems to us decidedly old fashioned. The fact is, that these older writers, who professed to point out the laws of human businesses, are accused of leaving out of view a full half of human nature; in insisting that men love gain, they are said to have quite forgotten that men sometimes love each other, that they are not only prehensile, but also a great many other things less aggressive and less selfish.

Those who make these charges want to leave nothing human out of their reckonings; they want to know 'all the facts,' and are ready, if necessary, to reduce every generalization of the older writers to the state—the wholly *excep-*

tional state—of a rule in German grammar.
Their protest is significant, their purpose heroic,
beyond a doubt; and what interesting questions
are not raised by their programme! How is the
world to contain the writings, statistical, historical, critical, which must be accumulated ere
this enormous diagnosis of trade and manufacture shall be completed in its details? And
after it shall have been completed in detail
who is to be born great enough in genius and
patience to reduce the mass to a system com-
prehensible by ordinary mortals? Moreover,
who is going surety that these new economists
will not be dreadful defaulters before they get
through handling these immense assets of human nature, which Mill confessed himself
unable to handle without wrecking his book-
keeping? Are they assured of the eventual
collaboration of some Shakespeare who will set
before the world all the standard types of economic character? Let the world hope so. Even
those who cannot answer the questions I have
broached ought to bid such sturdy workers
'God speed!'

The most interesting reflection suggested by
the situation is, that political economists are
being harassed by the same discipline of experience that, one day or another, sobers all con-
structors of systems. They cannot build in the
air and then escape chagrin because men only

gaze at their structures, and will not live in them. Closet students of politics are constantly undergoing new drill in the same lesson: the world is an inexorable schoolmaster; it will have none of any thought which does not recognize *it*. Sometimes theorists like Rousseau, being near enough the truth to deceive even those who knew something of it, are so unfortunate as to induce men to rear fabrics of government after their aerial patterns out of earth's stuffs, with the result of bringing every affair of weight crashing about their ears, to the shaking of the world. But there are not many such coincidences as Rousseau and his times, happily; and other closet politicians, more commonly cast and more ordinarily placed than he, have had no such perilous successes.

There is every reason to believe that in countries where men vote as well as write books, political writers at any rate give an honest recognition of act to these facts. They do not vote their opinions, they vote their party tickets; and they are the better citizens by far for doing so. Inside their libraries they go with their masters in thought—mayhap go great lengths with Adolph Wagner, or hold stiffly back, 'man *versus* the state,' with Spencer; outside their libraries they 'go with their party.' In a word, like sensible men, they frankly recognize the difference between what is possible in thought and what is practicable in action.

But the trouble is, that when they turn from voting to writing they call many of their abstract reflections on government studies of *politics*, and thereby lose the benefit of some very wholesome aids to just thought. Even when they draw near the actual life of living governments, as they frequently do, and read and compare statutes and constitutions, they stop short of asking and ascertaining what the men of the street think and say of institutions and laws; what little, as well as what big, influences brought particular laws into existence; how much of each law actually lives in the regulation of public function or private activity, how much of it has degenerated into 'dead letter;' in brief, just what things it is —what methods, what habits, what human characteristics and social conditions—that make the appearance of politics outside the library so different from its appearance inside that quiet retreat; what it is that constitutes 'practical politics' a peculiar province. And yet these are the questions most necessary to be answered in order to reach the heart of their study.

Every one who has read great treatises on government which were not merely speculative in their method must have been struck by their exhaustive knowledge of statutes, of judicial

precedents, and of legal and constitutional
history; and equally by their tacit ignorance
of anything more than this gaunt skeleton of
institutions. Their best pages are often those
on which a modest asterisk, an unobtrusive
numeral, or a tiny dagger sticking high in the
stately text, carries the eye down to a foot-note,
packed close in small print, in which some hint
is let drop of the fact that institutions have a
daily as well as an epochal life, from which the
student might 'learn something to his advantage.'

The inherent weakness of such a method is
shown by the readiness with which it is discredited when once a better one is put beside it.
What modern writer on political institutions
has not felt, either directly or indirectly, the
influence of de Tocqueville and Bagehot? Both
these inimitable writers were men of extraordinary genius, and, whatever they might have
written about, their writings would have been
admiringly preserved, if only for the wonder of
their luminous qualities. But their political
works live, not only as models of effective style,
but also as standards of stimulating wisdom;
because Bagehot and de Tocqueville were not
merely students, but also *men of the world*, for
whom the only acceptable philosophy of politics
was a generalization from actual daily observation of men and things. They could see institu-

tions writ small in the most trivial turns of
politics, and read constitutions more clearly
in a biography than in a statute-book. They
were men who, had they written history, would
have written the history of peoples, and not of
courts or parliaments merely. Their methods
have, therefore, because of their essential sanity,
gone far toward discrediting all others; they
have leavened the whole mass of political
literature. Was it not Bagehot, for instance,
who made it necessary for Professor Dicey to
entitle his recent admirable work "The Law of
the Constitution," that no one might think he
mistook it for the *Life* of the Constitution?

Who has not wished that Burke had fused
the permanent thoughts of his splendid sentences of wisdom together into a noble whole, an
incomparable treatise whereby every mind that
loved liberty might be strengthened and fertil-
ized? He has handled affairs, and could pluck
out the heart of their mystery with a skill that
seldom blundered; he spoke hardly a word of
mere hearsay or speculation. He, it would
seem, better than any other, could have shown
writers on politics the difference between knowledge and insight, between an acquaintance with
public law and a real mastery of the principles
of government.

Not that all 'practical politicians' would be
the best instructors in the deep—though they

might be in the hidden—things of politics.
Far from it. They are too thickly crowded
by daily detail to see permanent outlines, too
much pushed about by a thousand little influences to detect accurately the force or the
direction of the big and lasting influences.
They 'cannot see the forest for the trees.' They
are no more fitted to be instructors *because*
they are practical politicians than lawyers are
fitted to fill law-school chairs because they are
active practitioners. They must be something
else besides to qualify them for the high function of teaching, and must be that something
else in so masterful a fashion that no distraction
of active politics can for a moment withdraw
their vision from the great and continuous
principles of their calling.

The active statesman is often an incomparable teacher, however, when he is himself least
conscious that he is teaching at all, when he
has no thought of being didactic, but has simply
a heart full of the high purpose of leading his
fellow-countrymen to do those things which he
conceives to be right. Read the purposes of
men like Patrick Henry and Abraham Lincoln,
men untutored of the schools—read their words
of leadership, and say whether there be anything wiser than their home-made wisdom.

It is such reflections as these—whether my
examples be well chosen or not—which seem

to me to lead directly to the right principle of study for every one who would go beyond the law and know the life of states. Not every state lets statutes die by mere disuse, as Scotland once did; and if you are going to read constitutions with only lawyers for your guides, be they never so learned, you must risk knowing only the anatomy of institutions, never learning anything of their biology.

"Men of letters and of thought," says Mr. Sidney Colvin, where one would least expect to find such a remark—in a "Life of Walter Savage Landor"—

"Men of letters and of thought are habitually too much given to declaiming at their ease against the delinquencies of men of action and affairs. The inevitable friction of practical politics generates heat enough already, and the office of the thinker and critic should be to supply not heat, but light. The difficulties which attend his own unmolested task, the task of seeking after and proclaiming salutary truths, should teach him to make allowance for the still more urgent difficulties which beset the politician —the man obliged, amidst the clash of interests and temptations, to practise from hand to mouth, and at his peril, the most uncertain and at the same time the most indispensable of the experimental arts."

Excellent! But why stop there? Must the man of letters and of thought observe the friction of politics only to make due allowance for the practical politician, only to keep his

34

own placid conclusions free from any taint of scorn or cavil at men whose lives are thrown amidst affairs to endure the buffetings of interest and resist the tugs of temptation? Is not a just understanding of the conditions of practical politics also an indispensable pre-requisite to the discovery and audible proclama-tion of his own 'salutary truths?' No truth which does not on all its sides touch human life can ever reach the heart of politics; and men of 'unmolested tasks,' of mere library calm, simply cannot think the thoughts which will tell amidst the noise of affairs. An alert and sym-pathetic perception of the infinite shifts of circumstance and play of motive which control the actual conduct of government ought to permeate the thinking, as well as check the criticisms, of writers on politics.

In a word, ought not the 'man of the world' and the 'man of books' to be merged in each other in the student of politics? Was not John Stuart Mill the better student for having served the East India Company and sat in the House of Commons? Are not Professor Bryce and Mr. John Morley more to be trusted in their books because they have proved themselves worthy to be trusted in the Cabinet?

The success of great popular preachers con-tains a lesson for students of politics who would themselves convert men to a saving doctrine.

The preacher has, indeed, an incalculable advantage over the student of politics in having as his text-book that Bible which speaks of the human heart with a Maker's knowledge of the thing He has made; by knowing his book he knows the deepest things of daily life. But the great preacher reaches the heart of his hearers not by knowledge, but by sympathy—by showing himself a brother-man to his fellow-men. And this is just the principle which the student of politics must heed. He must frequent the street, the counting-house, the drawing-room, the club-house, the administrative offices, the halls—yes, and the lobbies—of legislatures. He must cross-examine the experience of government officials; he must hear the din of conventions, and see their intrigues; he must witness the scenes of election day. He must know how men who are not students regard government and its affairs. He will get many valuable suggestions from such men on occasion; better than that, he will learn the available approaches to such men's thoughts. Government is meant for the good of ordinary people, and it is for ordinary people that the student should elucidate its problems; let him be anxious to keep within earshot of such.

This is not to commend the writer on politics to narrow 'practical' views and petty comment; it is not to ask him to find a philosophy of

government which will fit the understanding
and please the taste of the 'ward politician:'
it is only to ask him to keep his generalizations
firmly bottomed on fact and experience. His
philosophy will not overshoot the hearts of
men because it is feathered with high thought
unless it be deliberately shot in air. Thoughts
do not fail of acceptance because they are not
commonplace enough, but because they are not
true enough; and, in the sort of writing about
which we are here speaking, truth is a thing
which can be detected better by the man who
knows life than by the man who knows only
logic. You cannot lift truth so high that men
cannot reach it; the only caution to be observed
is, that you do not ask them to climb where they
cannot go without leaving *terra firma*.

Nor is the student, who naturally and
properly loves books, to leave books and sit all
his time in wiseacre observation amidst busy
men. His books are his balance—or, rather,
his ballast. And of course the men of his own
day are not the only men from whom he can
learn politics. Government is as old as man;
men have always been politicians; the men of
to-day are only politicians of a particular school;
the past furnishes examples of politicians of
every other school, and there is as much to be
learned about government from them as from
their successors.

Carlyle had the sort of eye for which one should pray when seeking to find men alive and things actual in the records left of them. Who has not profited by his humorous familiarity with the foibles and personal habits of the men who lived about the court of the Hohenzollerns? Who has not learned more than any other man could have told him of Prussian administration under its first great organizer by looking with Carlyle into the sociable informalities of Frederick William's 'tobacco parliament?' Carlyle knew these men well enough to joke with and rail at them. He twitted them with their family secrets, and, knowing what clay they were of, was not awed by their state ceremonials. Yet he saw them, as he himself bitterly complains, only through the medium of crabbed documents and dry-as-dust books, with no seer like himself to help him in his interpretations. It was hard straining of the eyes to see so far back through the dense and murky atmosphere of formal record and set history; but he saw, nevertheless, because he did not need to be told all in order to know all; the dryest of historians could hardly avoid dropping some hint which would suffice Carlyle more than would tomes of 'profane history.'

If you know what you are looking for and are not expecting to find it advertised in the newspapers, but lying somewhere beneath the

surface of things, the dullest fool may often
help you to its discovery. It needs a good nose
to do the thing, but look how excellent is the
game to which a casual scent may bring you in
such a domain as the study of politics. There
are whole worlds of fact waiting to be discovered
by inference. Do not expect to find the life of
constitutions painted in the great 'standard
authorities,' but, following with becoming patience their legal anatomy of institutions, watch
their slightest movement toward an illustrative
foot-note, and try to find under that the scent
you are in quest of. If they cite an instance,
seek the recital of the same case elsewhere,
where it is told with a different purpose; if it
promise well there, hunt it further still, and
make sure you catch every glimpse it affords of
men's actual dealings with government. If your
text mention names of consequence, seek them
out in biographies, and scan there the personal
relations of men with affairs, for hints of the
methods by which governments are operated
from day to day. You will not need any incentive to read all their gossip, in letters and journals, and so see governors as men; but do more:
endure official interviews and sessions of Parliament with them; collate their private letters
and their public despatches—there's no telling
when or where you shall strike fresh trails of the
game you seek. Interview judges off the bench,

courtiers away from court, officers off duty.
Go to France and live next door a prefect in the
provinces; go to London and try to find out
how things of weight are talked about in the
smoking-room of the House of Commons.

Such excursions must, of course, lead the
student far afield; he will often get quite out of
sight of his starting-point, the 'standard authority;' but he will not on that account be lost.
The fact is, that all literature teems with suggestions on this topic of politics. Just as the
chance news item, the unstudied traveller's
reminiscence, the passing social or financial
scandal,* and every hint of any present contact
of men with law or authority, illuminates
directly, or by inference, the institutions of our
own day, similar random rays thrown across
the pages of old books by the unpremeditated
words of writers quite guiltless of such instructive intent may light up, for those who are alert
to see such things, the most intimate secrets of
state. If it be beyond hoping for to find a *whole*
Greville for every age of government, there may
be found Grevillian scraps, at least, in the
literature of almost every time. From men as
far back and as well remembered as Cicero,
down to men as recent and as easily forgotten

---

* Did not the Dilke trial in London, for instance, help us
to understand at least one influence that may sometimes
make a lawyer Home Secretary?

as several who might be named, politicians have loved to explain to posterity the part they took in conspicuous affairs; and that portion of posterity which studies politics by inference ought to be profoundly thankful to them for yielding to the taste.

Approach the life of States by such avenues, and you shall be convinced of the organic nature of political society. View society from what point you will, you always catch sight of some part of government; man is so truly a 'political animal' that you cannot examine him at all without seeing the points—points of his very structure—whereat he touches and depends upon, or upholds, the State.

In 1850, while Governor-General of Canada, Lord Elgin writes to Lord Grey:

"Our Reciprocity measure was pressed by us in Washington last session, just as a railway bill, in 1845 or 1846, would have been passed in Parliament. There was no Government to deal with, . . . it was all a matter of canvassing this member of Congress or the other."*

What? 'No Government to deal with?' Here's a central truth to be found in none of the 'standard authorities,' and yet to be seen by a practised diplomatist all the way from Canada. About the same date M. Bacourt came to this country to represent the French

* Letters and Journals of Lord Elgin, p. 121.

Government and be made wretched by the
crude deportment of the Americans. His chief
concern was to get away to some country where
people were less unconventionally at their ease
in drawing-rooms; but he turned, when necessary, to the business of his legation; and whenever he did so he found that "here diplomatic
affairs are not treated as everywhere else, where
we communicate with the Minister of Foreign
Affairs and arrange the matter with him alone."
He must 'arrange' the matter with several
committees of Congress. He must go to see
Mrs. Kennedy and Mrs. Winthrop, whose
"husbands are members of the House of Representatives, and on the committee having charge
of commercial affairs, in which" he "is interested," for "they say that these gentlemen are
very particular about visits from foreign ministers to their wives."* Just Lord Elgin's testi-
mony. Again the 'standard authorities' are
added to, and that in a quarter where we should
least expect to find them supplemented. We
need despair of no source.

These are only near and easily recognized
illustrations of the errant mode of study I am
expounding and advocating. Other systems
besides our own receive similar chance illumination in the odd corners of all sorts of books.
Now and again you strike mines like the

* Souvenirs of a Diplomat, pp. 189, 281.

"Mémoires of Madame de Rémusat," the "Letters" of Walpole, or the "Diary" of a Pepys or an Evelyn; at other periods you must be content to find only slender veins of the ore of familiar observation and intimate knowledge of affairs for which you are delving; but your search will seldom be altogether futile. Some newly opened archive office may offer *cahiers*, such as revealed to de Tocqueville, more than all other records, the *ancien régime*. Some elder Hamerton may tell you of the significant things to be seen 'round his house.' All correspondence and autobiography will repay perusal, even when not so soaked in affairs as the letters of Cromwell, or so reminiscent of politics as the "Memoirs of Samuel Romilly."

Politics is the life of the State, and nothing which illustrates that life, nothing which reveals any habit contracted by man as a political animal, comes amiss in the study of politics. Public law is the formal basis of the political life of society, but it is not always an expression of its vital principle. We are inclined, oftentimes, to take laws and constitutions too seriously, to put implicit faith in their professions without examining their conduct. Do they affect to advance liberty, for instance? We ought to go, in person or in imagination, amongst the people whom they command, and see for ourselves whether those people enjoy

liberty. With reference to laws and constitutions of our own day, we can learn such things
best by supplementing books and study by
travel and observation. The best taught class
in modern public law would be a travelling
class. Other times than our own we must
perforce be content to see through other men's
eyes.

In other words, statute-books and legal
commentaries are all very well in the study of
politics, if only you quite thoroughly understand that they furnish only the crude body
colors for your picture of the state's life, upon
which all your finer luminous and atmospheric
effects are afterwards to be worked. It is high
time to recognize the fact that politics can be
effectually expounded only by means of the
highest literary methods. Only master workers
in language and in the grouping and interpretation of heterogeneous materials can achieve the
highest success in making real *in words* the
complex life of states. If I might act as the
interpreter of the new-school economists of
whom I have already spoken, I trust with due
reverence, I should say that this is the thought
which, despite their too frequent practical contempt for artistic literary form, is possessing
them. John Stuart Mill and Ricardo made a sort
of logic of political economy; in order to simplify their processes, they deliberately stripped

man of all motives save self-interest alone,
and the result was evidently '*doctrinaire*'—was
not a picture of life, but a theorem of trade.
Hence 'the most dismal of all sciences;' hence
Sidney Smith's exhortation to his friend not to
touch the hard, unnatural thing. The new-
school economists revolt, and say they want 'a
more scientific method.' What they really
want is a higher literary method. They want
to take account of how a man's wife affects his
trade, how his children stiffen his prudence,
how his prejudices condition his enterprise,
how his lack of imagination limits his market,
how strongly love of home holds him back from
the good wages that might be had by emigra-
tion, how despotically the opinion of his neighbors forbids his insisting upon a cash business,
how his position in local society prescribes the
commodities he is *not* to deal in; in brief, how
men actually do labor, plan, and get gain.
They are, therefore, portentously busy amass-
ing particulars about the occupations, the
habits, the earnings, the whole economic life
of all classes and conditions of men. But these
things are only the raw material of poetry and
the literary art, and without the intervention
of literary art must remain raw material. To
make anything of them, the economist must
become a literary artist and bring his discoveries
home to our imaginations—make these innu-

merable details of his pour in a concentrated fire upon the central citadels of men's understandings. A single step or two would then bring him within full sight of the longed for time when political economy is to dominate legislation.

It has fallen out that, by turning its thoughts toward becoming a science, politics, like political economy, has joined its literature to those books of *natural* science which boast a brief authority, and then make way for what is 'latest.' Unless it be of the constitution of those rare books which mark an epoch in scientific thought, a 'scientific work' may not expect to outlive the prevailing fashion in ladies' wraps. But books on politics are in the wrong company when they associate with works among which so high a rate of mortality obtains. The 'science' proper to them, as distinguished from that which is proper to the company they now affect, is a science whose very expositions are as deathless as itself. It is the science of the life of man in society. Nothing which elucidates that life ought to be reckoned foreign to its art; and no true picture of that life can ever perish out of literature. Ripe scholarship in history and jurisprudence is not more indispensable to the student of politics than are a constructive imagination and a poet's eye for the detail of human incident. The heart of his task is insight

THE STUDY OF POLITICS

and interpretation; no literary power that he can bring to bear upon it will be greater than he needs. Arthur Young's way of observing, Bagehot's way of writing, and Burke's way of philosophizing would make an ideal combination for the work he has to do. His materials are often of the most illusive sort, the problems which he has to solve are always of the most confounding magnitude and variety.

It is easy for him to say, for instance, that the political institutions of one country will not suit another country; but how infinitely difficult is it to answer the monosyllables How? and Why? To reply to the Why he must make out all the contrasts in the histories of the two countries. But it depends entirely upon what sort of eye he has whether those contrasts will contain for him vital causes of the effect he is seeking to expound. He may let some anecdote escape him which gleams with the very spark needed to kindle his exposition. In looking only for grave political facts he may overlook some apparently trivial outlying detail which contains the very secret he would guess. He may neglect to notice what men are most talked about by the people; whose photographs are most frequently to be seen on the walls of peasant cottages; what books are oftenest on their shelves. Intent upon intrigue and legislation, he may pass over with only a laugh some

47

piquant gossip about legislator or courtier
without the least suspicion that it epitomizes
a whole scheme of government. He may admire
self-government so much as to forget that it is
a very coarse, homely thing when alive, and so
may really never know anything valuable about
it. The man who thinks the polls disagreeable
and uninteresting places has no business taking
up a pen to write about government. The man
who despises the sheriff because he is coarse
and uncouth, and who studies the sheriff's
functions only from the drawing-room or the
library, will realize the life of government no
better than he realizes the vanity of 'good
form.'

If politics were to be studied as a great
department of human conduct, not to be
understood by a scholar who is not also a man
of the world, its literature might be made as
imperishable as that of the imagination. There
might then enter into it that individuality
which is immortality. That personal equation
which constitutes the power of all books which
have aught of force in them would then rescue
books on politics from the dismal category of
'treatises,' and exalt them to the patriciate of
literature. The needed reaction against the
still 'orthodox' methods of discoursing upon
laws and constitutions, like that already set
afoot against the 'orthodox' political economists,

should be a 'literary movement'—a movement from formalism to life. In order really to know anything about government, you must *see it alive;* and the object of the writer on politics should be nothing less than this, to paint government to the life, to make it live again upon his page.

49

III

POLITICAL SOVEREIGNTY

50
51
52

POLITICAL SOVEREIGNTY

THE conception of political sovereignty is one of those interesting portions of doctrine which belong in common to several distinct branches of study. No systematic discussion of any part of the science of politics can advance very far without it; and it is even more indispensable to the student of legal systems than to the student of politics. It is a question central to the life of states and to the validity of law.

And it is rendered the more interesting by the fact that it is a critical question, used by all schools alike as a capital test of orthodoxy. No man who cares a whit about his standing among students of law or of politics can afford to approach it lightly. Whatever he says about it he must needs say with a profound sense of responsibility. He must undertake the discussion of it with the same sort of gravity, with the same deep sense of personal risk, that the political economist evinces when he ventures an opinion about Value or hazards a theory of

Distribution. When once he has committed himself to an opinion concerning it, he may be sure that with a large and influential number of his fellow-students he can never thereafter pass for a man of undoubted scholarship or unclouded sense.

If it is awkward, under such circumstances, that the conception should be so indispensable, it doubtless has the advantage of forcing boldness upon us. If for nothing else than for the sake of a *modus vivendi*, we must out with whatever notion it is that we have accepted or invented with reference to the nature and lodgement of sovereignty. It is, on the whole, safer to be explicit than to hedge.

And yet it is not easy to be explicit; for there are no suitable terms to be explicit with. One no sooner begins to examine the field and the matter of controversy than he begins to suspect that it is all a question of terminology. After being hurried in bewilderment through one of Browning's short poems without being permitted to be quite sure at any point of the full meaning, we are led in our disappointment to wonder, with Mr. Birrell, if it can be the punctuation. In what we read of sovereignty we are led to wonder if it can be the *words* that confuse us. It must be evident to every one who has not been sophisticated by the terms themselves, or committed beyond retrieval by the controversial use of them, that when, for example, the people of the United States and the Czar of Russia are put together in the same class as sovereigns, language has been forced to a very artificial use, and one term made to cover radically different things. There is clearly a striking contrast between these two sovereigns in character, in method, and in power. Doubtless an excellent way by which to enter our subject would be through an examination of this difference. But another way is more direct.

Let us begin with an accepted definition of sovereignty. It is both decent and convenient to take that of Austin, that celebrated definition which he received through Bentham from Hobbes. Austin conceived a sovereign very concretely, as a person or body of persons existing in an independent political society and accorded the habitual obedience of the bulk of the members of that society, while itself subordinate to no political superior. Law he defined to be the explicit or implicit command of such a person or body of persons, addressed to the members of the community, its inferiors or subjects. He took it for granted that in every independent community supreme political authority did actually vest in some such determinate sovereign person or body of persons.

By the very term used to describe it, more-

over, this sovereignty is supremacy—is subject
to no limitation. Every law is a command, not
only, but the command of a supreme authority;
and it would be a singular contradiction in
terms to speak of this supreme power as limited
by law. How can the supreme author of law
within a state himself be subject to law: how
can the creature bind the creator? How can
one refrain from smiling at the logical incapacity
of those who speak of limitations to sovereignty,
or, more absurdly still, of divisions of sovereignty? Is there a hierarchy of supremacies:
can there be a co-ordination of creators?

Austin had studied in Bonn while it was the
residence of such men as Niebuhr, Schlegel,
Arndt, Welcher, Mackeldey, and Heffter, and
at a period when controversy touching some of
the fundamental questions concerning the province and method of jurisprudence was in its
keen youth. His thought was mature, indeed,
before he went abroad, and nature had very
imperatively commanded of what sort that
thought should be by giving him a mind framed
for abstract conception and sharp logical processes; but contact with German thinking
contributed many important elements to his
mental equipment. Thibaut became scarcely
less his master than Bentham. It was inevitable that it should be Thibaut rather
than Savigny. Savigny believed that all law

was rooted in old habit, and that legislation could modify law successfully and beneficially only by consenting to the secondary *rôle* of supplementing, formulating, or at most guiding custom. He was at weapons drawn with the school of Thibaut, which proposed to lay legislative hands on the entire body of German law, make a code which should be common to all the German States, and so help to make Germany a national unit. To attempt thus to systematize law, where by natural development it was unsystematic, seemed to Savigny a deliberate effort to render it artificial. Law, he maintained, did not often grow into a logical system, but was the product of daily accretions of habit and sluggish formations of thought, which followed no system of philosophy. It was not the business of legal science to force it into logical categories; it was its function, rather, to give a clear explanation of the principles and order of its life and a satisfactory working analysis of its several parts and conceptions. Thibaut, on the other hand, believed it to be the legitimate function of the jurist to make piecemeal law up into organic wholes, rendering it clear where it had been obscure, correcting its inconsistencies, trimming away its irregularities, reducing the number of its exceptional provisions, discovering and filling in its gaps, running it through with threads of system, giving it elegance of style and completeness of method. He thought it possible to change law from a system of habits into a system of commands. These were, of course, the ideas which were most attractive, most congenial, to the mind of Austin.

But, however natural such conceptions may have been to Austin, it must certainly be regarded as singular that, although rejected on the Continent, where sovereignty had throughout the most important formative periods of European history been quite unequivocally lodged in unmistakable sovereigns, these notions should have been accepted in England, the land where law had been least subject to doctrine, most observant of times and circumstances, most piecemeal in its manner of construction, least like a set of commands, and most like a set of habits and conventions. Doubtless we are to remember, however, that the feudal theory of law had long been held with perfect confidence by English lawyers in calm despite of fact. Probably it is true that the English mind (our own), with its practical habit, likes nice systems well enough because of their appearance of completeness, has a sense of order which enjoys logic, without having any curiosity or capacity for the examination of premises. The Englishman has always been found ready to accept, from those

who had the leisure to amuse themselves in
that way, interesting explanations of his institutions which did not at all fit the actual facts.
It has caused him no inconvenience, for he has
not perceived the lack of adjustment between
his actual transactions and the theory he has
accepted concerning them. He has, of course,
not troubled himself to alter his institutions
to suit his philosophy. That philosophy satisfied his thought and inconvenienced neither
Parliament nor the law courts. And so he had
no doubt Austin was right.

Austin's logic is unrelenting, and the loyalty
of his followers unflinching. Sir Henry Maine
having shown that throughout the greater part
of history the world has been full of independent
political societies possessing no law-making
sovereign at all, and it having become notorious
that legislation has everywhere played a late
and comparatively subordinate part in the
production of law, the latest writers of the
Austinian school have reduced jurisprudence
to a merely formal science, professing to care
nothing for the actual manner in which law may
originate, nothing even for most of the motives
which induce men to obey law, provided you
will but concede that there is, among a great
many other imperative motives, one which is
universally operative, namely, the fear of the
compulsion of physical force, and that there is

at least one sovereign function, namely, the application of that physical force in the carrying out of the law. They ask to be allowed to confine themselves to such a definition of positive law as will limit it to "rules which are *enforced* by a political superior in his capacity as such." They take for their province only a systematic description of the forms and method "of the influence of government upon human conduct" through the operation of law. They thus virtually abandon the attempt to find any universal doctrines respecting the *rôle* of government as a *maker* of laws. For them government is not a creative agent, but only an instrumentality for the effectuation of legal rules already in existence. So hard is the principle of life to get at that they give over all attempts to find it, and, turning away from the larger topics of the biology, restrict themselves to the morphology, of law.

When it came to pointing out the body of persons with which sovereignty was lodged in particular states of complex constitutional structure, Austin was sometimes very unsatisfactory. Sovereignty is lodged in England, he says, in the king, the peers, and—*not* the House of Commons, but—the electorate. For he holds the House of Commons to be merely a trustee of the electors, notwithstanding the fact that the electors exercise their right of franchise under laws which Parliament itself enacted and may change. In the United States he "believes" it to be lodged "in the States' governments, as forming an aggregate body;" and he explains that by the government of a state he does not mean its "ordinary legislature, but the body of its citizens which appoints its ordinary legislature, and which, the Union apart, is properly sovereign therein." Apparently he is led thus to go back of the House of Commons and the legislatures of our states to the electorates by which they are chosen, because of his conception of sovereignty as *unlimited.* If he stopped short of the electors, some part of his sovereign body would be subject to political superiors. If he were to go beyond the electors, to the larger body of the people—to the women and the children and the men who cannot vote—he would come upon, not a 'determinate,' but an indeterminate body of persons.

Our own writers, however, having made bold to embrace the dogma of popular sovereignty with a certain fervor of patriotism, have no hesitation about taking the additional step. They maintain, with Lieber, that "according to the views of free men," sovereignty "can dwell with society, the nation, only." Writers like the late Judge Jameson, of Chicago, declare that they have very definite ideas of what this means. They think that Mr. Bryce expounded the doctrine when he wrote his chapter on "Government by Public Opinion." "When the true sovereign has spoken," says Judge Jameson, "at public meetings, by the press, or by personal argument or solicitation, the electorate, when it acts, either registers the behests of the people or ceases betimes further to represent them." "The pressure of public opinion consciously brought to bear upon the electorate," he declares to be, even when "inarticulate" (whatever inarticulate pressure may be), "a clear and legitimate exercise of sovereign power;" and he thinks that Mr. Herbert Spencer meant the same thing when he declared that "that which, from hour to hour, in every country, governed despotically or otherwise, produces the obedience making political action possible, is the accumulated and organized sentiment felt towards inherited institutions made sacred by tradition," inasmuch as Mr. Spencer proceeds to say with all plainness, "Hence it is undeniable that, taken in its widest acceptation, the feeling of the community is the sole source of political power; in those communities, at least, which are not under foreign domination. It is so at the outset of social life, and it still continues substantially so." And yet, if Mr. Spencer means the same thing that Judge Jameson means, what are we to think of the present fraternization of France

62

and Russia? If the people be sovereign in France and the Czar sovereign in Russia, it is doubtless quite conceivable that one sovereign should love another; but if it be true, as Judge Jameson makes Mr. Spencer say, that it is the people, even in Russia, who are, after all, sovereign, what are we to think of the fondness of the French sovereign for a government which is holding the Russian sovereign in subjection? If this be correct thinking, it puts us into awkward quandaries, troubling our logic as well as condemning our lives.

Apply this doctrine of our masters in American law to our actual political conditions, and see how far it simplifies the matter. In the United States (so runs the orthodox creed) the People is sovereign—the verb is singular because the people, under this doctrine, constitute a unit. And yet it is notorious that they never have acted as a unit, nor ever can act as a unit under our existing constitution. They have always acted, and must always act, in state groups. And in state groups what action do they take? They assent to constitutional provisions, or refuse to assent to them; and they select certain persons to act as law-makers, as judges, or as executive officers of government. Do they choose policies? No. Do they frame constitutional provisions? Certainly not; they only accept or reject them. In the only case in which they speak directly, concerning specific provisions of law, they neither command nor originate. They receive or decline what is offered them. They must wait until they are asked. They have neither initiative nor opportunity to construct. They must be consulted concerning government, but they do not conduct it.

Nor is it otherwise, upon last analysis, in Switzerland, where the *Referendum* exists, where, that is, the people vote upon specific measures of ordinary legislation not only, but where they are also provided with means of imperative initiative in legislation. By petitions bearing a certain large number of signatures they can propose definite legislation, compel action upon the matter of their petitions by their legislatures, and an ultimate submission of the question to popular vote. But see what this is, when examined. The eyes of the community, the men of observation and progress, get up a petition; that is, an indeterminate body and a minority demand that certain laws be formulated and put to the vote. The thing is done, but the measure defeated, let us suppose, at the polls. The eyes of the community have desired certain things, have offered them to the slow digestive organs, and they have been rejected. Are the digestive organs, then, sovereign, and not the initiative parts, the eyes and the reason? Is it sovereign to stomach a thing, and not sovereign to purpose a thing?

But turn the chase in another direction, if peradventure we may yet run the sovereign people to cover. The more absolute democratic theorists decline to restrict the sovereign body to the electorate, to those who have formal votes. Voters are simply the agents of the community, they say. The press and the pulpit, the private argument and the curtain lecture, command—voters, if they are faithful, obey. Others, no less democratic, but more precise, seek for a more determinate body, content themselves with the qualified voters, and think with relief that all difficulties are removed. The electorate is sovereign.

But is the electorate a more determinate body than the population? Does registration afford us any more certain results than the census yields? Do the electors act in determinate numbers? Is there a quorum? Have they any choice but to act under the forms and within the limits assigned by law? Can they command without invitation, or assent without suggestion? Are not the agencies which Judge Jameson calls sovereign after all more active, more self-directed, freer to criticise, to suggest, to insist? The newspapers, the clergymen, the mass-meeting orators, the urgent friends, the restless, ambitious wives, the pert and forward children can at any rate keep on talking in the intervals, when the electors are reduced to silence, patiently awaiting an opportunity to vote. Certainly, if we can accept this miscellaneous sovereign of men-women-and-children, the history of sovereignty is much simplified. This determinate body of persons, the free population, is always present, and always has been present, under all constitutions. All that we have to inquire is, What means had they for expressing their will? How were their dispositions and judgments made to tell upon the consciousness of those who framed the laws? True, this sovereign body has its points of resemblance to the god Baal. Those who call upon it call in vain, if it be not the season appointed for voting; there is no voice, nor any that answer, nor any that regardeth. No fire consumes the sacrifice. Perhaps the People is talking, or is pursuing, or is in a journey, or peradventure it sleepeth, and must be awaked.

Surely this is a singular undertaking, this mad pursuit of a sovereign amidst the obvious phenomena of politics! If laws be indeed commands, the commands of a determinate person or body of persons, it ought to be possible to discover this determinate source of authority without much curious research. And yet it would seem that it demands ingenious analysis. Look how uneasily Mr. Sidgwick casts about in the last chapter of his recent "Elements of Politics," to find Supreme Political Power—which is his name for sovereignty. He has been looking forward to this inquiry, not without nervousness, throughout the chapters which precede. Political power is exercised, he perceives, through some organ of government; but he cannot conceive that the power of this organ is its own power. He engages in a study of dynamics. What moves this organ: whence does it derive its power? How is it influenced? Is it itself commanded, overawed, constrained from any quarter? This is a door to the metaphysics of government. Taking a prince as a simple and normal organ of government, he analyzes the subjection of princes to their ministers, to priests, to mistresses, to the violent protests of an insubordinate people. No influence that the prince can throw off without losing his own authority, he thinks, can be a sovereign influence; but any influence which can threaten his power if he resist is a sovereign influence, the true depository of supreme political power. Sovereignty thus becomes a catalogue of influences.

Can we accept these singular processes? If a physicist were to discard all the separate laws, all the differential analysis of his science, and were to reduce its entire body of principles to some general statement of the correlation of forces, he would hardly be conceived to have done physics a service. If in our study of anatomy we should turn away from structural adjustment and functional force to take account of the thousand and one influences which in individual cases affect the organs from without, we should obviously be abandoning the science itself. It seems to me that we do a very like thing if, in studying the structural forces and organic actions of society, its organs of origination and command, its organs of execution, its superior and its subordinate authorities, its habitual modes of structural life, we abandon all attempts at differentiation, throw all analysis into hotch-potch, and reduce everything to terms of the general forces which mould and govern society as a whole. We confuse our thought in our effort to simplify it. We lose, we do not gain, by putting powers of radically different sorts together into the same categories, and driving them abreast, as if they pulled together, in the same propositions.

There is no unlimited power, except the sum of all powers. Our legal theorists have sought unlimited sovereignty by a process of summation; have made it consist in the combined forces of the community. Sovereignty, if it be a definite and separable thing at all, is not unlimited power; is not identical with the powers of the community. It is not the general vitality of the organism, but the specific originative power of certain organs. Sovereigns have always been subject in greater or less degree to the community; have always been organs of the state; have never been the state itself. But they have been sovereigns none the less; they, and not the community over which they presided.

It is necessary, if there is to be any clear thinking at all upon this subject, to distinguish very sharply two radically different things; namely, the powers and processes of governing, on the one hand, from the relations of the people to those powers and processes, on the other. Those relations are relations of assent and obedience; and the degree of assent and obedience marks in every case the limits, that is, the sphere, of sovereignty. Sovereignty is the daily operative power of framing and giving efficacy to laws. It is the originative, directive, governing power. It lives; it plans; it executes. It is the organic origination by the state of its law and policy; and the sovereign power is the highest originative organ of the state. It is none the less sovereign because it must be observant of the preferences of those whom it governs. The obedience of the subject has always limited the power of the sovereign. "The Eastern politicians never do anything,"

69

says Burke, "without the opinion of the astrologers on the fortunate moment. . . . Statesmen of a more judicious prescience look for the fortunate moment too; but they seek it, not in the conjunctions and oppositions of planets, but in the conjunctions and oppositions of men and things." This is the covert admission of the Austinian definition itself: the sovereign power is that to which "the bulk of the community *is habitually obedient*." When we discuss, with Mr. Sidgwick, the influences which tell upon the action of the originative organs of the state, we are not discussing sovereignty, but the natural and universal limitations of sovereignty, the structural checks and balances of the organism. There is no hope for theory if we neglect these obvious distinctions.

At all times and under all systems there have been two sets of phenomena visible in government: the phenomena of command and the phenomena of obedience, the phenomena of governing and the phenomena of being governed. Obedience, moreover, is not always an automatic or unconscious thing. It is a submission of the will—an acquiescence which is the product either of choice, of necessity, or of habit. This has been observed from the first; was observed by Bodin, from whom we get our word sovereignty, and much of our conception of the thing, sovereignty. He perceived that the

70

supremacy of the sovereign—even of the mediæval French sovereign before his eyes—was in fact limited, the frontiers of sovereignty being marked by certain antecedent rights, by divers established prerogatives of property and vested privilege—not a scientific, but a natural frontier, lying along the old mountains of habit, the well-known rivers of precedent.

We know that the history of politics has been the history of liberty; a history of the enlargement of the sphere of independent individual action at the expense of the sphere of dictatorial authority. It has revealed a process of differentiation. Certain freedoms of opinion and utterance, of choice of occupation and of allegiance, of fair trial and equitable condemnation, have been blocked out as inviolable territories, lying quite beyond the jurisdiction of political sovereignty. Beginning with that singular and interesting order of the classical states of the ancient world, under which the individual was merged in the community and liberty became identical with a share in the exercise of the public power, we witness something like a gradual disintegration, a resolution of the state into its constituent elements, until at length those who govern and those who are governed are no longer one and the same, but stand face to face treating with one another, agreeing upon terms of command and obedience, as at Runny-

mede. Conditions of submission have been
contested, and, as liberty has gained upon authority, have been jealously formulated. The
procedure and the prerogatives of authority
have been agreed upon; liberty has encroached
upon sovereignty and set bounds to it. The
process is old; only some of its results are new.
What both political philosophers and political
revolutionists have sought for time out of mind
has been a final definition for that part of the
Austinian conception which concerns the *habitual obedience* of the community. These defini-
tions, in their practical shape as institutions, we
now call constitutions. At last peoples have
become conscious of their relations to the highest powers of the state, and have sought to
give permanence and certainty to those relations by setting the conditions of their subordination fast in stubborn practices or in the
solemn covenants of written documents. A
constitution government has always had; but
not until this latest age these deliberate formu-
lations of principle and practice which determine
the whole organization and action of the State,
the domain of authority, the neutral territory of
liberty, the postulates of obedience.

Constitutions are definitive rather than creative. They sum up experiences. They register
consents. Assuredly Mr. Spencer is right when
he declares that that which in every country,

under whatever system governed, "produces the obedience making political action possible, is the accumulated and organized sentiment of the community towards inherited institutions," and that "the feeling of the community is the sole source of political power." But this does not mean what Judge Jameson reads into it, that sovereignty and the feeling of the community are one and the same thing; that the conditions of sovereignty and the exercise of sovereignty are identical. Sovereignty has at all times and under all systems of government been dependent upon the temper and disposition of the people. The will of the community, the inclinations and desires of the body politic, as a whole are always, in the last analysis, the foundation, as they are also in many instances the direct and immediate source, of law. But these preferences of the general body are exercised by way of approval or disapproval, acquiescence or resistance; they are not agencies of initial choice. The sanctioning judgments of a people are passive, dormant, waiting to have things put to them, unable themselves to suggest anything, because without organs of utterance or suggestion. I cannot predicate sovereignty of my physical parts, but must ascribe it to my will, notwithstanding the fact that my physical parts must assent to the purposes of my will, and that my will is dependent upon their obedience. The organism unquestionably dominates the organs; but there are organs, nevertheless, organs of origination, which direct and rule with a sovereign presidency.

A written constitution adopted by popular vote affords, perhaps. some of the nicest tests of theory. Here we have the most specific form of popular assent. In such a document the powers of the government are explicitly set forth and specifically lodged; and the means by which they may be differently constituted or bestowed are definitively determined. Now we know that these documents are the result of experience, the outcome of a contest of forces, the fruits of struggle. Nations have taken knowledge of despotism. They have seen authority abused and have refused to submit; have perceived justice to be arbitrary and hidden away in secret tribunals, and have insisted that it be made uniform and open; have seen ministers chosen from among favorites, and have demanded that they be taken from among representatives of the people; have found legislation regardful of classes, and have clamored to have laws made by men selected without regard to class; have felt obedience irksome because government was disordered in form and confused in respect of responsibility, and have insisted that responsibility be fixed and forms of order and publicity observed. Sometimes

74

only a steady practice has accomplished all this; sometimes documentary securities have been demanded. These documentary securities are written constitutions.

It is easy, as it is also impressive, to believe that a written constitution proceeds from the people, and constitutes their sovereign behest concerning government. But of course it does not. It proceeds always either from some ordinary or from some extraordinary organ of the state; its provisions are the fruit of the debated determinations of a comparatively small deliberative body, acting usually under some form of legal commission. It is accepted as a whole and without discrimination by the diffused, undeliberative body of voters.

What confuses our view is the fact that these formal documentary statements of the kinds and degrees of obedience to which the people assent, the methods of power to which they submit, the sort of responsibility upon which they insist, have become, from the very necessity of their nature, a distinct and superior sort of precise and positive law. We seek the sovereign who utters them. But they are not the utterances of a sovereign. They are the covenants of a community. Time out of mind communities have made covenants with their sovereigns. When despotism in France was 'tempered by epigram,' the sharp tongues of the wits spoke, after a sort, the constitution of the country—a positive law whose sanction was ridicule. But the wits were not sovereign; the *salons* did not conduct government. Our written constitutions are only very formal statements of the standards to which the people, upon whom government depends for support, will hold those who exercise the sovereign power.

I do not, of course, deny the power of the people. Ultimately they condition the action of those who govern; and it is salutary that it should be so. It is wise also, if it be not indispensable, that the extent and manner of their control should be explicitly set forth and definitively agreed upon in documents of unmistakable tenor. I say simply that such control is no new thing. It is only the precise formulation of it that is new.

If it seem to be after all a question of words, a little closer scrutiny will disclose the fact that it is much more than that. Mr. Ritchie, of Oxford University, in an able article on "The Conception of Sovereignty," contributed to the *Annals of the American Academy of Political and Social Science* (January, 1891), perceiving some part of the distinction that I have pointed out, and wishing to realize it in his thought, proposes to distinguish three several kinds of sovereigns: viz., a nominal sovereign—the English queen, for example; a legal sovereign—the law-making body; and a political sovereign—the voters, whom we might call the sovereign of appeal. But why not confine ourselves to substantives, if we may, and avoid the quicksands of adjectives? Sovereignty is something quite definite; so also is power; so also is control. Sovereignty is the highest political power in the state, lodged in active organs, for the purposes of governing. Sovereign power is a positive thing; control a negative thing. Power belongs to government, is lodged in organs of initiative; control belongs to the community, is lodged with the voters. To call these two things by the same name is simply to impoverish language by making one word serve for a variety of meanings.

It is never easy to point out in our complex modern governments the exact organs in which sovereignty is lodged. On the whole, however, it is always safe to ascribe sovereignty to the highest originative or law-making body of the state,—the body by whose determinations both the tasks to be carried out by the Administration and the rules to be applied by the courts are fixed and warranted. Even where the courts utter authoritative interpretations of what we call the fundamental law—the law that is embodied in constitutions—they are rather the organs through which the limitations of sovereignty are determined than organs of sovereignty itself. They declare the principles of that higher, constituent law which is set above sovereignty, which expresses the restrictions set about the exercise of sovereign authority. Such restrictions exist in all states, but they are given definite formulation only in some. As for the Executive, that is the agent, not the organ, of sovereignty.

But, even if it be comparatively easy thus to fix upon the organs of sovereignty in a unitary state, what shall we say of a federal state? How apply our analysis to that? One is tempted to declare, with Dr. Merkel, of Strassburg, that federal states give direct contradiction of fact to prevailing theories respecting the necessity for unity of power, indivisibility of sovereignty. Here, as he says, we have organs and authorities in possession of powers exclusively their own, for the furtherance of functions necessary to the ends of the state as a whole, existing side by side with organs also in full possession of powers exclusively their own, for the furtherance of the local and special functions of the member states. We know, moreover, that these two sets of organs are in fact co-ordinate; that the powers of the states were not derived from the federal authority, were even antecedent to the powers of the federal government, and historically quite independent of them. And yet no one who ponders either the life or the formal structure of a federal state can fail to perceive that there is, after all, an essential unity in it, the virtual creaton of a central sovereignty. The constituent act—the manner in which the government was created—can, I conceive, have nothing to do with our analysis in this matter. The way in which the federal state came into existence is immaterial to the question of sovereignty within it after it has been created. Originative life and action, the characteristic attributes of sovereignty, come after that. Character and choice are postponed to birth, sovereignty to the creation of the body politic. The constituent act creates a thing capable of exercising sovereignty. After the creative law has done its part, by whatever process, then the functions of independent life begin. Thereafter, in all federal states, even the amendment of the fundamental law becomes an organic act, depending, practically without exception, upon the initiative of the chief originative organ of the federal state. Confederations are here out of the question. They are, of course, associations of sovereigns. In the federal state self-determination with respect to their law as a whole has been lost by the member states. They cannot extend, they cannot even determine, their own powers conclusively without appeal to the federal authorities. They are unquestionably subject to a political superior. They are fused, subordinated, superior. Though they do not exercise their powers by virtue of delegation, though their powers are indeed inherent and in a very important sense independent, they are yet inferior to a body whose own powers are in reality self-determined, however much that self-determination may be hedged about and clogged by the forms of the fundamental federal law. They are still states, because their powers are original and inherent, not derivative; because their political rights are not also legal duties; and because they can apply to their commands the full imperative sanctions of law. But their sphere is limited by the presiding and sovereign powers of a state superordinated to them, the extent of whose authority is determined, under constitutional forms and guarantees, by itself. They have dominion; but it has sovereignty. For with the federal state lie the highest powers of originative legal determination, the ultimate authority to warrant change and sanction jurisdiction.

Our thought is embarrassed throughout such an analysis by the very fact which invalidates the Austinian conception and makes a fresh analysis necessary. Very little law literally originates in command, though its formulation and enforcement must unquestionably be effected through the commanding authorities of the state. It is their function to direct, to lead, rather than to command. They originate forms, but they do not discover principles. In a very profound sense law proceeds from the community. It is the result of its undeliberate as well as of its deliberate developments, of its struggles, class against class, interest against interest, and of its compromises and adjustments of opinion. It follows, slowly, its ethical judgments, more promptly its material necessities. But law issues thus from the body of the community only in vague and inchoate form. It must be taken out of the sphere of voluntary and uncertain action and made precise and invariable. It becomes positive law by receiving definition and being backed by an active and recognized power within the state. The sovereign organ of a state is, therefore, very properly said to be its law-*making* organ. It transmutes selected tendencies into stiff and urgent rules. It exercises a sovereign choice in so doing. It determines which tendencies shall be accepted, which checked and denied efficacy. It forms the purposes of the state, avoiding revolution if it form them wisely and with a true insight. This is sovereignty:—to sit at the helm and steer, marking out such free courses for the stanch craft as wind and weather will permit. This is the only sort of sovereignty that can be exercised in human affairs. But the pilot is sovereign, and not the weather.

IV
CHARACTER OF DEMOCRACY
IN THE UNITED STATES

82
83
84

CHARACTER OF
DEMOCRACY IN THE
UNITED STATES

EVERYTHING apprises us of the fact that
we are not the same nation now that we
were when the government was formed. In
looking back to that time, the impression is
inevitable that we started with sundry wrong
ideas about ourselves. We deemed ourselves
rank democrats, whereas we were in fact only
progressive Englishmen. Turn the leaves of
that sage manual of constitutional interpretation and advocacy, the *Federalist*, and note the
perverse tendency of its writers to refer to
Greece and Rome for precedents,—that Greece
and Rome which haunted all our earlier and
even some of our more mature years. Recall,
too, that familiar story of Daniel Webster which
tells of his coming home exhausted from an
interview with the first President-elect Harri-
son, whose Secretary of State he was to be,
and explaining that he had been obliged in the

course of the conference, which concerned the inaugural address about to be delivered, to kill nine Roman consuls whom it had been the intention of the good conqueror of Tippecanoe publicly to take into office with him. The truth is that we long imagined ourselves related in some unexplained way to all ancient republicans. Strangely enough, too, we at the same time accepted the quite incompatible theory that we were related also to the French philosophical radicals. We claimed kinship with democrats everywhere, with all democrats. We can now scarcely realize the atmosphere of such thoughts. We are no longer wont to refer to the ancients or to the French for sanction of what we do. We have had abundant experience of our own by which to reckon.

"Hardly any fact in history," says Mr. Bagehot, writing about the middle of the century, "is so incredible as that forty and a few years ago England was ruled by Mr. Perceval. It seems almost the same as being ruled by the *Record* newspaper." (Mr. Bagehot would now probably say the *Standard* newspaper.) "He had the same poorness of thought, the same petty conservatism, the same dark and narrow superstition." "The mere fact of such a premier being endured shows how deeply the whole national spirit and interest was absorbed in the contest with Napoleon, how little we understood the sort of man who should regulate its conduct,—'in the crisis of Europe,' as Sydney Smith said, 'he safely brought the Curates' Salaries Improvement Bill to a hearing;' and it still more shows the horror of all innovation which the recent events of French history had impressed on our wealthy and comfortable classes. They were afraid of catching revolution, as old women of catching cold. Sir Archibald Alison to this day holds that revolution is an infectious disease, beginning no one knows how, and going on no one knows where. There is but one rule of escape, explains the great historian: 'Stay still; don't move; do what you have been accustomed to do; and consult your grandmother on everything.'"

Almost equally incredible to us is the ardor of revolution that filled the world in those first days of our national life,—the fact that one of the rulers of the world's mind in that generation was Rousseau, the apostle of all that is fanciful, unreal, and misleading in politics. To be ruled by him was like taking an account of life from Mr. Rider Haggard. And yet there is still much sympathy in this timid world for the dull people who felt safe in the hands of Mr. Perceval, and, happily, much sympathy also, though little justification, for such as caught a generous elevation of spirit from the speculative enthusiasm of Rousseau.

For us who stand in the dusty matter-of-fact world of to-day, there is a touch of pathos in recollections of the ardor for democratic liberty that filled the air of Europe and America a century ago with such quickening influences. We may sometimes catch ourselves regretting that the inoculations of experience have closed our systems against the infections of hopeful revolution.

"Bliss was it in that dawn to be alive,
  But to be young was very heaven!   O times
  In which the meagre, stale, forbidding ways
  Of custom, law, and statute took at once
  The attraction of a country in romance!
  When Reason seemed the most to assert her rights,
  When most intent on making of herself
  A prime Enchantress, to assist the work
  Which then was going forward in her name!
  Not favored spots alone, but the whole earth,
  The beauty wore of promise, that which sets
  (As at some moment might not be unfelt
  Among the bowers of paradise itself)
  The budding rose above the rose full blown."

Such was the inspiration which not Wordsworth alone, but Coleridge also, and many another generous spirit whom we love, caught in that day of hope.

It is common to say, in explanation of our regret that the dawn and youth of democracy's day are past, that our principles are cooler now and more circumspect, with the coolness and circumspection of advanced years. It seems to some that our enthusiasms have become tamer and more decorous because our sinews have hardened; that as experience has grown idealism has declined. But to speak this is to speak with the old self-deception as to the character of our politics. If we are suffering disappointment, it is the disappointment of an awakening: we were dreaming. For we never had any business hearkening to Rousseau or consorting with Europe in revolutionary sentiment. The government which we founded one hundred years ago was no type of an experiment in advanced democracy, as we allowed Europe and even ourselves to suppose; it was simply an adaptation of English constitutional government. If we suffered Europe to study our institutions as instances in point touching experimentation in politics, she was the more deceived. If we began the first century of our national existence under a similar impression ourselves, there is the greater reason why we should start out upon a new century of national life with more accurate conceptions.

To this end it is important that the following, among other things, should be kept prominently in mind:—

(1) That there are certain influences astir in this century which make for democracy the world over, and that these influences owe their

origin in part to the radical thought of the last century; but that it was not such forces that made us democratic, nor are we responsible for them.

(2) That, so far from owing our government to these general influences, we began, not by carrying out any theory, but by simply carrying out a history,—inventing nothing, only establishing a specialized species of English government; that we founded, not democracy, but constitutional government in America.

(3) That the government which we thus set up in a perfectly normal manner has nevertheless changed greatly under our hands, by reason both of growth and of the operation of the general democratic forces,—the European, or rather world-wide, democratic forces of which I have spoken.

(4) That two things, the great size to which our governmental organism has attained, and, still more, this recent exposure of its character and purposes to the common democratic forces of the age of steam and electricity, have created new problems of organization, which it behooves us to meet in the old spirit, but with new measures.

I

First, then, for the forces which are bringing in democratic temper and method the world over. It is matter of familiar knowledge what these forces are, but it will be profitable to our thought to pass them once more in review. They are freedom of thought and the diffusion of enlightenment among the people. Steam and electricity have co-operated with systematic popular education to accomplish this diffusion. The progress of popular education and the progress of democracy have been inseparable. The publication of their great encyclopædia by Diderot and his associates in France in the last century, was the sure sign of the change that was setting in. Learning was turning its face away from the studious few towards the curious many. The intellectual movement of the modern time was emerging from the narrow courses of scholastic thought, and beginning to spread itself abroad over the extended, if shallow, levels of the common mind. The serious forces of democracy will be found, upon analysis, to reside, not in the disturbing doctrines of eloquent revolutionary writers, not in the turbulent discontent of the pauperized and oppressed, so much as in the educational forces of the last hundred and fifty years, which have elevated the masses in many countries to a plane of understanding and of orderly, intelligent purpose more nearly on a level with the average man of the classes that have hitherto been permitted to govern. The movements towards democracy which have mastered all the other political tendencies of our day are not older than the middle of the last century; and that is just the age of the now ascendant movement towards systematic popular education.

Yet organized popular education is only one of the quickening influences that have been producing the general enlightenment which is everywhere becoming the promise of general liberty. Rather, it is only part of a great whole, vastly larger than itself. Schools are but separated seed-beds, in which the staple thoughts of the steady and stay-at-home people are prepared and nursed. Not much of the world, moreover, goes to school in the school-house. But through the mighty influences of commerce and the press the world itself has become a school. The air is alive with the multitudinous voices of information. Steady trade winds of intercommunication have sprung up which carry the seeds of education and enlightenment, wheresoever planted, to every quarter of the globe. No scrap of new thought can escape being borne away from its place of birth by these all-absorbing currents. No idea can be kept exclusively at home, but is taken up by the trader, the reporter, the traveller, the missionary, the explorer, and is given to all the world, in the newspaper, the novel, the memoir, the poem, the treatise, till every community may know, not only itself, but all the world as well, for the small price of learning to read and keeping its ears open. All the world, so far as its news and its most insistent thoughts are concerned, is fast being made every man's neighbor.

Carlyle unquestionably touched one of the obvious truths concerning modern democracy when he declared it to be the result of printing. In the newspaper press a whole population is made critic of all human affairs; democracy is 'virtually extant,' and 'democracy virtually extant will insist on becoming palpably extant." Looked at in the large, the newspaper press is a type of democracy, bringing all men without distinction under comment made by any man without distinction; every topic is reduced to a common standard of news; everything is noted and argued about by everybody. Nothing could give surer promise of popular power than the activity and alertness of thought which are made through such agencies to accompany the training of the public schools. The activity may often be misdirected or unwholesome, may sometimes be only feverish and mischievous, a grievous product of narrow information and hasty conclusion; but it is none the less a stirring and potent activity. It at least marks the initial stages of effective thought. It makes men conscious of the existence and interest of affairs lying outside the dull round of their own daily lives. It gives them nations, instead of neighborhoods, to look upon and think about. They catch glimpses of the international connections of their trades, of the universal application of law, of the endless variety of life, of diversities of race, of a world teeming with men like themselves, and yet full of strange customs, puzzled by dim omens, stained by crime, ringing with voices familiar and unfamiliar.

And all this a man can nowadays get without stirring from home, by merely spelling out the print that covers every piece of paper about him. If men are thrown, for any reason, into the swift and easy currents of travel, they find themselves brought daily face to face with persons native of every clime, with practices suggestive of whole histories, with a thousand things which challenge curiosity, inevitably provoking inquiries such as enlarge knowledge of life and shake the mind imperatively loose from old preconceptions.

These are the forces which have established the drift towards democracy. When all sources of information are accessible to all men alike, when the world's thought and the world's news are scattered broadcast where the poorest may find them, the non-democratic forms of government must find life a desperate venture. Exclusive privilege needs privacy, but cannot have it. Kingship of the elder patterns needs sanctity, but can find it nowhere obtainable in a world of news items and satisfied curiosity. The many will no longer receive submissively the thought of a ruling few, but insist upon having opinions of their own. The reaches of public opinion have been infinitely extended; the number of voices that must be heeded in legislation and in executive policy has been infinitely multiplied. Modern influences have inclined every man to clear his throat for a word in the world's debates. They have popularized everything they have touched.

In the newspapers, it is true, there is very little concert between the writers; little but piecemeal opinion is created by their comment and argument; there is no common voice amidst their counsellings. But the aggregate voice thunders with tremendous volume; and that aggregate voice is 'public opinion.' Popular education and cheap printing and travel vastly thicken the ranks of thinkers everywhere where their influence is felt, and by rousing the multitude to take knowledge of the affairs of government prepare the time when the multitude will, so far as possible, take charge of the affairs of government,—the time when, to repeat Carlyle's phrase, democracy will become palpably extant.

But, mighty as such forces are, democratic as they are, no one can fail to perceive that they

are inadequate to produce of themselves such a
government as ours. There is little in them of
constructive efficacy. They could not of themselves build any government at all. They are
critical, analytical, questioning, quizzing forces;
not architectural, not powers that devise and
build. The influences of popular education, of
the press, of travel, of commerce, of the innumerable agencies which nowadays send knowledge
and thought in quick pulsations through every
part and member of society, do not necessarily
mould men for effective endeavor. They may
only confuse and paralyze the mind with their
myriad stinging lashes of excitement. They
may only strengthen the impression that 'the
world's a stage,' and that no one need do more
than sit and look on through his ready glass, the
newspaper. They overwhelm one with impressions, but do they give stalwartness to his
manhood? Do they make his hand any steadier
on the plough, or his purpose any clearer with
reference to the duties of the moment? They
stream light about him, it may be, but do they
clear his vision? Is he better able to see because
they give him countless things to look at? Is he
better able to judge because they fill him with a
delusive sense of knowing everything? Activity
of mind is not necessarily strength of mind.
It may manifest itself in mere dumb show; it
may run into jigs as well as into strenuous work

at noble tasks. A man's farm does not yield its fruits the more abundantly in their season because he reads the world's news in the papers. A merchant's shipments do not multiply because he studies history. Banking is none the less hazardous to the banker's capital and taxing to his powers because the best writing of the best essayists is to be bought cheap.

II

Very different were the forces behind us. Nothing establishes the republican state save trained capacity for self-government, practical aptitude for public affairs, habitual soberness and temperateness of united action. When we look back to the moderate sagacity and stead-fass, self-contained habit in self-government of the men to whom we owe the establishment of our institutions in the United States, we are at once made aware that there is no communion between their democracy and the radical thought and restless spirit called by that name in Europe. There is almost nothing in common between popular outbreaks such as took place in France at her great Revolution and the establishment of a government like our own. Our memories of the year 1789 are as far as possible removed from the memories which Europe retains of that pregnant year. We manifested one hundred years ago what Europe lost, namely, self-command, self-possession. Democracy, in Europe outside of closeted Switzerland, has acted always in rebellion, as a destructive force: it can scarcely be said to have had, even yet, any period of organic development. It has built such temporary governments as it has had opportunity to erect on the old foundations and out of the discredited materials of centralized rule, elevating the people's representatives for a season to the throne, but securing almost as little as ever of that every-day local self-government which lies so near to the heart of liberty. Democracy in America, on the other hand, and in the English colonies has had, almost from the first, a truly organic growth. There was nothing revolutionary in its movements; it had not to overthrow other polities; it had only to organize itself. It had not to create, but only to expand, self-government. It did not need to spread propaganda: it needed nothing but to methodize its ways of living.

In brief, we were doing nothing essentially new a century ago. Our strength and our facility alike inhered in our traditions; those traditions made our character and shaped our institutions. Liberty is not something that can be created by a document; neither is it something which, when created, can be laid away in a document, a completed work. It is an organic principle,—a principle of life, renewing and being renewed. Democratic institutions are never done; they are like living tissue, always a-making. It is a strenuous thing, this of living the life of a free people; and our success in it depends upon training, not upon clever invention.

Our democracy, plainly, was not a body of doctrine; it was a stage of development. Our democratic state was not a piece of developed theory, but a piece of developed habit. It was not created by mere aspirations or by new faith; it was built up by slow custom. Its process was experience, its basis old wont, its meaning national organic oneness and effective life. It came, like manhood, as the fruit of youth. An immature people could not have had it, and the maturity to which it was vouchsafed was the maturity of freedom and self-control. Such government as ours is a form of conduct, and its only stable foundation is character. A particular form of government may no more be adopted than a particular type of character may be adopted: both institutions and character must be developed by conscious effort and through transmitted aptitudes.

Governments such as ours are founded upon discussion, and government by discussion comes as late in political as scientific thought in intellectual development. It is a habit of state life created by long-established circumstance, and is possible for a nation only in the adult age of its political life. The people who successfully maintain such a government must have gone through a period of political training which shall have prepared them by gradual steps of acquired privilege for assuming the entire control of their affairs. Long and slowly widening experience in local self-direction must have prepared them for national self-direction. They must have acquired adult self-reliance, self-knowledge, and self-control, adult soberness and deliberateness of judgment, adult sagacity in self-government, adult vigilance of thought and quickness of insight. When practised, not by small communities, but by wide nations, democracy, far from being a crude form of government, is possible only amongst peoples of the highest and steadiest political habit. It is the heritage of races purged alike of hasty barbaric passions and of patient servility to rulers, and schooled in temperate common counsel. It is an institution of political noonday, not of the half-light of political dawn. It can never be made to sit easily or safely on first generations, but strengthens through long heredity. It is poison to the infant, but tonic to the man. Monarchies may be made, but democracies must grow.

It is a deeply significant fact, therefore, again and again to be called to mind, that only in the

United States, in a few other governments begotten of the English race, and in Switzerland, where old Teutonic habit has had the same persistency as in England, have examples yet been furnished of successful democracy of the modern type. England herself is close upon democracy. Her backwardness in entering upon its full practice is no less instructive as to the conditions prerequisite to democracy than is the forwardness of her offspring. She sent out to all her colonies which escaped the luckless beginning of being made penal settlements, comparatively small, homogeneous populations of pioneers, with strong instincts of self-govern-ment, and with no social materials out of which to build government otherwise than democrati-cally. She herself, meanwhile, retained masses of population never habituated to participation in government, untaught in political principle either by the teachers of the hustings or of the school-house. She has had to approach democ-racy, therefore, by slow and cautious extensions of the franchise to those prepared for it; while her better colonies, born into democracy, have had to receive all comers within their pale. She has been paring down exclusive privileges and levelling classes; the colonies have from the first been asylums of civil equality. They have assimilated new while she has prepared old populations.

Erroneous as it is to represent government as only a commonplace sort of business, little elevated in method above merchandising, and to be regulated by counting-house principles, the favor easily won for such views among our own people is very significant. It means self-reliance in government. It gives voice to the eminently modern democratic feeling that government is no hidden cult, to be left to a few specially prepared individuals, but a common, every-day concern of life, even if the biggest such concern. It is this self-confidence, in many cases mistaken, no doubt, which is gradually spreading among other peoples, less justified in it than are our own.

One cannot help marvelling that facts so obvious as these should have escaped the perception of some of the sagest thinkers and most thorough historical scholars of our day. Yet so it is. Sir Henry Maine, even, the great interpreter to Englishmen of the historical forces operative in law and social institutions, has utterly failed, in his plausible work on "Popular Government," to distinguish the democracy, or rather the popular government, of the English race, which is bred by slow circumstance and founded upon habit, from the democracy of other peoples, which is bred by discontent and founded upon revolution. He has missed that most obvious teaching of events, that successful democracy differs from unsuccessful in being a product of history,—a product of forces not suddenly become operative, but slowly working upon whole peoples for generations together. The level of democracy is the level of every-day habit, the level of common national experiences, and lies far below the elevations of ecstasy to which the revolutionist climbs.

III

While there can be no doubt about the derivation of our government from habit rather than from doctrine, from English experience rather than from European thought; while it is evident that our institutions were originally but products of a long, unbroken, unperverted constitutional history; and certain that we shall preserve our institutions in their integrity and efficiency only so long as we keep true in our practice to the traditions from which our first strength was derived, there is, nevertheless, little doubt that the forces peculiar to the new civilization of our day, and not only these, but also the restless forces of European democratic thought and anarchic turbulence brought to us in such alarming volume by immigration, have deeply affected and may deeply modify the forms and habits of our politics.

All vital governments—and by vital govern-

ments I mean those which have life in their outlying members as well as life in their heads—all
systems in which self-government lives and
retains its self-possession, must be governments
by neighbors, by peoples not only homogeneous,
but characterized within by the existence among
their members of a quick sympathy and an easy
neighborly knowledge of each other. Not foreseeing steam and electricity or the diffusion of
news and knowledge which we have witnessed,
our fathers were right in thinking it impossible
for the government which they had founded to
spread without strain or break over the whole
of the continent. Were not California now as
near neighbor to the Atlantic States as Massachusetts then was to New York, national self-
government on our present scale would assuredly hardly be possible, or conceivable even.
Modern science, scarcely less than our pliancy
and steadiness in political habit, may be said to
have created the United States of to-day.

Upon some aspects of this growth it is very
pleasant to dwell, and very profitable. It is
significant of a strength which it is inspiring to
contemplate. The advantages of bigness ac-
companied by abounding life are many and
invaluable. It is impossible among us to hatch
in a corner any plot which will affect more than
a corner. With life everywhere throughout the
continent, it is impossible to seize illicit power

over the whole people by seizing any central offices. To hold Washington would be as useless to a usurper as to hold Duluth. Self-government cannot be usurped.

A French writer has said that the autocratic ascendency of Andrew Jackson illustrated anew the long-credited tendency of democracies to give themselves over to one hero. The country is older now than it was when Andrew Jackson delighted in his power, and few can believe that it would again approve or applaud childish arrogance and ignorant arbitrariness like his; but even in his case, striking and ominous as it was, it must not be overlooked that he was suffered only to strain the Constitution, not to break it. He held his office by orderly election; he exercised its functions within the letter of the law; he could silence not one word of hostile criticism; and, his second term expired, he passed into private life as harmlessly as did James Monroe. A nation that can quietly reabsorb a vast victorious army is no more safely free and healthy than is a nation that could reabsorb such a President as Andrew Jackson, sending him into seclusion at the Hermitage to live without power, and die almost forgotten.

A huge, stalwart body politic like ours, with quick life in every individual town and county, is apt, too, to have the strength of variety of judgment. Thoughts which in one quarter kindle enthusiasm may in another meet coolness or arouse antagonism. Events which are fuel to the passions of one section may be but as a passing wind to another section. No single moment of indiscretion, surely, can easily betray the whole country at once. There will be entire populations still cool, self-possessed, unaffected. Generous emotions sometimes sweep whole peoples, but, happily, evil passions, sinister views, base purposes, do not and cannot. Sedition cannot surge through the hearts of a wakeful nation as patriotism can. In such organisms poisons diffuse themselves slowly; only healthful life has unbroken course. The sweep of agitations set afoot for purposes unfamiliar or uncongenial to the customary popular thought is broken by a thousand obstacles. It may be easy to reawaken old enthusiasms, but it must be infinitely hard to create new ones, and impossible to surprise a whole people into unpremeditated action.

It is well to give full weight to these great advantages of our big and strenuous and yet familiar way of conducting affairs; but it is imperative at the same time to make very plain the influences which are pointing toward changes in our politics—changes which threaten loss of organic wholeness and soundness. The union of strength with bigness depends upon the maintenance of character, and it is just the character of the nation which is being most deeply affected and modified by the enormous immigration which, year after year, pours into the country from Europe. Our own temperate blood, schooled to self-possession and to the measured conduct of self-government, is receiving a constant infusion and yearly experiencing a partial corruption of foreign blood. Our own equable habits have been crossed with the feverish humors of the restless Old World. We are unquestionably facing an ever-increasing difficulty of self-command with ever-deteriorating materials, possibly with degenerating fibre. We have so far succeeded in retaining

"Some sense of duty, something of a faith,
    Some reverence for the laws ourselves have made,
    Some patient force to change them when we will,
    Some civic manhood firm against the crowd;"

But we must reckon our power to continue to do so with a people made up of "minds cast in every mould of race,—minds inheriting every basis of environment, warped by the diverse histories of a score of different nations, warmed or chilled, closed or expanded, by almost every climate on the globe."

What was true of our early circumstances is not true of our present. We are not now simply carrying out under normal conditions the principles and habits of English constitutional history. Our tasks of construction are not done. We have not simply to conduct, but also to preserve and freshly adjust our government. Europe has sent her habits to us, and she has sent also her political philosophy, a philosophy which has never been purged by the cold bath of practical politics. The communion which we did not have at first with her heated and mistaken ambitions, with her radical, speculative habit in politics, with her readiness to experiment in forms of government, we may possibly have to enter into now that we are receiving her populations. Not only printing and steam and electricity have gotten hold of us to expand our English civilization, but also those general, and yet to us alien, forces of democracy of which mention has already been made; and these are apt to tell disastrously upon our Saxon habits in government.

IV

It is thus that we are brought to our fourth and last point. We have noted (1) the general forces of democracy which have been sapping old forms of government in all parts of the world; (2) the error of supposing ourselves indebted to those forces for the creation of our government, or in any way connected with them in our origins; and (3) the effect they have nevertheless had upon us as parts of the general influences of the age, as well as by reason of our vast immigration from Europe. What, now, are the new problems which have been prepared for our solution by reason of our growth and of the effects of immigration? They may require as much political capacity for their proper solution as any that confronted the architects of our government.

These problems are chiefly problems of organization and leadership. Were the nation homogeneous, were it composed simply of later generations of the same stock by which our institutions were planted, few adjustments of the old machinery of our politics would, perhaps, be necessary to meet the exigencies of growth. But every added element of variety, particularly every added element of foreign variety, complicates even the simpler questions of politics. The dangers attending that variety which is heterogeneity in so vast an organism as ours are, of course, the dangers of disintegration— nothing less; and it is unwise to think these dangers remote and merely contingent because they are not as yet very menacing. We are conscious of oneness as a nation, of vitality, of strength, of progress; but are we often conscious of common thought in the concrete things of national policy? Does not our legislation wear the features of a vast conglomerate? Are we conscious of any national leadership? Are we not, rather, dimly aware of being pulled in a score of directions by a score of crossing influences, a multitude of contending forces?

This vast and miscellaneous democracy of ours must be led; its giant faculties must be schooled and directed. Leadership cannot belong to the multitude; masses of men cannot be self-directed, neither can groups of communities. We speak of the sovereignty of the people, but that sovereignty, we know very well, is of a peculiar sort; quite unlike the sovereignty of a king or of a small, easily concerting group of confident men. It is judicial merely, not creative. It passes judgment or gives sanction, but it cannot direct or suggest. It furnishes standards, not policies. Questions of government are infinitely complex questions, and no multitude can of themselves form clear-cut, comprehensive, consistent conclusions touching them. Yet without such conclusions, without single and prompt purposes, government cannot be carried on. Neither legislation nor administration can be done at the ballot box. The people can only accept the governing act of representatives. But the size of the modern democracy necessitates the exercise of persuasive power by dominant minds in the shaping of popular judgments in a very different way from that in which it was exercised in former times. "It is said by emi-

nent censors of the press," said Mr. Bright on
one occasion in the House of Commons, "that
this debate will yield about thirty hours of talk,
and will end in no result. I have observed that
all great questions in this country require thirty
hours of talk many times repeated before they
are settled. There is much shower and much
sunshine between the sowing of the seed and the
reaping of the harvest, but the harvest is generally reaped after all." So it must be in all self-
governing nations of to-day. They are not a
single audience within sound of an orator's
voice, but a thousand audiences. Their actions
do not spring from a single thrill of feeling, but
from slow conclusions following upon much
talk. The talk must gradually percolate
through the whole mass. It cannot be sent
straight through them so that they are electri-
fied as the pulse is stirred by the call of a trumpet. A score of platforms in every neighborhood
must ring with the insistent voice of controversy; and for a few hundreds who hear what is
said by the public speakers, many thousands
must read of the matter in the newspapers,
discuss it interjectionally at the breakfast-table,
desultorily in the street-cars, laconically on the
streets, dogmatically at dinner; all this with a
certain advantage, of course. Through so many
stages of consideration passion cannot possibly
hold out. It gets chilled by over-exposure. It

finds the modern popular state organized for giving and hearing counsel in such a way that those who give it must be careful that it is such counsel as will wear well. Those who hear it handle and examine it enough to test its wearing qualities to the utmost. All this, however, when looked at from another point of view, but illustrates an infinite difficulty of achieving energy and organization. There is a certain peril almost of disintegration attending such phenomena.

Every one now knows familiarly enough how we accomplished the wide aggregations of self-government characteristic of the modern time, how we have articulated governments as vast and yet as whole as continents like our own. The instrumentality has been representation, of which the ancient world knew nothing, and lacking which it always lacked national integration. Because of representation and the railroads to carry representatives to distant capitals, we have been able to rear colossal structures like the government of the United States as easily as the ancients gave political organization to a city; and our great building is as stout as was their little one.

But not until recently have we been able to see the full effects of thus sending men to legislate for us at capitals distant the breadth of a continent. It makes the leaders of our politics, many of them, mere names to our consciousness instead of real persons whom we have seen and heard, and whom we know. We have to accept rumors concerning them, we have to know them through the variously colored accounts of others; we can seldom test our impressions of their sincerity by standing with them face to face. Here certainly the ancient pocket republics had much the advantage of us: in them citizens and leaders were always neighbors; they stood constantly in each other's presence. Every Athenian knew Themistocles's manner, and gait, and address, and felt directly the just influence of Aristides. No Athenian of a later period needed to be told of the vanities and fopperies of Alcibiades, any more than the elder generation needed to have described to them the personality of Pericles.

Our separation from our leaders is the greater peril, because democratic government more than any other needs organization in order to escape disintegration; and it can have organization only by full knowledge of its leaders and full confidence in them. Just because it is a vast body to be persuaded, it must know its persuaders; in order to be effective, it must always have choice of men who are impersonated policies. Just because none but the finest mental batteries, with pure metals and unadulterated acids, can send a current through so huge and yet so rare a medium as democratic opinion, it is the more necessary to look to the excellence of these instrumentalities. There is no permanent place in democratic leadership except for him who 'hath clean hands and a pure heart.' If other men come temporarily into power among us, it is because we cut our leadership up into so many small parts, and do not subject any one man to the purifying influences of centered responsibility. Never before was consistent leadership so necessary; never before was it necessary to concert measures over areas so vast, to adjust laws to so many interests, to make a compact and intelligible unit out of so many fractions, to maintain a central and dominant force where there are so many forces.

It is a noteworthy fact that the admiration for our institutions which has during the past few years so suddenly grown to large proportions among publicists abroad is almost all of it directed to the restraints we have effected upon the action of government. Sir Henry Maine thought our federal Constitution an admirable reservoir, in which the mighty waters of democracy are held at rest, kept back from free destructive course. Lord Rosebery has wondering praise for the security of our Senate against usurpation of its functions by the House of Representatives. Mr. Goldwin Smith supposes the saving act of organization for a democracy to be the drafting and adoption of a written constitution. Thus it is always the static, never the dynamic, forces of our government which are praised. The greater part of our foreign admirers find our success to consist in the achievement of stable safeguards against hasty or retrogressive action; we are asked to believe that we have succeeded because we have taken Sir Archibald Alison's advice, and have resisted the infection of revolution by staying quite still.

But, after all, progress is motion, government is action. The waters of democracy are useless in their reservoirs unless they may be used to drive the wheels of policy and administration. Though we be the most law-abiding and law-directed nation in the world, law has not yet attained to such efficacy among us as to frame, or adjust, or administer itself. It may restrain, but it cannot lead us; and I believe that unless we concentrate legislative leadership—leadership, that is, in progressive policy—unless we give leave to our nationality and practice to it by such concentration, we shall sooner or later suffer something like national paralysis in the face of emergencies. We have no one in Congress who stands for the nation. Each man stands but for his part of the nation; and so management and combination, which may be

effected in the dark, are given the place that
should be held by centred and responsible
leadership, which would of necessity work in the
focus of the national gaze.

What is the valuable element in monarchy
which causes men constantly to turn to it as to
an ideal form of government, could it but be
kept pure and wise? It is its cohesion, its
readiness and power to act, its abounding loyalty to certain concrete things, to certain visible
persons, its concerted organization, its perfect
model of progressive order. Democracy abounds
with vitality; but how shall it combine with its
other elements of life and strength this power of
the governments that know their own minds
and their own aims? We have not yet reached
the age when government may be made impersonal.

The only way in which we can preserve our
nationality in its integrity and its old-time
originative force in the face of growth and imported change is by concentrating it; by putting
leaders forward, vested with abundant authority in the conception and execution of policy.
There is plenty of the old vitality in our national
character to tell, if we will but give it leave.
Give it leave, and it will the more impress and
mould those who come to us from abroad.
I believe that we have not made enough of
leadership.

> "A people is but the attempt of many
>   To rise to the completer life of one;
> And those who live as models for the mass
>   Are singly of more value than they all."

We shall not again have a true national life until we compact it by such legislative leadership as other nations have. But once thus compacted and embodied, our nationality is safe. An acute English historical scholar has said that "the Americans of the United States are a nation because they once obeyed a king;" we shall remain a nation only by obeying leaders.

> "Keep but the model safe,
>   New men will rise to study it."

V
GOVERNMENT UNDER THE CONSTITUTION

118
119
120

GOVERNMENT UNDER THE CONSTITUTION

IT is by no means wholly to our advantage
that our constitutional law is contained in
definitive written documents. The fact that
it is thus formulated and rendered fixed and
definite has seriously misled us, it is to be feared,
as to the true function and efficacy of constitutional law. That law is not made more valid
by being written, but only more explicit; it is
not rendered more sacred, but only more definite
and secure. Written constitutions are simply
more or less successful generalizations of political experience. Their tone of authority does
not at all alter the historical realities and
imperative practical conditions of government.
They determine forms, utter distinct purposes,
set the powers of the state in definite hierarchy;
but they do not make the forms they originate
workable, or the purposes they utter feasible.
All that must depend upon the men who become
governors and upon the people over whom they
are set in authority. Laws can have no other

life than that which is given them by the men who administer and the men who obey them. Constitutional law affords no exception to the rule. The Constitution of the United States, happily, was framed by exceptional men thoroughly schooled in the realities of government. It consists, accordingly, not of principles newly invented, to be put into operation by means of devices originated for the occasion, but of sound pieces of tested experience. It has served its purpose beneficently, not because it was written, but because it has proved itself accordant in every essential part with tried principles of government—principles tested by the race for whose use it was intended, and therefore already embedded in their lives and practices. Its strength will be found, upon analysis, to lie in its definiteness and in its power to restrain rather than in any unusual excellence of its energetic parts. For the right operation of these it has had to depend, like other constitutions, upon the virtue and discretion of the people and their ministers. "The public powers are carefully defined; the mode in which they are to be exercised is fixed; and the amplest securities are taken that none of the more important constitutional arrangements shall be altered without every guarantee of caution and every opportunity for deliberation. . . . It would seem that, by a wise constitution, democracy may be made nearly as calm as water in a great artificial reservoir.''*

We possess, therefore, not a more suitable constitution than other countries, but a constitution which is perfectly definite and which is preserved by very formidable difficulties of amendment against inconsiderate change. The difference between our own case and that of Great Britain upon which we have most reason to congratulate ourselves is that here public opinion has definite *criteria* for its conservatism; whereas in England it has only shifting and uncertain precedent. In both countries there is the same respect for law. But there is not in England the same certainty as to what the law of the constitution is. We have a fundamental law which is written, and which in its main points is read by all alike in a single accepted sense. There is no more quarrel about its main intent than there is in England about the meaning of Magna Charta. Much of the British constitution, on the contrary, has not the support of even a common statute. It may, in respect of many vital parts of it, be interpreted or understood in half a dozen different ways, *and amended by the prevalent understanding*. We are not more free than the English; we are only more secure.

* Sir Henry Maine: Popular Government (Am. ed.), pp. 110, 111.

The definiteness of our Constitution, nevertheless, apart from its outline of structural arrangements and of the division of functions among the several departments of the government, is negative rather than affirmative. Its very enumeration of the powers of Congress is but a means of indicating very plainly what Congress can *not* do. It is significant that one of the most important and most highly esteemed of the many legal commentaries on our government should be entitled "Constitutional Limitations." In expounding the restrictions imposed by fundamental law upon state and federal action, Judge Cooley is allowed to have laid bare the most essential parts of our constitutional system. It was a prime necessity in so complex a structure that bounds should be set to authority. The 'may-nots' and the 'shall-nots' of our constitutions, consequently, give them their distinctive form and character. The strength which preserves the system is the strength of self-restraint.

And yet here again it must be understood that mere definiteness of legal provision has no saving efficacy of its own. These distinct lines run between power and power will not of their own virtue maintain themselves. It is not in having such a constitution but in obeying it that our advantage lies. The vitality of such provisions consists wholly in the fact that they receive our

acquiescence. They rest upon the legal conscience, upon what Mr. Grote would have
called the 'constitutional morality,' of our race.
They are efficient because we are above all
things law-abiding. The prohibitions of the
law do not assert themselves as taskmasters
set over us by some external power. They are
of our own devising. We are self-restrained.

This legal conscience manifestly constitutes
the only guarantee, for example, of the division
of powers between the state and federal governments, that chief arrangement of our constitutional system. The integrity of the powers
possessed by the states has from the first de-
pended solely upon the conservatism of the
federal courts. State functions have certainly
not decayed; but they have been preserved,
not by virtue of any forces of self-defence of
their own, but because the national government
has been vouchsafed the grace of self-restraint.
What curtailment their province might suffer
has been illustrated in several notable cases
in which the Supreme Court of the United States
has confirmed to the general government exten-
sive powers of punishing state judicial and
executive officers for disobedience to state laws.
Although the federal courts have generally held
Congress back from aggressions upon the states,
they have nevertheless once and again counte-
nanced serious encroachments upon state powers;

and their occasional laxity of principle on such
points is sufficiently significant of the fact that
there is no *balance* between the state and federal
governments, but only the safeguard of a
customary 'constitutional morality' on the part
of the federal courts. The actual encroachments
upon state rights which those courts have permitted, under the pressure of strong political
interests at critical periods, were not, however,
needed to prove the potential supremacy of the
federal government. They only showed how
that potential supremacy would on occasion
become actual supremacy. There is no guarantee but that of conscience that justice will be
accorded a suitor when his adversary is both
court and opposing litigant. So strong is the
instinct of those who administer our governments to keep within the sanction of the law,
that even when the last three amendments to
the Constitution were being forced upon the
southern states by means which were revolutionary the outward forms of the Constitution
were observed. It was none the less obvious,
however, with what sovereign impunity the
national government might act in stripping
those forms of their genuineness. As there are
times of sorrow or of peril which try men's souls
and lay bare the inner secrets of their characters,
so there are times of revolution which act as fire
in burning away all but the basic elements of

constitutions. It is then, too, that dormant powers awake which are not afterwards readily lulled to sleep again.

Such was certainly the effect of the civil war upon the Constitution of the Union. The implying of powers, once cautious, is now become bold and confident. In the discussions now going forward with reference to federal regulation of great corporations, and with reference to federal aid to education, there are scores of writers and speakers who tacitly assume the power of the federal government to act in such matters, for one that urges a constitutional objection. Constitutional objections, before the war habitual, have, it would seem, permanently lost their prominence.

The whole energy of origination under our system rests with Congress. It stands at the front of all government among us; it is the single affirmative voice in national policy. First or last, it determines what is to be done. The President, indeed, appoints officers and negotiates treaties, but he does so subject to the 'yes' of the Senate. Congress organizes the executive departments, organizes the army, organizes the navy. It audits, approves, and pays expenses. It conceives and directs all comprehensive policy. All else is negation. The President says 'no' in his vetoes; the Supreme Court says 'no' in its restraining decisions. And it is as much the law of public opinion as the law of the Constitution that restrains the action of Congress.

It is the habit both of English and American writers to speak of the constitution of Great Britain as if it were 'writ in water,' because nothing but the will of Parliament stands between it and revolutionary change. But is there nothing back of the will of Parliament? Parliament dare not go faster than the public thought. There are vast barriers of conservative public opinion to be overrun before a ruinous speed in revolutionary change can be attained. In the last analysis, our own Constitution has no better safeguard. We have, as I have already pointed out, the salient advantage of knowing just what the standards of our Constitution are. They are formulated in a written code, wherein all men may look and read; whereas many of the designs of the British system are to be sought only in a cloud-land of varying individual readings of affairs. From the constitutional student's point of view, there are, for instance, as many different Houses of Lords as there are writers upon the historical functions of that upper chamber. But the public opinion of Great Britain is no more a juggler of precedents than is the public opinion of this country. Perhaps the absence of a written constitution makes it even less a fancier of logical refinements. The arrangements of the

British constitution have, for all their theoretical instability, a very firm and definite standing in the political habit of Englishmen: and the greatest of those arrangements can be done away with only by the extraordinary force of conscious revolution.

It is wholesome to observe how much of our own institutions rests upon the same basis, upon no other foundations than those that are laid in the opinions of the people. It is within the undoubted constitutional power of Congress, for example, to overwhelm the opposition of the Supreme Court upon any question by increasing the number of justices and refusing to confirm any appointments to the new places which do not promise to change the opinion of the court. Once, at least, it was believed that a plan of this sort had been carried deliberately into effect. But we do not think of such a violation of the spirit of the Constitution as possible, simply because we share and contribute to that public opinion which makes such outrages upon constitutional morality impossible by standing ready to curse them. There is a close analogy between this virtual inviolability of the Supreme Court and the integrity hitherto vouchsafed to the English House of Lords. There may be an indefinite creation of peers at any time that a strong ministry chooses to give the sovereign its imperative advice in favor of such a course. It was, doubtless, fear of the final impression that would be made upon public opinion by action so extraordinary, as much as the timely yielding of the Lords upon the question at issue, that held the ministry back from such a measure, on one notable occasion. Hitherto that ancient upper chamber has had in this regard the same protection that shields our federal judiciary.

It is not essentially a different case as between Congress and the Executive. Here, too, at the very center of the Constitution, Congress stands almost supreme, restrained by public opinion rather than by law. What with the covetous admiration of the presidency recently manifested by some alarmed theorists in England, and the renewal prestige lately given that office by the prominence of the question of civil service reform, it is just now particularly difficult to apply political facts to an analysis of the President's power. But a clear conception of his real position is for that very reason all the more desirable. While he is a dominant figure in politics would seem to be the best time to scrutinize and understand him.

It is clearly misleading to use the ascendant influence of the President in effecting the objects of civil service reform as an illustration of the constitutional size and weight of his office. The principal part in making administration pure, business-like, and efficient must always, under any conceivable system of government, be taken by the executive. It was certainly taken by the executive in England thirty years ago; and that much in opposition to the will of Parliament. The prominence of our President in administrative reform furnishes no sufficient ground for attributing a singularity of executive influence to the government of this country.

In estimating the actual powers of the President it is no doubt best to begin, as almost all writers in England and America now habitually begin, with a comparison between the executives of the two kindred countries. Whilst Mr. Bagehot has done more than any other thinker to clear up the facts of English constitutional practice, he has also, there is reason to believe, done something toward obscuring those facts. Everybody, for instance, has accepted as wholly true his description of the ministry of the Crown as merely an executive committee of the House of Commons; and yet that description is only partially true. An English Cabinet represents, not the Commons only, but also the Crown. Indeed, it is itself 'the Crown.' All executive prerogatives are prerogatives which it is within the discretion of the Cabinet itself to make free use of. The fact that it is generally the disposition of ministers to defer to the opinion of Parliament in the use of the prerogative, does not make that use the less a privilege strictly beyond the sphere of direct parliamentary control, to be exercised independently of its sanction, even secretly on occasion, when ministers see their way clear to serving the state thereby. "The ministry of the day," says a perspicacious expounder of the English system,* "appears in Parliament, on the one hand, as personating the Crown in the legitimate exercise of its recognized prerogatives; and on the other hand, as the mere agent of Parliament itself, in the discharge of the executive and administrative functions of government cast upon them by law." Within the province of the prerogative "lie the stirring topics of foreign negotiations, the management of the army and navy, public finance, and, in some important respects, colonial administration." Very recent English history furnishes abundant and striking evidence of the vitality of the prerogative in these fields in the hands of the gentlemen who 'personate the Crown' in Parliament. "No subject has been more eagerly discussed of late," declares Mr. Amos (page 187), "than that of the province of Parliament in respect of the making of treaties and the declaration of war. No prerogative of the Crown is more undisputed than that of taking the initiative in all negotia-

* Mr. Sheldon Amos: Fifty Years of the English Constitution, p. 338.

tions with foreign governments, conducting
them throughout, and finally completing them
by the signature and ratification of a treaty.
. . . It is a bare fact that during the progress of
the British diplomatic movements which ter-
minated in the Treaty of Berlin of 1878, or more
properly in the Afghan war of that year,"—
including the secret treaty by which Turkey
ceded Cyprus to England, and England assumed the protectorate of Asia Minor,—
"Parliament never had an opportunity of expressing its mind on any one of the important
and complicated engagements to which the
country was being committed, or upon the
policy of the war upon the northwest frontier
of India. The subjects were, indeed, over and
over again discussed in Parliament, but always
subsequent to irreparable action having been
taken by the government" (page 188). Had
Mr. Amos lived to take his narrative of constitutional affairs beyond 1880, he would have had
equally significant instances of ministerial initiative to adduce in the cases of Egypt and
Burmah.

The unfortunate campaign in the Soudan
was the direct outcome of the purchase of the
Suez Canal shares by the British government
in 1875. The result of that purchase was that
"England became pledged in a wholly new and
peculiar way to the support of the existing

Turkish and Egyptian dominion in Egypt; that large English political interests were rendered subservient to the decisions of local tribunals in a foreign country; and that English diplomatic and political action in Egypt, and indeed in Europe, was trammelled, or at least indirectly influenced, by a narrow commercial interest which could not but weigh, however slightly, upon the apparent purity and simplicity of the motives of the English government." And yet the binding engagements which involved all this were entered into "despite the absence of all assistance from, or consent of, Parliament."* Such exercises of the prerogatives of the Crown receive additional weight from "the almost recognized right of evolving an army of almost any size from the Indian seed-plot, of using reserve forces without communication to Parliament in advance, and of obtaining large votes of credit for prospective military operations of an indefinite character, the nature of which Parliament is allowed only dimly to surmise" (page 392). The latest evidence of the 'almost recognized' character of such rights was the war preparations made by England against Russia in 1885. If to such powers of committing the country irrevocably to far-reaching foreign policies, of inviting or precipitating war, and of using Indian troops without embarrassment

* Amos, page 384.

from the trammels of the Mutiny Act, there be added the great discretionary functions involved in the administration of colonial affairs, some measure may be obtained of the power wielded by ministers, not as the mere agents of Parliament, but as personating the Crown. Such is in England the independence of action possible to the executive.

As compared with this, the power of the President is insignificant. Of course, as everybody says, he is more powerful than the sovereign of Great Britain. If relative personal power were the principle of etiquette, Mr. Cleveland would certainly not have to lift his hat to the Queen, because the Queen is not the English executive. The prerogatives of the Crown are still much greater than the prerogatives of the presidency; they are exercised, however, not by the wearer of the crown, but by the ministry of the Crown.

As Sir Henry Maine rightly says, the framers of our Constitution, consciously or unconsciously, made the President's office like the King's office under the English constitution of their time,—the constitution, namely, of George III., who chose his advisers with or without the assent of Parliament. They took care, however, to pare down the model where it seemed out of measure with the exercise of the people's liberty. They allowed the President to choose his minis-

135

ters freely, as George then seemed to have established his right to do; but they made the confirmation of the Senate a necessary condition to his appointments. They vested in him the right of negotiating treaties with foreign governments; but he was not to sign and ratify treaties until he had obtained the sanction of the Senate. That oversight of executive action which Parliament had not yet had the spirit or the inclination to exert, and which it had forfeited its independence by not exerting, was forever secured to our federal upper chamber by the fundamental law. The conditions of mutual confidence and co-operation between executive and legislature now existing in England had not then been developed, and consequently could not be reproduced in this country. The posture and disposition of mutual wariness which were found existing there were made constitutional here by express written provision. In short, the transitional relations of the Crown and Parliament of that day were crystallized in our Constitution, such guarantees of executive good faith and legislative participation in the weightier determinations of government as were lacking in the model being sedulously added in the copy.

The really subordinate position of the presidency is hidden from view partly by that dignity which is imparted to the office by its conspicuous place at the front of a great government, and its security and definiteness of tenure; partly by the independence apparently secured to it by its erection into an entirely distinct and separate 'branch' of the government; and partly by those circumstances of our history which have thrust our Presidents forward, during one or two notable periods, as real originators of policy and leaders in affairs. The President has never been powerful, however, except at such times as he has had Congress at his back. While the new government was a-making—and principally because it was a-making—Washington and his secretaries were looked to by Congress for guidance; and during the presidencies of several of Washington's immediate successors the continued prominence of questions of foreign policy and of financial management kept the officers of the government in a position of semi-leadership. Jackson was masterful with or without right. He entered upon his presidency as he entered upon his campaign in Florida, without asking too curiously for constitutional warrant for what he was to undertake. In the settlement of the southern question Congress went for a time on all-fours with the President. He was powerful because Congress was acquiescent.

But such cases prove rather the usefulness than the strength of the presidency. Congress has, at several very grave crises in national affairs, been seasonably supplied with an energetic leader or agent in the person of the President. At other times, when Congress was in earnest in pushing views not shared by the President, our executives have either been overwhelmed, as Johnson was, or have had to decline upon much humbler services. Their negotiations with foreign governments are as likely to be disapproved as approved; their budgets are cut down like a younger son's portion; their appointments are censured and their administrations criticised without chance for a counter-hearing. They create nothing. Their veto is neither revisory nor corrective. It is merely obstructive. It is, as I have said, a simple blunt negation, oftentimes necessarily spoken without discrimination against a good bill because of a single bad clause in it. In such a contest between origination and negation origination must always win, or government must stand still.

In England the veto of the Crown has not passed out of use, as is commonly said. It has simply changed its form. It does not exist as an imperative, obstructive 'no,' uttered by the sovereign. It has passed over into the privilege of the ministers to throw their party weight, reinforced by their power to dissolve Parliament, against measures of which they disapprove. It is a much-tempered instrument, but for that reason all the more flexible and useful. The old, blunt, antagonistic veto is no longer needed. It is needed here, however, to preserve the presidency from the insignificance of merely administrative functions. Since executive and legislature cannot come into relations of mutual confidence and co-operation, the former must be put in a position to maintain a creditable competition for consideration and dignity.

A clear-headed, methodical, unimaginative President like Mr. Cleveland unaffectedly recognizes the fact that all creating, originating power rests with Congress, and that he can do no more than direct the details of such projects as he finds commended by its legislation. The suggestions of his message he acknowledges to be merely suggestions, which must depend upon public opinion for their weight. If Congress does not regard them, it must reckon with the people, not with him. It is his duty to tell Congress what he thinks concerning the pending questions of the day; it is not his duty to assume any responsibility for the effect produced on Congressmen.

The English have transformed their Crown into a Ministry, and in doing so have recognized both the supremacy of Parliament and the *rôle* of leadership in legislation properly belonging to a responsible executive. The result has been that they have kept a strong executive without abating either the power or the independence of the representative chamber in respect of its legislative function. We, on the contrary, have left our executive separate, as the Constitution made it; chiefly, it is to be suspected, because the explicit and confident gifts of function contained in that positive instrument have blinded us by their very positiveness to the real subordination of the executive resulting from such a separation. We have supposed that our President was great because his powers were specific, and that our Congress was not supreme because it could not lay its hands directly upon his office and turn him out. In fact, neither the dignity and power of the executive nor the importance of Congress is served by the arrangement. Being held off from authoritative suggestion in legislation, the President becomes, under ordinary circumstances, merely a ministerial officer; whilst Congress, on its part, deprived of such leadership, becomes a legislative mass meeting instead of a responsible co-operating member of a well-organized government. Being under the spell of the Constitution, we have been unable to see the facts which written documents can neither establish nor change.

Singularly enough, there is sharp opposition to the introduction into Congress of any such leadership on the part of the executive as the

Ministers of the Crown enjoy in Parliament, on
the ground of the increase of power which would
accrue as a result to the legislature. It is said
that such a change would, by centring party
and personal responsibility in Congress, give
too great a prominence to legislation; would
make Congress the object of too excited an
interest on the part of the people. Legislation
in Parliament, instead of being piecemeal,
tessellated work, such as is made up in Congress
of the various fragments contributed by the
standing committees, is, under each Ministry, a
continuous, consistent, coherent whole; and,
instead of bearing the sanction of both national
parties, is the peculiar policy of only one of
them. It is thought that, if such coherence of
plan, definiteness and continuity of aim, and
sanction of party were to be given the work of
Congress, the resulting concentration of popular
interest and opinion would carry Congress over
all the barriers of the Constitution to an undisputed throne of illimitable power. In short,
the potential supremacy of Congress is thought
to be kept within bounds, not by the constitutional power of the executive and the judiciary,
its co-ordinate branches, but by the intrinsic
dulness and confusion of its own proceedings.
It cannot make itself interesting enough to be
great.

But this is a two-edged argument, which one

must needs handle with great caution. It is evidently calculated to destroy every argument constructed on the assumption that it is written laws which are effective to the salvation of our constitutional arrangements; for it is itself constructed on the opposite assumption, that it is the state of popular interest in the nation which balances the forces of the government. It would, too, serve with equal efficacy against any scheme whatever for reforming the present methods of legislation in Congress, with which almost everybody is dissatisfied. Any reform which should tend to give to national legislation that uniform, open, intelligent, and responsible character which it now lacks, would also create that popular interest in the proceedings of Congress which, it is said, would unhinge the Constitution. Democracy is so delicate a form of government that it must break down if given too great facility or efficacy of operation. No one body of men must be suffered to utter the voice of the people, lest that voice become, through it, directly supreme.

The fact of the overtopping power of Congress, however, remains. The houses create all governmental policy, with that wide latitude of 'political discretion' in the choice of means which the Supreme Court unstintingly accords them. Congress has often come into conflict with the Supreme Court by attempting to extend the province of the federal government as against the states; but it has seldom, I believe, been brought effectually to book for any alleged exercise of powers as against its directly competing branch, the executive. Having by constitutional grant the last word as to foreign relations, the control of the finances, and even the oversight of executive appointments, Congress exercises what powers of direction and management it pleases, as fulfilling, not as straining, the Constitution. Government lives in the origination, not in the defeat, of measures of government. The President obstructs by means of his 'no;' the houses govern by means of their 'yes.' He has killed some policies that are dead; they have given birth to all policies that are alive.

But the measures born in Congress have no common lineage. They have not even a traceable kinship. They are fathered by a score or two of unrelated standing committees: and Congress stands godfather to them all, without discrimination. Congress, in effect, parcels out its great powers amongst groups of its members, and so confuses its plans and obscures all responsibility. It is a leading complaint of Sir Henry Maine's against the system in England, which is just under his nose, that it confers the preliminary shaping and the initiation of all legislation upon the Cabinet, a body which deliberates and resolves in strict secrecy,—and so reminds him, remotely enough, of the Spartan Ephors and the Venetian Council of Ten. He commends, by contrast, that constitution (our own, which he sees at a great distance) which reserves to the legislature itself the origination and drafting of its measures. It is hard for us, who have this commended constitution under our noses, to perceive wherein we have the advantage. British legislation is for the most part originated and shaped by a single committee, acting in secret, whose proposals, when produced, are eagerly debated and freely judged by the sovereign legislative body. Our legislation is framed and initiated by a great many committees, deliberating in secret, whose proposals are seldom debated and only perfunctorily judged by the sovereign legislative body. It is impossible to mistake the position and privileges of the British Cabinet, so great and conspicuous and much discussed are they. They simplify the whole British system for men's comprehension by merely standing at the centre of it. But our own system is simple only in appearance. It is easy to see that our legislature and executive are separate, and that the legislature matures its own measures by means of committees of its own members. But it may readily escape superficial observation that our legislature, instead of being served, is ruled by its committees;

that those committees prepare their measures in private; that their number renders their privacy a secure secrecy, by making them too many to be watched, and individually too insignificant to be worth watching; that their division of prerogatives results in a loss, through diffusion, of all actual responsibility; and that their co-ordination leads to such a competition among them for the attention of their respective houses that legislation is rushed, when it is not paralyzed.

It is thus that, whilst all real power is in the hands of Congress, that power is often thrown out of gear and its exercise brought almost to a standstill. The competition of the committees is the clog. Their reports stand in the way of each other, and so the complaint is warranted that Congress can get nothing done. Interests which press for attention in the nation are reported upon by the appropriate committee, perhaps, but the report gets pushed to the wall. Or they are not reported upon. They are brought to the notice of Congress, but they go to a committee which is unfavorable. The progress of legislation depends both upon the fortunes of competing reports and upon the opinions held by particular committees.

The same system of committee government prevails in our state legislatures, and has led to some notable results, which have recently been pointed out in a pamphlet entitled *American Constitutions*, contributed to the Johns Hopkins series of Studies in History and Political Science by Mr. Horace Davis. In the state legislatures, as in Congress, the origination and control of legislation by standing committees has led to haphazard, incoherent, irresponsible law-making, and to a universal difficulty about getting anything done. The result has been that state legislatures have been falling into disrepute in all quarters. They are despised and mistrusted, and many states have revised their constitutions in order to curtail legislative powers and limit the number and length of legislative sessions. There is in some states an apparent inclination to allow legislators barely time enough to provide moneys for the maintenance of the governments. In some instances necessary powers have been transferred from the legislatures to the courts; in others to the governors. The intent of all such changes is manifest. It is thought safer to entrust power to a law court, performing definite functions under clear laws and in accordance with strict judicial standards, or to a single conspicuous magistrate, who can be watched and cannot escape responsibility for his official acts, than to entrust it to a numerous body which burrows towards its ends in committee-rooms, getting its light through lobbies: and which has a thousand devices for juggling away responsibility, as well as scores of antagonisms wherewith to paralyze itself.

Like fear and distrust have often been felt and expressed of late years concerning Congress, for like reasons. But so far no attempt has been made to restrict either the powers or the time of Congress. Amendments to the Constitution are difficult almost to the point of impossibility, and the few definite schemes nowadays put forward for a revision of the Constitution involve extensions rather than limitations of the powers of Congress. The fact is that, though often quite as exasperating to sober public opinion as any state legislature, Congress is neither so much distrusted nor so deserving of distrust. Its high place and vast sphere in the government of the nation cause its members to be more carefully chosen, and its proceedings to be more closely watched, and frequently controlled by criticism. The whole country has its eyes on Congress, and Congress is aware of the fact. It has both the will and the incentive to be judicious and patriotic. Newspaper editors have constantly to be saying to their readers, 'Look what our state legislators are doing;' they seldom have to urge, 'Look what Congress is doing.' It cannot, indeed, be watched easily, or to much advantage. It requires a distinct effort to watch it. It has no dramatic contests of party leaders to attract notice. Its methods are so much after the fashion of the game of hide-and-seek that the eye of the ordinary man is quite baffled in trying to understand or follow them, if he try only at leisure moments. But, at the same time, the interests handled by Congress are so vast that at least the newspapers and the business men, if no others, must watch its legislation as best they may. However hard it may be to observe, it is too influential in great affairs to make it safe for the country to give over trying to observe it.

But though Congress may always be watched, and so in a measure controlled, despite its clandestine and confusing methods, those methods must tend to increase the distrust with which Congress is widely regarded; and distrust cannot but enervate, belittle, and corrupt this will-centre of the Constitution. The question is not merely, How shall the methods of Congress be clarified and its ways made purposeful and responsible? There is this greater question at stake: How shall the essential arrangements of the Constitution be preserved? Congress is the purposing, designing, aggressive power of the national government. Disturbing and demoralizing influences in the organism, if there be any, come out from its restless energies. Damaging encroachments upon ground forbidden to the federal government generally originate in measures of its planning. So long as it continues to be governed by unrelated standing committees, and to take its resolves in accordance with no clear plan, no single, definite purpose, so long as what it does continues to be neither evident nor interesting, so long must all its exertions of power be invidious; so long must its competition with the executive or the judiciary seem merely jealous and always underhand; so long must it remain virtually impossible to control it through public opinion. As well ask the stranger in the gallery of the New York Stock Exchange to judge of the proceedings on the floor. As well ask a man who has not time to read all the newspapers in the Union to judge of passing sentiment in all parts of the country. Congress in its composition is the country in miniature. It realizes Hobbes's definition of liberty as political power divided into small fragments. The standing committees typify the individuals of the nation. Congress is better fitted for counsel than the voters simply because its members are less than four hundred instead of more than ten million.

It has been impossible to carry out the programme of the Constitution; and, without careful reform, the national legislature will even more dangerously approach the perilous model of a mass meeting. There are several ways in which Congress can be so integrated as to impart to its proceedings system and party responsibility. That may be done by entrusting the preparation and initiation of legislation to a single committee in each house, composed of the leading men of the majority in that house. Such a change would not necessarily affect the present precedents as to the relations between the executive and the legislature. They might still stand stiffly apart. Congress would be integrated and invigorated, however, though the whole system of the government would not be. To integrate that, some common meeting-ground of public consultation must be provided for the executive and the houses. That can be accomplished only by the admission to Congress, in whatever capacity,—whether simply to answer proper questions and to engage in debate, or with the full privileges of membership,—of official representatives of the executive who understand the administration and are interested and able to defend it. Let the tenure of ministers have what disconnection from legislative responsibility may seem necessary to the preservation of the equality of House and Senate, and the separation of administration from legislation; light would at least be thrown upon administration; it would be given the same advantages of public suggestion and un-hampered self-defence that Congress, its competitor has: and Congress would be constrained to apply system and party responsibility to its proceedings.

The establishment in the United States of what is known as 'ministerial responsibility' would unquestionably involve some important changes in our constitutional system. I am strongly of the opinion that such changes would not be too great a price to pay for the advantages secured us by such a government. Ministerial responsibility supplies the only conditions which have yet proved efficacious, in the political experience of the world, for vesting recognized leadership in men chosen for their abilities by a natural selection of debate in a sovereign assembly of whose contests the whole country is witness. Such survival of the ablest in debate seems the only process available for selecting leaders under a popular government. The mere fact that such a contest proceeds with such a result is the strongest possible incentive to men of first-rate powers to enter legislative service; and popular governments, more than any other governments, need leaders so placed that, by direct contact with both the legislative and the executive departments of the government, they shall see the problems of government at first hand; and so trained that they shall at the same time be, not mere administrators, but also men of tact and eloquence, fitted to persuade masses of men and to draw about themselves a loyal following.

If we borrowed ministerial responsibility from England, we should, too, unquestionably enjoy an infinite advantage over the English in the use of it. We should sacrifice by its adoption none of that great benefit and security which our federal system derives from a clear enumeration of powers and an inflexible difficulty of amendment. If anything would be definite under Cabinet government, responsibility would be definite; and, unless I am totally mistaken in my estimate of the legal conscience of the people of this country,—which seems to me to be the heart of our whole system,— definite responsibility will establish rather than shake those arrangements of our Constitution which are really our own, and to which our national pride properly attaches, namely, the distinct division of powers between the state and federal governments, the slow and solemn formalities of constitutional change, and the interpretative functions of the federal courts. If we are really attached to these principles, the concentration of responsibility in government will doubly insure their preservation. If we are not, they are in danger of destruction in any case.

But we cannot have ministerial responsibility in its fulness under the Constitution as it stands.

The most that we can have is distinct legislative responsibility, with or without any connection of co-operation or of mutual confidence between the executive and Congress. To have so much would be an immense gain. Changes made to this end would leave the federal system still an unwieldy mechanism of counteracting forces, still without unity or flexibility; but we should at least have made the very great advance of fastening upon Congress an even more positive form of accountability than now rests upon the President and the courts. Questions of vast importance and infinite delicacy have constantly to be dealt with by Congress; and there is an evident tendency to widen the range of those questions. The grave social and economic problems now thrusting themselves forward, as the result of the tremendous growth and concentration of our population, and the consequent sharp competition for the means of livelihood, indicate that our system is already aging, and that any clumsiness, looseness, or irresponsibility in governmental action must prove a source of grave and increasing peril. There are already commercial heats and political distempers in our body politic which warn of an early necessity for carefully prescribed physic. Under such circumstances, some measure of legislative reform is clearly indispensable. We cannot afford to put up any longer with such legislation as we may happen upon. We must look and plan ahead. We must have legislation which has been definitely forecast in party programmes and explicitly sanctioned by the public voice. Instead of the present arrangements for compromise, piecemeal legislation, we must have coherent plans from recognized party leaders, and means for holding those leaders to a faithful execution of their plans in clear-cut Acts of Congress.

154

MERE LITERATURE
AND OTHER ESSAYS
BY
WOODROW WILSON

MERE LITERATURE.

I.

"MERE LITERATURE."

A SINGULAR phrase this, "mere literature," — the irreverent invention of a scientific age. Literature we know, but "mere" literature? We are not to read it as if it meant *sheer* literature, literature in the essence, stripped of all accidental or ephemeral elements, and left with nothing but its immortal charm and power. "Mere literature" is a serious sneer, conceived in all honesty by the scientific mind, which despises things that do not fall within the categories of demonstrable knowledge. It means *nothing but literature*, as who should say, "mere talk," "mere fabrication," "mere pastime." The scientist, with his head comfortably and excusably full of knowable things, takes nothing seriously and with his hat off, except human knowledge. The creations of the human spirit are, from his point of view, incalculable vagaries, irresponsible phenomena, to be regarded

only as play, and, for the mind's good, only as
recreation, — to be used to while away the tedium
of a railway journey, or to amuse a period of rest
or convalescence; mere byplay, mere make-believe.

And so very whimsical things sometimes happen,
because of this scientific and positivist spirit of the
age, when the study of the literature of any language is made part of the curriculum of our colleges. The more delicate and subtle purposes of
the study are put quite out of countenance, and
literature is commanded to assume the phrases and
the methods of science. It would be very painful
if it should turn out that schools and universities
were agencies of Philistinism; but there are some
things which should prepare us for such a discovery. Our present plans for teaching everybody
involve certain unpleasant things quite inevitably.
It is obvious that you cannot have universal education without restricting your teaching to such things
as can be universally understood. It is plain that
you cannot impart "university methods" to thousands, or create "investigators" by the score,
unless you confine your university education to
matters which dull men can investigate, your laboratory training to tasks which mere plodding dili-
gence and submissive patience can compass. Yet,
if you do so limit and constrain what you teach,

you thrust taste and insight and delicacy of perception out of the schools, exalt the obvious and the merely useful above the things which are only imaginatively or spiritually conceived, make education an affair of tasting and handling and smelling, and so create Philistia, that country in which they speak of "mere literature." I suppose that in Nirvana one would speak in like wise of "mere life."

The fear, at any rate, that such things may happen cannot fail to set us anxiously pondering certain questions about the systematic teaching of literature in our schools and colleges. How are we to impart classical writings to the children of the general public? "Beshrew the general public!" cries Mr. Birrell. "What in the name of the Bodleian has the general public got to do with literature?" Unfortunately, it has a great deal to do with it; for are we not complacently forcing the general public into our universities, and are we not arranging that all its sons shall be instructed how they may themselves master and teach our literature? You have nowadays, it is believed, only to heed the suggestions of pedagogics in order to know how to impart Burke or Browning, Dryden or Swift. There are certain practical difficulties, indeed; but there are ways of overcoming them. You must have strength if you would handle with real mastery the firm fibre of these men ; you must have a heart, moreover, to feel their warmth, an eye to see what they see, an imagination to keep them company, a pulse to experience their delights. But if you have none of these things, you may make shift to do without them. You may count the words they use, instead, note the changes of phrase they make in successive revisions, put their rhythm into a scale of feet, run their allusions — particularly their female allusions — to cover, detect them in their previous reading. Or, if none of these things please you, or you find the big authors difficult or dull, you may drag to light all the minor writers of their time, who are easy to understand. By setting an example in such methods you render great services in certain directions. You make the higher degrees of our universities available for the large number of respectable men who can count, and measure, and search diligently ; and that may prove no small matter. You divert attention from thought, which is not always easy to get at, and fix attention upon language, as upon a curious mechanism, which can be perceived with the bodily eye, and which is worthy to be studied for its own sake, quite apart from anything it may mean. You encourage the examination of forms, grammatical and metrical,

which can be quite accurately determined and quite
exhaustively catalogued. You bring all the visible
phenomena of writing to light and into ordered
system. You go further, and show how to make
careful literal identification of stories somewhere
told ill and without art with the same stories told
over again by the masters, well and with the trans-
figuring effect of genius. You thus broaden the
area of science; for you rescue the concrete phenomena of the expression of thought — the necessary syllabification which accompanies it, the inevitable juxtaposition of words, the constant use of
particles, the habitual display of roots, the inveterate repetition of names, the recurrent employment
of meanings heard or read — from their confusion
with the otherwise unclassifiable manifestations of
what had hitherto been accepted, without critical
examination, under the lump term "literature,"
simply for the pleasure and spiritual edification to
be got from it.

An instructive differentiation ensues. In contrast with the orderly phenomena of speech and
writing, which are amenable to scientific processes
of examination and classification, and which take
rank with the orderly successions of change in
nature, we have what, for want of a more exact
term, we call "mere literature," — the literature

which is not an expression of form, but an expression of spirit. This is a fugitive and troublesome thing, and perhaps does not belong in well-conceived plans of universal instruction; for it offers many embarrassments to pedagogic method. It escapes all scientific categories. It is not pervious to research. It is too wayward to be brought under the discipline of exposition. It is an attribute of so many different substances at one and the same time, that the consistent scientific man must needs put it forth from his company, as without responsible connections. By "mere literature" he means mere evanescent color, wanton trick of phrase, perverse departures from categorical statement,— something *all* personal equation, such stuff as dreams are made of.

We must not all, however, be impatient of this truant child of fancy. When the schools cast her out, she will stand in need of friendly succor, and we must train our spirits for the function. We must be free-hearted in order to make her happy, for she will accept entertainment from no sober, prudent fellow who shall counsel her to mend her ways. She has always made light of hardship, and she has never loved or obeyed any, save those who were of her own mind,— those who were indulgent to her humors, responsive to her ways of

thought, attentive to her whims, content with her
"mere" charms. She already has her small following of devotees, like all charming, capricious
mistresses. There are some still who think that
to know her is better than a liberal education.

There is but one way in which you can take
mere literature as an education, and that is directly,
at first hand. Almost any media except her own
language and touch and tone are non-conducting.
A descriptive catalogue of a collection of paintings
is no substitute for the little areas of color and
form themselves. You do not want to hear about
a beautiful woman, simply, — how she was dressed,
how she bore herself, how the fine color flowed
sweetly here and there upon her cheeks, how her
eyes burned and melted, how her voice thrilled
through the ears of those about her. If you have
ever seen a woman, these things but tantalize and
hurt you, if you cannot see her. You want to be
in her presence. You know that only your own
eyes can give you direct knowledge of her. Nothing but her presence contains her life. 'T is
the same with the authentic products of literature.
You can never get their beauty at second hand, or
feel their power except by direct contact with them.

It is a strange and occult thing how this quality
of "mere literature" enters into one book, and is

absent from another; but no man who has once felt it can mistake it. I was reading the other day a book about Canada. It is written in what the reviewers have pronounced to be an " admirable, spirited style." By this I take them to mean that it is grammatical, orderly, and full of strong adjectives. But these reviewers would have known more about the style in which it is written if they had noted what happens on page 84. There a quotation from Burke occurs. " There is," says Burke, " but one healing, catholic principle of toleration which ought to find favor in this house. It is wanted not only in our colonies, but here. The thirsty earth of our own country is gasping and gaping and crying out for that healing shower from heaven. The noble lord has told you of the right of those people by treaty; but I consider the right of conquest so little, and the right of human nature so much, that the former has very little consideration with me. I look upon the people of Canada as coming by the dispensation of God under the British government. I would have us govern it in the same manner as the all-wise disposition of Providence would govern it. We know he suffers the sun to shine upon the righteous and the unrighteous; and we ought to suffer all classes to enjoy equally the right of worshiping God accord-

ing to the light he has been pleased to give them."
The peculiarity of such a passage as that is, that it
needs no context. Its beauty seems almost independent of its subject matter. It comes on that
eighty-fourth page like a burst of music in the
midst of small talk, — a tone of sweet harmony
heard amidst a rattle of phrases. The mild noise
was unobjectionable enough until the music came.
There is a breath and stir of life in those sentences
of Burke's which is to be perceived in nothing else
in that volume. Your pulses catch a quicker
movement from them, and are stronger on their
account.

It is so with all essential literature. It has a
quality to move you, and you can never mistake it,
if you have any blood in you. And it has also a
power to instruct you which is as effective as it is
subtle, and which no research or systematic method
can ever rival. 'T is a sore pity if that power cannot be made available in the classroom. It is not
merely that it quickens your thought and fills your
imagination with the images that have illuminated
the choicer minds of the race. It does indeed exercise the faculties in this wise, bringing them into
the best atmosphere, and into the presence of the
men of greatest charm and force; but it does a
great deal more than that. It acquaints the mind,

by direct contact, with the forces which really govern and modify the world from generation to generation.   There is more of a nation's politics to be
got out of its poetry than out of all its systematic
writers upon public affairs and constitutions. Epics
are better mirrors of manners than chronicles;
dramas oftentimes let you into the secrets of statutes; orations stirred by a deep energy of emotion
or resolution, passionate pamphlets that survive their
mission because of the direct action of their style
along permanent lines of thought, contain more
history than parliamentary journals.   It is not
knowledge that moves the world, but ideals, convictions, the opinions or fancies that have been held
or followed; and whoever studies humanity ought
to study it alive, practice the vivisection of reading
literature, and acquaint himself with something
more than anatomies which are no longer in use by
spirits.

There are some words of Thibaut, the great
jurist, which have long seemed to me singularly
penetrative of one of the secrets of the intellectual
life.   "I told him," he says, — he is speaking of
an interview with Niebuhr, — "I told him that I
owed my gayety and vigor, in great part, to my
love for the classics of all ages, even those outside
the domain of jurisprudence."   Not only the gayety

and vigor of his hale old age, surely, but also his insight into the meaning and purpose of laws and institutions. The jurist who does not love the classics of all ages is like a post-mortem doctor presiding at a birth, a maker of manikins prescribing for a disease of the blood, a student of masks setting up for a connoisseur in smiles and kisses. In narrating history, you are speaking of what was done by men; in discoursing of laws, you are seeking to show what courses of action, and what manner of dealing with one another, men have adopted. You can neither tell the story nor conceive the law till you know how the men you speak of regarded themselves and one another; and I know of no way of learning this but by reading the stories they have told of themselves, the songs they have sung, the heroic adventures they have applauded. I must know what, if anything, they revered; I must hear their sneers and gibes; must learn in what accents they spoke love within the family circle; with what grace they obeyed their superiors in station; how they conceived it politic to live, and wise to die; how they esteemed property, and what they deemed privilege; when they kept holiday, and why; when they were prone to resist oppression, and wherefore, — I must see things with their eyes, before I can comprehend their law books. Their jural re-

lationships are not independent of their way of living, and their way of thinking is the mirror of their
way of living.

It is doubtless due to the scientific spirit of the
age that these plain, these immemorial truths are
in danger of becoming obscured. Science, under
the influence of the conception of evolution, devotes
itself to the study of forms, of specific differences,
of the manner in which the same principle of life
manifests itself variously under the compulsions of
changes of environment. It is thus that it has become " scientific " to set forth the manner in which
man's nature submits to man's circumstances;
scientific to disclose morbid moods, and the conditions which produce them; scientific to regard
man, not as the centre or source of power, but as
subject to power, a register of external forces instead of an originative soul, and character as a
product of man's circumstances rather than a sign
of man's mastery over circumstance. It is thus
that it has become " scientific " to analyze language as itself a commanding element in man's life.
The history of word-roots, their modification under
the influences of changes wrought in the vocal
organs by habit or by climate, the laws of phonetic
change to which they are obedient, and their persistence under all disguises of dialect, as if they

were full of a self-originated life, a self-directed
energy of influence, is united with the study of
grammatical forms in the construction of scientific
conceptions of the evolution and uses of human
speech. The impression is created that literature
is only the chosen vessel of these forms, disclosing
to us their modification in use and structure from
age to age. Such vitality as the masterpieces of
genius possess comes to seem only a dramatization
of the fortunes of words. Great writers construct
for the adventures of language their appropriate
epics. Or, if it be not the words themselves that
are scrutinized, but the style of their use, that style
becomes, instead of a fine essence of personality, a
matter of cadence merely, or of grammatical and
structural relationships. Science is the study of
the forces of the world of matter, the adjustments,
the apparatus, of the universe; and the scientific
study of literature has likewise become a study of
apparatus, — of the forms in which men utter
thought, and the forces by which those forms have
been and still are being modified, rather than of
thought itself.

The essences of literature of course remain the
same under all forms, and the true study of literature is the study of these essences, — a study, not
of forms or of differences, but of likenesses, — like-

nesses of spirit and intent under whatever varieties of method, running through all forms of speech like the same music along the chords of various instruments. There is a sense in which literature is independent of form, just as there is a sense in which music is independent of its instrument. It is my cherished belief that Apollo's pipe contained as much eloquent music as any modern orchestra. Some books live; many die: wherein is the secret of immortality? Not in beauty of form, nor even in force of passion. We might say of literature what Wordsworth said of poetry, the most easily immortal part of literature: it is "the impassioned expression which is in the countenance of all science; it is the breath of the finer spirit of all knowledge." Poetry has the easier immortality because it has the sweeter accent when it speaks, because its phrases linger in our ears to delight them, because its truths are also melodies. Prose has much to overcome, — its plainness of visage, its less musical accents, its homelier turns of phrase. But it also may contain the immortal essence of truth and seriousness and high thought. It too may clothe conviction with the beauty that must make it shine forever. Let a man but have beauty in his heart, and, believing something with his might, put it forth arrayed as he sees it, the lights and shadows falling upon it on his page as they fall upon it in his heart, and he may die assured that that beauty will not pass away out of the world.

Biographers have often been puzzled by the contrast between certain men as they lived and as they wrote. Schopenhauer's case is one of the most singular. A man of turbulent life, suffering himself to be cut to exasperation by the petty worries of his lot, he was nevertheless calm and wise when he wrote, as if the Muse had rebuked him. He wrote at a still elevation, where small and temporary things did not come to disturb him. 'T is a pity that for some men this elevation is so far to seek. They lose permanency by not finding it. Could there be a deliberate regimen of life for the author, it is plain enough how he ought to live, not as seeking fame, but as deserving it.

> " Fame, like a wayward girl, will still be coy
> To those who woo her with too slavish knees ;
> But makes surrender to some thoughtless boy,
> And dotes the more upon a heart at ease.
>
> .   .   .   .
>
> " Ye love-sick bards, repay her scorn with scorn ;
> Ye love-sick artists, madmen that ye are,
> Make your best bow to her and bid adieu ;
> Then, if she likes it, she will follow you."

It behooves all minor authors to realize the possibility of their being discovered some day, and exposed to the general scrutiny. They ought to live as if conscious of the risk. They ought to purge their hearts of everything that is not genuine and capable of lasting the world a century, at least, if need be. Mere literature is made of spirit. The difficulties of style are the artist's difficulties with his tools. The spirit that is in the eye, in the pose, in mien or gesture, the painter must find in his color-box; as he must find also the spirit that nature displays upon the face of the fields or in the hidden places of the forest. The writer has less obvious means. Word and spirit do not easily consort. The language which the philologists set out before us with such curious erudition is of very little use as a vehicle for the essences of the human spirit. It is too sophisticated and self-conscious. What you need is, not a critical knowledge of language, but a quick feeling for it. You must recognize the affinities between your spirit and its idioms. You must immerse your phrase in your thought, your thought in your phrase, till each becomes saturated with the other. Then what you produce is as necessarily fit for permanency as if it were incarnated spirit.

And you must produce in color, with the touch of imagination which lifts what you write away from the dull levels of mere exposition. Black-

and-white sketches may serve some purposes of the artist, but very little of actual nature is in mere black-and-white. The imagination never works thus with satisfaction. Nothing is ever conceived completely when conceived so grayly, without suffusion of real light. The mind creates, as great Nature does, in colors, with deep chiaroscuro and burning lights. This is true not only of poetry and essentially imaginative writing, but also of the writing which seeks nothing more than to penetrate the meaning of actual affairs, — the writing of the greatest historians and philosophers, the utterances of orators and of the great masters of political exposition. Their narratives, their analyses, their appeals, their conceptions of principle, are all dipped deep in the colors of the life they expound. Their minds respond only to realities, their eyes see only actual circumstance. Their sentences quiver and are quick with visions of human affairs, — how minds are bent or governed, how action is shaped or thwarted. The great " constructive " minds, as we call them, are of this sort. They " construct " by seeing what others have not imagination enough to see. They do not always know more, but they always realize more. Let the singular reconstruction of Roman history and institutions by Theodor Mommsen serve as an illustration. Safe men distrust this great master. They cannot find what he finds in the documents. They will draw you truncated figures of the antique Roman state, and tell you the limbs cannot be found, the features of the face have nowhere been unearthed. They will cite you fragments such as remain, and show you how far these can be pieced together toward the making of a complete description of private life and public function in those first times when the Roman commonwealth was young; but what the missing sentences were they can only weakly conjecture. Their eyes cannot descry those distant days with no other aids than these. Only the greatest are dissatisfied, and go on to paint that ancient life with the materials that will render it lifelike, — the materials of the constructive imagination. They have other sources of information. They see living men in the old documents. Give them but the torso, and they will supply head and limbs, bright and animate as they must have been. If Mommsen does not quite do that, another man, with Mommsen's eye and a touch more of color on his brush, might have done it, — may yet do it.

It is in this way that we get some glimpse of the only relations that scholarship bears to literature. Literature can do without exact scholarship, or any scholarship at all, though it may impoverish itself thereby; but scholarship cannot do without literature. It needs literature to float it, to set it current, to authenticate it to the race, to get it out of closets, and into the brains of men who stir abroad. It will adorn literature, no doubt; literature will be the richer for its presence; but it will not, it cannot, of itself create literature. Rich stuffs from the East do not create a king, nor warlike trappings a conqueror. There is, indeed, a natural antagonism, let it be frankly said, between the standards of scholarship and the standards of literature. Exact scholarship values things in direct proportion as they are verifiable; but literature knows nothing of such tests. The truths which it seeks are the truths of self-expression. It is a thing of convictions, of insights, of what is felt and seen and heard and hoped for. Its meanings lurk behind nature, not in the facts of its phenomena. It speaks of things as the man who utters it saw them, not necessarily as God made them. The personality of the speaker runs throughout all the sentences of real literature. That personality may not be the personality of a poet: it may be only the personality of the penetrative seer. It may not have the atmosphere in which visions are seen, but only that in which men and affairs look keenly cut in outline, boldly massed in bulk, consummately grouped in detail, to the reader as to the writer. Sentences of perfectly clarified wisdom may be literature no less than stanzas of inspired song, or the intense utterances of impassioned feeling. The personality of the sunlight is in the keen lines of light that run along the edges of a sword no less than in the burning splendor of the rose or the radiant kindlings of a woman's eye. You may feel the power of one master of thought playing upon your brain as you may feel that of another playing upon your heart.

Scholarship gets into literature by becoming part of the originating individuality of a master of thought. No man is a master of thought without being also a master of its vehicle and instrument, style, that subtle medium of all its evasive effects of light and shade. Scholarship is material; it is not life. It becomes immortal only when it is worked upon by conviction, by schooled and chastened imagination, by thought that runs alive out of the inner fountains of individual insight and purpose. Colorless, or without suffusion of light from some source of light, it is dead, and will not twice be looked at; but made part of the life of a great mind, subordinated, absorbed, put forth with authentic stamp of currency on it, minted at some definite mint and bearing some sovereign image, it

will even outlast the time when it shall have ceased
to deserve the acceptance of scholars, — when it
shall, in fact, have become " mere literature."

Scholarship is the realm of nicely adjusted opinion. It is the business of scholars to assess evidence and test conclusions, to discriminate values
and reckon probabilities. Literature is the realm
of conviction and vision. Its points of view are as
various as they are oftentimes unverifiable. It
speaks individual faiths. Its groundwork is not
erudition, but reflection and fancy. Your thorough-
going scholar dare not reflect. To reflect is to let
himself in on his material; whereas what he wants
is to keep himself apart, and view his materials in
an air that does not color or refract. To reflect is
to throw an atmosphere about what is in your
mind, — an atmosphere which holds all the colors
of your life. Reflection summons all associations,
and they so throng and move that they dominate
the mind's stage at once. The plot is in their
hands. Scholars, therefore, do not reflect; they
label, group kind with kind, set forth in schemes,
expound with dispassionate method. Their minds
are not stages, but museums; nothing is done
there, but very curious and valuable collections are
kept there. If literature use scholarship, it is only
to fill it with fancies or shape it to new standards,
of which of itself it can know nothing.

True, there are books reckoned primarily books of science and of scholarship which have nevertheless won standing as literature; books of science such as Newton wrote, books of scholarship such as Gibbon's. But science was only the vestibule by which such a man as Newton entered the temple of nature, and the art he practiced was not the art of exposition, but the art of divination. He was not only a scientist, but also a seer; and we shall not lose sight of Newton because we value what he was more than what he knew. If we continue Gibbon in his fame, it will be for love of his art, not for worship of his scholarship. We some of us, nowadays, know the period of which he wrote better even than he did; but which one of us shall build so admirable a monument to ourselves, as artists, out of what we know? The scholar finds his immortality in the form he gives to his work. It is a hard saying, but the truth of it is inexorable: be an artist, or prepare for oblivion. You may write a chronicle, but you will not serve yourself thereby. You will only serve some fellow who shall come after you, possessing, what you did not have, an ear for the words you could not hit upon; an eye for the colors you could not see; a hand for the strokes you missed.

Real literature you can always distinguish by its

form, and yet it is not possible to indicate the form it should have. It is easy to say that it should have a form suitable to its matter ; but how suitable? Suitable to set the matter off, adorn, embellish it, or suitable simply to bring it directly, quick and potent, to the apprehension of the reader? This is the question of style, about which many masters have had many opinions ; upon which you can make up no safe generalization from the practice of those who have unquestionably given to the matter of their thought immortal form, an accent or a countenance never to be forgotten. Who shall say how much of Burke's splendid and impressive imagery is part and stuff of his thought, or tell why even that part of Newman's prose which is devoid of ornament, stripped to its shining skin, and running bare and lithe and athletic to carry its tidings to men, should promise to enjoy as certain an immortality? Why should Lamb go so quaintly and elaborately to work upon his critical essays, taking care to perfume every sentence, if possible, with the fine savor of an old phrase, if the same business could be as effectively done in the plain and even cadences of Mr. Matthew Arnold's prose? Why should Gibbon be so formal, so stately, so elaborate, when he had before his eyes the example of great Tacitus, whose direct, sententious style had

outlived by so many hundred years the very language in which he wrote? In poetry, who shall
measure the varieties of style lavished upon similar
themes? The matter of vital thought is not separable from the thinker; its forms must suit his
handling as well as fit his conception. Any style
is author's stuff which is suitable to his purpose and
his fancy. He may use rich fabrics with which to
costume his thoughts, or he may use simple stone
from which to sculpture them, and leave them
bare. His only limits are those of art. He may
not indulge a taste for the merely curious or fan-
tastic. The quaint writers have quaint thoughts;
their material is suitable. They do not merely
satisfy themselves as virtuosi, with collections of
odd phrases and obsolete meanings. They needed
twisted words to fit the eccentric patterns of their
thought. The great writer has always dignity, restraint, propriety, adequateness; what time he
loses these qualities he ceases to be great. His
style neither creaks nor breaks under his passion,
but carries the strain with unshaken strength. It
is not trivial or mean, but speaks what small meanings fall in its way with simplicity, as conscious of
their smallness. Its playfulness is within bounds;
its laugh never bursts too boisterously into a
guffaw. A great style always knows what it would

be at, and does the thing appropriately, with the larger sort of taste.

This is the condemnation of tricks of phrase, devices to catch the attention, exaggerations and loud talk to hold it. No writer can afford to strive after effect, if his striving is to be apparent. For just and permanent effect is missed altogether unless it be so completely attained as to seem like some touch of sunlight, perfect, natural, inevitable, wrought without effort and without deliberate purpose to be effective. Mere audacity of attempt can, of course, never win the wished for result; and if the attempt be successful, it is not audacious. What we call audacity in a great writer has no touch of temerity, sauciness, or arrogance in it. It is simply high spirit, a dashing and splendid display of strength. Boldness is ridiculous unless it be impressive, and it can be impressive only when backed by solid forces of character and attainment. Your plebeian hack cannot afford the showy paces; only the full-blooded Arabian has the sinew and proportion to lend them perfect grace and propriety. The art of letters eschews the bizarre as rigidly as does every other fine art. It mixes its colors with brains, and is obedient to great Nature's sane standards of right adjustment in all that it attempts.

You can make no catalogue of these features of great writing; there is no science of literature. Literature in its essence is mere spirit, and you must experience it rather than analyze it too formally. It is the door to nature and to ourselves. It opens our hearts to receive the experiences of great men and the conceptions of great races. It awakens us to the significance of action and to the singular power of mental habit. It airs our souls in the wide atmosphere of contemplation. "In these bad days, when it is thought more educationally useful to know the principle of the common pump than Keats' Ode on a Grecian Urn," as Mr. Birrell says, we cannot afford to let one single precious sentence of "mere literature" go by us unread or unpraised. If this free people to which we belong is to keep its fine spirit, its perfect temper amidst affairs, its high courage in the face of difficulties, its wise temperateness and wide-eyed hope, it must continue to drink deep and often from the old wells of English undefiled, quaff the keen tonic of its best ideals, keep its blood warm with all the great utterances of exalted purpose and pure principle of which its matchless literature is full. The great spirits of the past must command us in the tasks of the future. Mere literature will keep us pure and keep us strong.

Even though it puzzle or altogether escape scientific method, it may keep our horizon clear for us, and our eyes glad to look bravely forth upon the world.

II.

THE AUTHOR HIMSELF.

WHO can help wondering, concerning the modern
multitude of books, where all these companions of
his reading hours will be buried when they die;
which will have monuments erected to them; which
escape the envy of time and live? It is pathetic
to think of the number that must be forgotten,
after having been removed from the good places to
make room for their betters.

Much the most pathetic thought about books,
however, is that excellence will not save them.
Their fates will be as whimsical as those of the
humankind which produces them. Knaves find it
as easy to get remembered as good men. It is not
right living or learning or kind offices, simply and
of themselves, but — something else that gives
immortality of fame. Be a book never so scholarly, it may die; be it never so witty, or never so
full of good feeling and of an honest statement
of truth, it may not live.

When once a book has become immortal, we
think that we can see why it became so. It contained,

we perceive, a casting of thought which could not but arrest and retain men's attention; it said some things once and for all because it gave them their best expression. Or else it spoke with a grace or with a fire of imagination, with a sweet cadence of phrase and a full harmony of tone, which have made it equally dear to all generations of those who love the free play of fancy or the incomparable music of perfected human speech. Or perhaps it uttered with candor and simplicity some universal sentiment; perchance pictured something in the tragedy or the comedy of man's life as it was never pictured before, and must on that account be read and read again as not to be superseded. There must be something special, we judge, either in its form or in its substance, to account for its unwonted fame and fortune.

This upon first analysis, taking one book at a time. A look deeper into the heart of the matter enables us to catch at least a glimpse of a single and common source of immortality. The world is attracted by books as each man is attracted by his several friends. You recommend that capital fellow So-and-So to the acquaintance of others because of his discriminating and diverting powers of observation: the very tones and persons — it would seem the very selves — of every type of man live again in his mimicries and descriptions. He is the dramatist of your circle; you can never forget him, nor can any one else; his circle of acquaintances can never grow smaller. Could he live on and retain perennially that wonderful freshness and vivacity of his, he must become the most famous guest and favorite of the world. Who that has known a man quick and shrewd to see dispassionately the inner history, the reason and the ends, of the combinations of society, and at the same time eloquent to tell of them, with a hold on the attention gained by a certain quaint force and sagacity resident in no other man, can find it difficult to understand why we still resort to Montesquieu? Possibly there are circles favored of the gods who have known some fellow of infinite store of miscellaneous and curious learning, who has greatly diverted both himself and his friends by a way peculiar to himself of giving it out upon any and all occasions, item by item, as if it were all homogeneous and of a piece, and by his odd skill in making unexpected application of it to out-of-the-way, unpromising subjects, as if there were in his view of things mental no such disintegrating element as incongruity. Such a circle would esteem it strange were Burton not beloved of the world. And so of those, if any there be, who have known men of simple, calm, transparent natures, untouched by storm or perplexity, whose talk was full of such serious, placid reflection as seemed to mirror their own reverent hearts, — talk often prosy, but more often touchingly beautiful, because of its nearness to nature and the solemn truth of life. There may be those, also, who have felt the thrill of personal contact with some stormy peasant nature full of strenuous, unsparing speech concerning men and affairs. These have known why a Wordsworth or a Carlyle must be read by all generations of those who love words of first-hand inspiration. In short, in every case of literary immortality originative personality is present. Not origination simply, — that may be mere invention, which in literature has nothing immortal about it; but origination which takes its stamp and character from the originator, which is his spirit given to the world, which is himself outspoken.

Individuality does not consist in the use of the very personal pronoun, *I:* it consists in tone, in method, in attitude, in point of view; it consists in saying things in such a way that you will yourself be recognized as a force in saying them. Do we not at once know Lamb when he speaks? And even more formal Addison, does not his speech bewray and endear him to us? His personal charm is less distinct, much less fascinating, than that which goes with what Lamb speaks, but a charm he has sufficient for immortality. In Steele the matter is more impersonal, more mortal. Some of Dr. Johnson's essays, you feel, might have been written by a dictionary. It is impersonal matter that is dead matter. Are you asked who fathered a certain brilliant, poignant bit of political analysis? You say, Why, only Bagehot could have written that. Does a wittily turned verse make you hesitate between laughter at its hit and grave thought because of its deeper, covert meaning? Do you not know that only Lowell could do that? Do you catch a strain of pure Elizabethan music and doubt whether to attribute it to Shakespeare or to another? Do you not *know* the authors who still live?

Now, the noteworthy thing about such individuality is that it will not develop under every star, or in one place just as well as in another; there is an atmosphere which kills it, and there is an atmosphere which fosters it. The atmosphere which kills it is the atmosphere of sophistication, where cleverness and fashion and knowingness thrive: cleverness, which is froth, not strong drink; fashion, which is a thing assumed, not a thing of nature; and knowingness, which is naught.

Of course there are born, now and again, as

tokens of some rare mood of Nature, men of so intense and individual a cast that circumstance and surroundings affect them little more than friction affects an express train. They command their own development without even the consciousness that to command costs strength. These cannot be sophisticated ; for sophistication is subordination to the ways of your world. But these are the very greatest and the very rarest ; and it is not the greatest and the rarest alone who shape the world and its thought. That is done also by the great and the merely extraordinary. There is a rank and file in literature, even in the literature of immortality, and these must go much to school to the people about them.

It is by the number and charm of the individualities which it contains that the literature of any country gains distinction. We turn anywhither to know men. The best way to foster literature, if it may be fostered, is to cultivate the author himself, — a plant of such delicate and precarious growth that special soils are needed to produce it in its full perfection. The conditions which foster individuality are those which foster simplicity, thought and action which are direct, naturalness, spontaneity. What are these conditions ?

In the first place, a certain helpful ignorance.

It is best for the author to be born away from literary centres, or to be excluded from their ruling
set if he be born in them. It is best that he start
out with his thinking, not knowing how much has
been thought and said about everything. A certain
amount of ignorance will insure his sincerity, will
increase his boldness and shelter his genuineness,
which is his hope of power. Not ignorance of life,
but life may be learned in any neighborhood ; —
not ignorance of the greater laws which govern
human affairs, but they may be learned without a
library of historians and commentators, by imaginative sense, by seeing better than by reading ; — not
ignorance of the infinitudes of human circumstance,
but these may be perceived without the intervention
of universities ; — not ignorance of one's self and
of one's neighbor; but innocence of the sophistica-
tions of learning, its research without love, its knowledge without inspiration, its method without grace ;
freedom from its shame at trying to know many
things as well as from its pride of trying to know
but one thing ; ignorance of that faith in small confounding facts which is contempt for large reassur-
ing principles.

Our present problem is not how to clarify our
reasonings and perfect our analyses, but how to
reënrich and reënergize our literature. That litera-

ture is suffering, not from ignorance, but from sophistication and self-consciousness; and it is suffering hardly less from excess of logical method. Ratiocination does not keep us pure, render us earnest, or make us individual and specific forces in the world. Those inestimable results are accomplished by whatever implants principle and conviction, whatever quickens with inspiration, fills with purpose and courage, gives outlook, and makes character. Reasoned thinking does indeed clear the mind's atmospheres and lay open to its view fields of action; but it is loving and believing, sometimes hating and distrusting, often prejudice and passion, always the many things which we call the one thing, character, which create and shape our acting. Life quite overtowers logic. Thinking and erudition alone will not equip for the great tasks and triumphs of life and literature: the persuading of other men's purposes, the entrance into other men's minds to possess them forever. Culture broadens and sweetens literature, but native sentiment and unmarred individuality create it. Not all of mental power lies in the processes of thinking. There is power also in passion, in personality, in simple, native, uncritical conviction, in unschooled feeling. The power of science, of system, is executive, not stimulative. I do not find that I derive inspiration, but only information, from the learned historians and analysts of liberty; but from the sonneteers, the poets, who, speak its spirit and its exalted purpose, — who, recking nothing of the historical method, obey only the high method of their own hearts, — what may a man not gain of courage and confidence in the right way of politics?

It is your direct, unhesitating, intent, headlong man, who has his sources in the mountains, who digs deep channels for himself in the soil of his times and expands into the mighty river, to become a landmark forever; and not your " broad " man, sprung from the schools, who spreads his shallow, extended waters over the wide surfaces of learning, to leave rich deposits, it may be, for other men's crops to grow in, but to be himself dried up by a few score summer noons. The man thrown early upon his own resources, and already become a conqueror of success before being thrown with the literary talkers; the man grown to giant's stature in some rural library, and become exercised there in a giant's prerogatives before ever he has been laughingly told, to his heart's confusion, of scores of other giants dead and forgotten long ago; the man grounded in hope and settled in conviction ere he has discovered how many hopes time has seen buried, how many convictions cruelly given the lie direct by fate; the man who has carried his youth into middle age before going into the chill atmosphere of *blasé* sentiment; the quiet, stern man who has cultivated literature on a little oatmeal before thrusting himself upon the great world as a prophet and seer; the man who pronounces new eloquence in the rich dialect in which he was bred; the man come up to the capital from the provinces, — these are the men who people the world's mind with new creations, and give to the sophisticated learned of the next generation new names to conjure with.

If you have a candid and well-informed friend among city lawyers, ask him where the best masters of his profession are bred, — in the city or in the country. He will reply without hesitation, "In the country." You will hardly need to have him state the reason. The country lawyer has been obliged to study all parts of the law alike, and he has known no reason why he should not do so. He has not had the chance to make himself a specialist in any one branch of the law, as is the fashion among city practitioners, and he has not coveted the opportunity to do it. There would not have been enough special cases to occupy or remunerate him if he had coveted it. He has dared attempt the task of knowing the whole law, and yet without any sense of daring, but as a matter of course. In his own little town, in the midst of his own small library of authorities, it has not seemed to him an impossible task to explore all the topics that engage his profession ; the guiding principles, at any rate, of all branches of the great subject were open to him in a few books. And so it often happens that when he has found his sea legs on the sequestered inlets at home, and ventures, as he sometimes will, upon the great, troublous, and much-frequented waters of city practice in search of more work and larger fees, the country lawyer will once and again confound his city-bred brethren by discovering to them the fact that the law is a many-sided thing of principles, and not altogether a one-sided thing of technical rule and arbitrary precedent.

It would seem to be necessary that the author who is to stand as a distinct and imperative individual among the company of those who express the world's thought should come to a hard crystallization before subjecting himself to the tense strain of cities, the corrosive acids of critical circles. The ability to see for one's self is attainable, not by mixing with crowds and ascertaining how they look at things, but by a certain aloofness and self-

containment. The solitariness of some genius is
not accidental; it is characteristic and essential.
To the constructive imagination there are some immortal feats which are possible only in seclusion.
The man must heed first and most of all the suggestions of his own spirit; and the world can be
seen from windows overlooking the street better
than from the street itself.

Literature grows rich, various, full-voiced largely
through the re-discovery of truth, by thinking re-
thought, by stories re-told, by songs re-sung. The
song of human experience grows richer and richer
in its harmonies, and must grow until the full ac-
cord and melody are come. If too soon subjected
to the tense strain of the city, a man cannot expand ; he is beaten out of his natural shape by the
incessant impact and press of men and affairs. It
will often turn out that the unsophisticated man
will display not only more force, but more literary
skill even, than the trained *littérateur*. For one
thing, he will probably have enjoyed a fresher contact with old literature. He reads not for the sake
of a critical acquaintance with this or that author,
with no thought of going through all his writings
and "working him up," but as he would ride a
spirited horse, for love of the life and motion of it.

A general impression seems to have gained cur-

rency that the last of the bullying, omniscient
critics was buried in the grave of Francis Jeffrey;
and it is becoming important to correct the misap-
prehension.   There never was a time when there
was   more   superior   knowledge,   more   specialist
omniscience, among reviewers than there is to-day;
not pretended superior knowledge, but real.   Jeffrey's was very real of its kind.   For those who
write books, one of the special, inestimable advantages of lacking a too intimate knowledge of the
"world of letters" consists in not knowing all that
is known by those who review books, in ignorance
of the fashions among those who construct canons
of taste.   The modern critic is a leader of fashion.
He carries with him the air of a literary worldliness.   If your book be a novel, your reviewer will
know all previous plots, all former, all possible,
motives and situations.   You cannot write anything absolutely new for him, and why should you
desire to do again what has been done already?
If it be a poem, the reviewer's head already rings
with the whole gamut of the world's metrical music;
he can recognize any simile, recall all turns of
phrase, match every sentiment; why seek to please
him anew with old things?   If it concern itself
with the philosophy of politics, he can and will set
himself to test it by the whole history of its kind

from Plato down to Benjamin Kidd. How can it but spoil your sincerity to know that your critic will know everything? Will you not be tempted of the devil to anticipate his judgment or his pretensions by pretending to know as much as he?

The literature of creation naturally falls into two kinds : that which interprets nature or human action, and that which interprets self. Both of these may have the flavor of immortality, but neither unless it be free from self-consciousness. No man, therefore, can create after the best manner in either of these kinds who is an *habitue* of the circles made so delightful by those interesting men, the modern *literati*, sophisticated in all the fashions, ready in all the catches of the knowing literary world which centres in the city and the university. He cannot always be simple and straightforward. He cannot be always and without pretension himself, bound by no other man's canons of taste in speech or conduct. In the judgment of such circles there is but one thing for you to do if you would gain distinction : you must " beat the record ; " you must do certain definite literary feats better than they have yet been done. You are pitted against the literary " field." You are hastened into the paralysis of comparing yourself with others, and thus away from the health of unhesitating self-expression and directness of first-hand vision.

It would be not a little profitable if we could make correct analysis of the proper relations of learning — learning of the critical, accurate sort — to origination, of learning's place in literature. Although learning is never the real parent of literature, but only sometimes its foster-father, and although the native promptings of soul and sense are its best and freshest sources, there is always the danger that learning will claim, in every court of taste which pretends to jurisdiction, exclusive and preëminent rights as the guardian and preceptor of authors. An effort is constantly being made to create and maintain standards of literary worldliness, if I may coin such a phrase. The thorough man of the world affects to despise natural feeling; does at any rate actually despise all displays of it. He has an eye always on his world's best manners, whether native or imported, and is at continual pains to be master of the conventions of society; he will mortify the natural man as much as need be in order to be in good form. What learned criticism essays to do is to create a similar literary worldliness, to establish fashions and conventions in letters.

I have an odd friend in one of the northern coun-

ties of Georgia, — a county set off by itself among
the mountains, but early found out by refined people
in search of summer refuge from the unhealthful
air of the southern coast. He belongs to an excellent family of no little culture, but he was sur-
prised in the midst of his early schooling by the
coming on of the war ; and education given pause
in such wise seldom begins again in the schools.
He was left, therefore, to " finish " his mind as
best he might in the companionship of the books in
his uncle's library. These books were of the old
sober sort : histories, volumes of travels, treatises
on laws and constitutions, theologies, philosophies
more fanciful than the romances encased in neighbor volumes on another shelf. But they were books
which were used to being taken down and read ;
they had been daily companions to the rest of the
family, and they became familiar companions to my
friend's boyhood. He went to them day after day,
because theirs was the only society offered him in
the lonely days when uncle and brothers were at
the war, and the women were busy about the tasks
of the home. How literally did he make those
delightful old volumes his familiars, his cronies !
He never dreamed the while, however, that he was
becoming learned ; it never seemed to occur to him
that everybody else did not read just as he did, in just

such a library.   He found out afterwards, of course,
that he had kept much more of such company than
had the men with whom he loved to chat at the
post-office or around the fire in the village shops,
the habitual resorts of all who were socially inclined; but he attributed that to lack of time on
their part, or to accident, and has gone on thinking
until now that all the books that come within his
reach are the natural intimates of man.   And so
you shall hear him, in his daily familiar talk with
his neighbors, draw upon his singular stores of wise,
quaint learning with the quiet colloquial assurance,
" They tell me," as if books contained current
rumor ; and quote the poets with the easy unaffect-
edness with which others cite a common maxim of
the street !   He has been heard to refer to Dr.
Arnold of Rugby as " that school teacher over there
in England."

Surely one may treasure the image of this
simple, genuine man of learning as the image of a
sort of masterpiece of Nature in her own type of
erudition, a perfect sample of the kind of learning
that might beget the very highest sort of literature ;
the literature, namely, of authentic individuality.   It
is only under one of two conditions that learning
will not dull the edge of individuality : first, if one
never suspect that it is creditable and a matter of

pride to be learned, and so never become learned for the sake of becoming so; or, second, if it never suggest to one that investigation is better than reflection. Learned investigation leads to many good things, but one of these is not great literature, because learned investigation commands, as the first condition of its success, the repression of individuality.

His mind is a great comfort to every man who has one; but a heart is not often to be so conveniently possessed. Hearts frequently give trouble; they are straightforward and impulsive, and can seldom be induced to be prudent. They must be schooled before they will become insensible; they must be coached before they can be made to care first and most for themselves: and in all cases the mind must be their schoolmaster and coach. They are irregular forces; but the mind may be trained to observe all points of circumstance and all motives of occasion.

No doubt it is considerations of this nature that must be taken to explain the fact that our universities are erected entirely for the service of the tractable mind, while the heart's only education must be gotten from association with its neighbor heart, and in the ordinary courses of the world. Life is its only university. Mind is monarch.

whose laws claim supremacy in those lands which
boast the movements of civilization, and it must
command all the instrumentalities of education.
At least such is the theory of the constitution of
the modern world.   It is to be suspected that, as a
matter of fact, mind is one of those modern monarchs
who reign, but do not govern.   That old House of
Commons, that popular chamber in which the passions, the prejudices, the inborn, unthinking affections long ago repudiated by mind, have their full
representation, controls much the greater part of
the actual conduct of affairs.   To come out of the
figure, reasoned thought is, though perhaps the presiding, not yet the regnant force in the world.   In
life and in literature it is subordinate.   The future
may belong to it; but the present and past do not.
Faith and virtue do not wear its livery; friendship,
loyalty, patriotism, do not derive their motives from
it.   It does not furnish the material for those masses
of habit, of unquestioned tradition, and of treasured
belief which are the ballast of every steady ship of
state, enabling it to spread its sails safely to the
breezes of progress, and even to stand before the
storms of revolution.   And this is a fact which
has its reflection in literature.   There is a literature of reasoned thought; but by far the greater
part of those writings which we reckon worthy of

that great name is the product, not of reasoned thought, but of the imagination and of the spiritual vision of those who see, — writings winged, not with knowledge, but with sympathy, with sentiment, with heartiness. Even the literature of reasoned thought gets its life, not from its logic, but from the spirit, the insight, and the inspiration which are the vehicle of its logic. Thought presides, but sentiment has the executive powers ; the motive functions belong to feeling.

"Many people give many theories of literary composition," says the most natural and stimulating of English critics, "and Dr. Blair, whom we will read, is sometimes said to have exhausted the subject ; but, unless he has proved the contrary, we believe that the knack in style is to write like a human being. Some think they must be wise, some elaborate, some concise ; Tacitus wrote like a pair of stays ; some startle us, as Thomas Carlyle, or a comet, inscribing with his tail. But legibility is given to those who neglect these notions, and are willing to be themselves, to write their own thoughts in their own words, in the simplest words, in the words wherein they were thought. . . . Books are for various purposes, — tracts to teach, almanacs to sell, poetry to make pastry ; but this is the rarest sort of a book, — a book to read. As Dr. Johnson said, ' Sir, a good book is one you can hold in your hand, and take to the fire.' Now there are extremely few books which can, with any propriety, be so treated. When a great author, as Grote or Gibbon, has devoted a whole life of horrid industry to the composition of a large history, one feels one ought not to touch it with a mere hand, — it is not respectful. The idea of slavery hovers over the Decline and Fall. Fancy a stiffly dressed gentleman, in a stiff chair, slowly writing that stiff compilation in a stiff hand; it is enough to stiffen you for life."

It is devoutly to be wished that we might learn to prepare the best soils for mind, the best associations and companionships, the least possible sophistication. We are busy enough nowadays finding out the best ways of fertilizing and stimulating mind; but that is not quite the same thing as discovering the best soils for it, and the best atmospheres. Our culture is, by erroneous preference, of the reasoning faculty, as if that were all of us. Is it not the instinctive discontent of readers seeking stimulating contact with authors that has given us the present almost passionately spoken dissent from the standards set themselves by the realists in fiction, dissatisfaction with mere recording or observation? And is not realism working out upon itself the revenge its enemies would fain compass?

Must not all April Hopes exclude from their number the hope of immortality?

The rule for every man is, not to depend on the education which other men prepare for him, — not even to consent to it; but to strive to see things as they are, and to be himself as he is. Defeat lies in self-surrender.

III.

ON AN AUTHOR'S CHOICE OF COMPANY.

ONCE and again, it would seem, a man is born into the world belated. Strayed out of a past age, he comes among us like an alien, lives removed and singular, and dies a stranger. There was a touch of this strangeness in Charles Lamb. Much as he was loved and befriended, he was not much understood; for he drew aloof in his studies, affected a " self-pleasing quaintness " in his style, took no pains to hit the taste of his day, wandered at sweet liberty in an age which could scarcely have bred such another. " Hang the age! " he cried. " I will write for antiquity." And he did. He wrote as if it were still Shakespeare's day; made the authors of that spacious time his constant companions and study; and deliberately became himself " the last of the Elizabethans." When a new book came out, he said, he always read an old one.

The case ought, surely, to put us occasionally upon reflecting. May an author not, in some degree, by choosing his literary company, choose also his literary character, and so, when he comes to write, write himself back to his masters? May he not, by examining his own tastes and yielding himself obedient to his natural affinities, join what congenial group of writers he will? The question can be argued very strongly in the affirmative, and that not alone because of Charles Lamb's case. It might be said that Lamb was antique only in the forms of his speech; that he managed very cleverly to hit the taste of his age in the substance of what he wrote, for all the phraseology had so strong a flavor of quaintness and was not at all in the mode of the day. It would not be easy to prove that; but it really does not matter. In his tastes, certainly, Lamb was an old author, not a new one; a "modern antique," as Hood called him. He wrote for his own age, of course, because there was no other age at hand to write for, and the age he liked best was past and gone; but he wrote what he fancied the great generations gone by would have liked, and what, as it has turned out in the generosity of fortune, subsequent ages have warmly loved and reverently canonized him for writing; as if there were a casual taste that belongs to a day and generation, and also a permanent taste which is without date, and he had hit the latter.

Great authors are not often men of fashion. Fashion is always a harness and restraint, whether it be fashion in dress or fashion in vice or fashion in literary art; and a man who is bound by it is caught and formed in a fleeting mode. The great writers are always innovators; for they are always frank, natural, and downright, and frankness and naturalness always disturb, when they do not wholly break down, the fixed and complacent order of fashion. No genuine man can be deliberately in the fashion, indeed, in what he says, if he have any movement of thought or individuality in him. He remembers what Aristotle says, or if he does not, his own pride and manliness fill him with the thought instead. The very same action that is noble if done for the satisfaction of one's own sense of right or purpose of self-development, said the Stagirite, may, if done to satisfy others, become menial and slavish. " It is the object of any action or study that is all-important," and if the author's chief object be to please he is condemned already. The true spirit of authorship is a spirit of liberty which scorns the slave's trick of imitation. It is a masterful spirit of conquest within the sphere of ideas and of artistic form, — an impulse of empire and origination.

Of course a man may choose, if he will, to be less than a free author. He may become a reporter; for there is such a thing as reporting for books as

well as reporting for newspapers, and there have
been reporters so amazingly clever that their very
aptness and wit constitute them a sort of immor-
tals. You have proof of this in Horace Walpole,
at whose hands gossip and compliment receive a
sort of apotheosis. Such men hold the secret of
a kind of alchemy by which things trivial and temporary may be transmuted into literature. But
they are only inspired reporters, after all; and
while a man was wishing, he might wish to be more,
and climb to better company.

Every man must, of course, whether he will or
not, feel the spirit of the age in which he lives and
thinks and does his work; and the mere contact
will direct and form him more or less. But to wish
to serve the spirit of the age at any sacrifice of individual naturalness or conviction, however small,
is to harbor the germ of a destroying disease.
Every man who writes ought to write for immortality, even though he be of the multitude that die
at their graves; and the standards of immortality
are of no single age. There are many qualities
and causes that give permanency to a book, but
universal vogue during the author's lifetime is not
one of them. Many authors now immortal have
enjoyed the applause of their own generations;
many authors now universally admired will, let us

hope, pass on to an easy immortality. The praise
of your own day is no absolute disqualification;
but it may be if it be given for qualities which
your friends are the first to admire, for 't is likely
they will also be the last. There is a greater
thing than the spirit of the age, and that is the
spirit of the ages. It is present in your own day;
it is even dominant then, with a sort of accumulated power and mastery. If you can strike it,
you will strike, as it were, into the upper air of
your own time, where the forces are which run
from age to age. Lower down, where you breathe,
is the more inconstant air of opinion, inhaled, ex-
haled, from day to day, — the variant currents, the
forces that will carry you, not forward, but hither
and thither.

We write nowadays a great deal with our eyes
circumspectly upon the tastes of our neighbors, but
very little with our attention bent upon our own
natural, self-speaking thoughts and the very truth
of the matter whereof we are discoursing. Now
and again, it is true, we are startled to find how
the age relishes still an old-fashioned romance, if
written with a new-fashioned vigor and directness;
how quaint and simple and lovely things, as well
as what is altogether modern and analytic and
painful, bring our most judicious friends crowding,

purses in hand, to the book-stalls ; and for a while we are puzzled to see worn-out styles and past modes revived. But we do not let these things seriously disturb our study of prevailing fashions. These books of adventure are not at all, we assure ourselves, in the true spirit of the age, with its realistic knowledge of what men really do think and purpose, and the taste for them must be only for the moment or in jest. We need not let our surprise at occasional flurries and variations in the literary market cloud or discredit our analysis of the real taste of the day, or suffer ourselves to be betrayed into writing romances, however much we might rejoice to be delivered from the drudgery of sociological study, and made free to go afield with our imaginations upon a joyous search for hidden treasure or knightly adventure.

And yet it is quite likely, after all, that the present age is transient. Past ages have been. It is probable that the objects and interests now so near us, looming dominant in all the foreground of our day, will sometime be shifted and lose their place in the perspective. That has happened with the near objects and exaggerated interests of other days, so violently sometimes as to submerge and thrust out of sight whole libraries of books. It will not do to reckon upon the persistence of new

things.   'T were best to give them time to make
trial of the seasons.   The old things of art and
taste and thought are the permanent things.   We
know that they are because they have lasted long
enough to grow old; and we deem it safe to assess
the spirit of the age by the same test.   No age
adds a great deal to what it received from the age
that went before it; no time gets an air all its
own.   The same atmosphere holds from age to age;
it is only the little movements of the air that are
new.   In the intervals when the trades do not
blow, fleeting cross-winds venture abroad, the which
if a man wait for he may lose his voyage.

No man who has anything to say need stop and
bethink himself whom he may please or displease
in the saying of it.   He has but one day to write
in, and that is his own.   He need not fear that he
will too much ignore it.   He will address the men
he knows when he writes, whether he be conscious
of it or not; he may dismiss all fear on that score
and use his liberty to the utmost.   There are some
things that can have no antiquity and must ever be
without date, and genuineness and spirit are of
their number.   A man who has these must ever
be " timely," and at the same time fit to last, if he
can get his qualities into what he writes.   He may
freely read, too, what he will that is congenial, and

form himself by companionships that are chosen
simply because they are to his taste ; that is, if he
be genuine and in very truth a man of independent
spirit.   Lamb would have written "for antiquity"
with a vengeance had his taste for the quaint
writers of an elder day been an affectation, or
the authors he liked men themselves affected and
ephemeral.   No age this side antiquity would ever
have vouchsafed him a glance or a thought.   But
it was not an affectation, and the men he preferred were as genuine and as spirited as he was.
He was simply obeying an affinity and taking
cheer after his own kind.   A man born into the
real patriciate of letters may take his pleasure in
what company he will without taint or loss of
caste ;   may go confidently abroad in the free
world of books and choose his comradeships without fear of offense.

More than that, there is no other way in which
he can form himself, if he would have his power
transcend a single age.   He belittles himself who
takes from the world no more than he can get
from the speech of his own generation.   The only
advantage of books over speech is that they may
hold from generation to generation, and reach, not
a small group merely, but a multitude of men ;
and a man who writes without being a man of

letters is curtailed of his heritage. It is in this world of old and new that he must form himself if he would in the end belong to it and increase its bulk of treasure. If he has conned the new theories of society, but knows nothing of Burke; the new notions about fiction, and has not read his Scott and his Richardson; the new criminology, and wots nothing of the old human nature; the new religions, and has never felt the power and sanctity of the old, it is much the same as if he had read Ibsen and Maeterlinck, and had never opened Shakespeare. How is he to know wholesome air from foul, good company from bad, visions from nightmares? He has framed himself for the great art and handicraft of letters only when he has taken all the human parts of literature as if they were without date, and schooled himself in a catholic sanity of taste and judgment.

Then he may very safely choose what company his own work shall be done in, — in what manner, and under what masters. He cannot choose amiss for himself or for his generation if he choose like a man, without light whim or weak affectation; not like one who chooses a costume, but like one who chooses a character. What is it, let him ask himself, that renders a bit of writing a " piece of literature " ? It is reality. A " wood-note wild,"

sung unpremeditated and out of the heart; a description written as if with an undimmed and
seeing eye upon the very object described; an
exposition that lays bare the very soul of the
matter ; a motive truly revealed ; anger that is
righteous and justly spoken; mirth that has its
sources pure ; phrases to find the heart of a thing,
and a heart seen in things for the phrases to find ;
an unaffected meaning set out in language that is
its own, — such are the realities of literature.
Nothing else is of the kin. Phrases used for their
own sake; borrowed meanings which the borrower
does not truly care for; an affected manner; an
acquired style ; a hollow reason ; words that are
not fit ; things which do not live when spoken, —
these are its falsities, which die in the handling.

The very top breed of what is unreal is begotten by imitation. Imitators succeed sometimes,
and flourish, even while a breath may last ; but
"imitate and be damned" is the inexorable
threat and prophecy of fate with regard to the
permanent fortunes of literature. That has been
notorious this long time past. It is more worth
noting, lest some should not have observed it, that
there are other and subtler ways of producing
what is unreal. There are the mixed kinds of
writing, for example. Argument is real if it come

vital from the mind ; narrative is real if the thing
told have life and the narrator unaffectedly see it
while he speaks ; but to narrate and argue in the
same breath is naught. Take, for instance, the
familiar example of the early history of Rome.
Make up your mind what was the truth of the
matter, and then, out of the facts as you have disen-
tangled them, construct a firmly touched narrative,
and the thing you create is real, has the confidence
and consistency of life. But mix the narrative
with critical comment upon other writers and their
variant versions of the tale, show by a nice elabo-
ration of argument the whole conjectural basis of
the story, set your reader the double task of doubt-
ing and accepting, rejecting and constructing, and
at once you have touched the whole matter with
unreality. The narrative by itself might have had
an objective validity ; the argument by itself an
intellectual firmness, sagacity, vigor, that would
have sufficed to make and keep it potent ; but
together they confound each other, destroy each
other's atmosphere, make a double miscarriage.
The story is rendered unlikely, and the argument
obscure. This is the taint which has touched all
our recent historical writing. The critical discussion and assessment of the sources of information,
which used to be a thing for the private mind of

the writer, now so encroach upon the open text
that the story, for the sake of which we would believe the whole thing was undertaken, is oftentimes fain to sink away into the foot-notes. The
process has ceased to be either pure exegesis or
straightforward narrative, and history has ceased
to be literature.

Nor is this our only sort of mixed writing.
Our novels have become sociological studies, our
poems vehicles of criticism, our sermons political
manifestos. We have confounded all processes in
a common use, and do not know what we would be
at. We can find no better use for Pegasus than
to carry our vulgar burdens, no higher key for
song than questionings and complainings. Fancy
pulls in harness with intellectual doubt; enthusiasm walks apologetically alongside science. We
try to make our very dreams engines of social reform. It is a parlous state of things for literature,
and it is high time authors should take heed what
company they keep. The trouble is, they all want
to be " in society," overwhelmed with invitations
from the publishers, well known and talked about
at the clubs, named every day in the newspapers,
photographed for the news-stalls ; and it is so hard
to distinguish between fashion and form, costume
and substance, convention and truth, the things

that show well and the things that last well; so
hard to draw away from the writers that are new
and talked about and note those who are old and
walk apart, to distinguish the tones which are
merely loud from the tones that are genuine, to
get far enough away from the press and the hub-
bub to see and judge the movements of the crowd!

Some will do it. Choice spirits will arise and
make conquest of us, not "in society," but with
what will seem a sort of outlawry. The great
growths of literature spring up in the open, where
the air is free and they can be a law unto themselves. The law of life, here as elsewhere, is the
law of nourishment: with what was the earth
laden, and the atmosphere? Literatures are renewed, as they are originated, by uncontrived impulses of nature, as if the sap moved unbidden in
the mind. Once conceive the matter so, and
Lamb's quaint saying assumes a sort of gentle
majesty. A man should " write for antiquity " as
a tree grows into the ancient air, — this old air
that has moved upon the face of the world ever
since the day of creation, which has set the law of
life to all things, which has nurtured the forests
and won the flowers to their perfection, which has
fed men's lungs with life, sped their craft upon the
seas, borne abroad their songs and their cries,

blown their forges to flame, and buoyed up whatever they have contrived. 'T is a common medium, though a various life; and the figure may serve the author for instruction.

The breeding of authors is no doubt a very occult thing, and no man can set the rules of it; but at least the sort of " ampler ether " in which they are best brought to maturity is known. Writers have liked to speak of the Republic of Letters, as if to mark their freedom and equality; but there is a better phrase, namely, the Community of Letters; for that means intercourse and comradeship and a life in common. Some take up their abode in it as if they had made no search for a place to dwell in, but had come into the freedom of it by blood and birthright. Others buy the freedom with a great price, and seek out all the sights and privileges of the place with an eager thoroughness and curiosity. Still others win their way into it with a certain grace and aptitude, next best to the ease and dignity of being born to the right. But for all it is a bonny place to be. Its comradeships are a liberal education. Some, indeed, even there, live apart; but most run always in the market-place to know what all the rest have said. Some keep special company, while others keep none at all. But all feel the atmosphere and life of the place in their several degrees.

No doubt there are national groups, and Shake-speare is king among the English, as Homer is among the Greeks, and sober Dante among his gay countrymen. But their thoughts all have in common, though speech divide them; and sovereignty does not exclude comradeship or embarrass freedom. No doubt there is many a willful, ungoverned fellow endured there without question, and many a churlish cynic, because he possesses that patent of genuineness or of a wit which strikes for the heart of things, which, without further test, secures citizenship in that free company. What a gift of tongues is there, and of prophecy! What strains of good talk, what counsel of good judgment, what cheer of good tales, what sanctity of silent thought! The sight-seers who pass through from day to day, the press of voluble men at the gates, the affectation of citizenship by mere sojourners, the folly of those who bring new styles or affect old ones, the procession of the generations, disturb the calm of that serene community not a whit. They will entertain a man a whole decade, if he happen to stay so long, though they know all the while he can have no permanent place among them.

'T would be a vast gain to have the laws of that community better known than they are. Even the first principles of its constitution are singularly unfamiliar. It is not a community of writers, but a community of letters. One gets admission, not because he writes, — write he never so cleverly, like a gentleman and a man of wit, — but because he is literate, a true initiate into the secret craft and mystery of letters. What that secret is a man may know, even though he cannot practice or appropriate it. If a man can see the permanent element in things, — the true sources of laughter, the real fountains of tears, the motives that strike along the main lines of conduct, the acts which display the veritable characters of men, the trifles that are significant, the details that make the mass, — if he know these things, and can also choose words with a like knowledge of their power to illuminate and reveal, give color to the eye and passion to the thought, the secret is his, and an entrance to that immortal communion.

It may be that some learn the mystery of that insight without tutors ; but most must put themselves under governors and earn their initiation. While a man lives, at any rate, he can keep the company of the masters whose words contain the mystery and open it to those who can see, almost with every accent ; and in such company it may at last be revealed to him, — so plainly that he may, if he will, still linger in such comradeship when he is dead.

It would seem that there are two tests which admit to that company, and that they are conclusive. The one is, Are you individual? the other, Are you conversable? "I beg pardon," said a grave wag, coming face to face with a small person of most consequential air, and putting glass to eye in calm scrutiny — " I beg pardon; but are you anybody in particular?" Such is very much the form of initiation into the permanent communion of the realm of letters. Tell them, No, but that you have done much better — you have caught the tone of a great age, studied taste, divined opportunity, courted and won a vast public, been most timely and most famous; and you shall be pained to find them laughing in your face. Tell them you are earnest, sincere, consecrate to a cause, an apostle and reformer, and they will still ask you, " But are you anybody in particular?" They will mean, " Were you your own man in what you thought, and not a puppet? Did you speak with an individual note and distinction that marked you able to think as well as to speak, — to be yourself in thoughts and in words also?" " Very well, then; you are welcome enough."

" That is, if you be also conversable." It is

plain enough what they mean by that, too. They
mean, if you have spoken in such speech and spirit
as can be understood from age to age, and not in
the pet terms and separate spirit of a single day
and generation. Can the old authors understand
you, that you would associate with them? Will
men be able to take your meaning in the differing
days to come? Or is it perishable matter of the
day that you deal in — little controversies that
carry no lasting principle at their heart; experimental theories of life and science, put forth for
their novelty and with no test of their worth; pic-
tures in which fashion looms very large, but human
nature shows very small; things that please everybody, but instruct no one; mere fancies that are
an end in themselves? Be you never so clever an
artist in words and in ideas, if they be not the
words that wear and mean the same thing, and
that a thing intelligible, from age to age, the ideas
that shall hold valid and luminous in whatever day
or company, you may clamor at the gate till your
lungs fail and get never an answer.

For that to what you seek admission is a veritable "community." In it you must be able to be,
and to remain, conversable. How are you to test
your preparation meanwhile, unless you look to
your comradeships now while yet it is time to

learn? Frequent the company in which you may learn the speech and the manner which are fit to last. Take to heart the admirable example you shall see set you there of using speech and manner to speak your real thought and be genuinely and simply yourself.

IV.

A LITERARY POLITICIAN.

"LITERARY politician" is not a label much in vogue, and may need first of all a justification, lest even the man of whom I am about to speak should decline it from his very urn. I do not mean a politician who affects literature; who seems to appreciate the solemn moral purpose of Wordsworth's Happy Warrior, and yet is opposed to ballot reform. Neither do I mean a literary man who affects politics; who earns his victories through the publishers, and his defeats at the hands of the men who control the primaries. I mean the man who has the genius to see deep into affairs, and the discretion to keep out of them, — the man to whom, by reason of knowledge and imagination and sympathetic insight, governments and policies are as open books, but who, instead of trying to put haphazard characters of his own into those books, wisely prefers to read their pages aloud to others. A man this who knows politics, and yet does not handle policies.

There is, no doubt, a very widespread skepticism
as to the existence of such a man. Many people
would ask you to prove him as well as define him;
and that, as they assume, upon a very obvious
principle. It is a rule of universal acceptance in
theatrical circles that no one can write a good play
who has no practical acquaintance with the stage.
A knowledge of greenroom possibilities and of
stage machinery, it is held, must go before all successful attempts to put either passion or humor
into action on the boards, if pit and gallery are to
get a sense of reality from the performance. No
wonder that Sheridan's plays were effective, for
Sheridan was both author and actor; but abundant wonder that simple Goldsmith succeeded with
his exquisite "She Stoops to Conquer," — unless
we are to suppose that an Irishman of the last century, like the Irishman of this, had some sixth
sense which enabled him to understand other people's business better than his own; for poor Goldsmith could not act (even off the stage), and his
only connection with the theatre seems to have been
his acquaintance with Garrick. Lytton, we know,
had Macready constantly at his elbow, to give and
enforce suggestions calculated to render plays play-
able. And in our own day, the authors of what
we indulgently call "dramatic literature" find

themselves constantly obliged to turn tragedies into comedies, comedies into farces, to satisfy the managers; for managers know the stage, and pretend to know all possible audiences also. The writer for the stage must be playwright first, author second.

Similar principles of criticism are not a little affected by those who play the parts, great and small, on the stage of politics. There is on that stage, too, it is said, a complex machinery of action and scene-shifting, a greenroom tradition and practice as to costume and make-up, as to entry and exit, necessities of concession to footlights and of appeal to the pit, quite as rigorous and quite as proper for study as are the concomitants of that other art which we frankly call acting. This is an idea, indeed, accepted in some quarters outside the political playhouse as well as within it. Mr. Sydney Colvin, for example, declares very rightly that: —

" Men of letters and of thought are habitually too much given to declaiming at their ease against the delinquencies of men of action and affairs. The inevitable friction of practical politics," he argues, " generates heat enough already, and the office of the thinker and critic should be to supply not heat, but light. The difficulties which attend his own unmolested task — the task of seeking after and proclaiming salutary truths — should teach him to make allowance for the far more urgent difficulties which beset the politican; the man obliged, amidst the clash of interests and temptations, to practice from hand to mouth, and at his peril, the most uncertain and at the same time the most indispensable of the experimental arts."

Mr. Colvin is himself of the class of men of letters and of thought; he accordingly puts the case against his class much more mildly than the practical politician would desire to see it put. Practical politicians are wont to regard closeted writers upon politics with a certain condescension, dashed with slight traces of uneasy concern. "Literary men can say strong things of their age," observes Mr. Bagehot, "for no one expects that they will go out and act on them. They are a kind of ticket-of-leave lunatics, from whom no harm is for the moment expected; who seem quiet, but on whose vagaries a practical public must have its eye." I suppose that the really serious, practical man in politics would see nothing of satirical humor in such a description. He would have you note that, although traced with a sharp point of wit, the picture is nevertheless true. He can cite you a score of instances illustrative of the danger of putting faith in the political judgments of those who are not politicians bred in the shrewd and moving world of political management.

The genuine practical politician, such as (even our enemies being the witnesses) we must be acknowledged to produce in great numbers and perfection in this country, reserves his acidest contempt for the literary man who assumes to utter judgments touching public affairs and political institutions. If he be a reading man, as will sometimes happen, he is able to point you, in illustration of what you are to expect in such cases, to the very remarkable essays of the late Mr. Matthew Arnold on parliamentary policy and the Irish question. If he be not a reading man, as sometimes happens, he is able to ask, much to your confusion, " What does a fellow who lives inside a library know about politics, anyhow? " You have to admit, if you are candid, that most fellows who live in libraries know little enough. You remember Macaulay, and acknowledge that, although he made admirable speeches in Parliament, held high political office, and knew all the considerable public men of his time, he did imagine the creation to have been made in accordance with Whig notions ; did hope to find the judgments of Lord Somers some day answering mankind as standards for all possible times and circumstances. You recall Gibbon, and allow, to your own thought at least, that, had he not remained silent in his seat, a very few of his sentences would probably have sufficed to freeze the House of Commons stiff.   The ordinary literary man, even though he be an eminent historian, is ill enough fitted to be a mentor in affairs of government.   For, it must be admitted, things are for the most part very simple in books, and in practical life very complex. Not all the bindings of a library inclose the various world of circumstance.

But the practical politician should discriminate.   Let him find a man with an imagination which, though it stands aloof, is yet quick to conceive the very things in the thick of which the politician struggles.   To that man he should resort for instruction.   And that there is occasionally such a man we have proof in Bagehot, the man who first clearly distinguished the facts of the English constitution from its theory.

Walter Bagehot is a name known to not a few of those who have a zest for the juiciest things of literature, for the wit that illuminates and the knowledge that refreshes.   But his fame is still singularly disproportioned to his charm; and one feels once and again like publishing him, at least to all spirits of his own kind.   It would be a most agreeable good fortune to introduce Bagehot to men who have not read him!   To ask your friend to know Bagehot is like inviting him to seek pleasure.

Occasionally, a man is born into the world whose mission it evidently is to clarify the thought of his generation, and to vivify it; to give it speed where it is slow, vision where it is blind, balance where it is out of poise, saving humor where it is dry, — and such a man was Walter Bagehot. When he wrote of history, he made it seem human and probable; when he wrote of political economy, he made it seem credible, entertaining, — nay, engaging even; when he wrote criticism, he wrote sense. You have in him a man who can jest to your instruction, who will beguile you into being informed beyond your wont and wise beyond your birthright. Full of manly, straightforward meaning, earnest to find the facts that guide and strengthen conduct, a lover of good men and seers, full of knowledge and a consuming desire for it, he is yet genial withal, with the geniality of a man of wit, and alive in every fibre of him, with a life he can communicate to you. One is constrained to agree, almost, with the verdict of a witty countryman of his, who happily still lives to cheer us, that when Bagehot died he " carried away into the next world more originality of thought than is now to be found in the three Estates of the Realm."

An epitome of Bagehot's life can be given very briefly. He was born in February, 1826, and

died in March, 1877, — the month in which one
would prefer to die. Between those two dates he had
much quaint experience as a boy, and much sober
business experience as a man. He wrote essays
on poets, prose writers, statesmen, whom he would,
with abundant insight, but without too much respect of persons ; also books on banking, on the
early development of society, and on English politics, kindling a flame of interest with these dry
materials such as made men stare who had often described the facts of society themselves, but who had
never dreamed of applying fire to them, as Bagehot
did, to make them give forth light and wholesome
heat. He set the minds of a few fortunate friends
aglow with the delights of the very wonderful tongue
which nature had given him through his mother.
And then he died, while his power was yet young.
Not a life of event or adventure, but a life of deep
interest, none the less, because a life in which those
two things of our modern life, commonly deemed
incompatible, business and literature, namely, were
combined without detriment to either ; and from
which, more interesting still, politics gained a profound expounder in one who was no politician and
no party man, but, as he himself said, " between
sizes in politics."

Mr. Bagehot was born in the centre of Somer-

setshire, that southwestern county of old England
whose coast towns look across Bristol Channel to
the highlands of Wales: a county of small farms,
and pastures that keep their promise of fatness to
many generous milkers; a county broken into ab-
rupt hills, and sodden moors hardly kept from the
inroads of the sea, as well as rural valleys open to
the sun; a county visited by mists from the sea,
and bathed in a fine soft atmosphere all its own;
visited also by people of fashion, for it contains
Bath; visited now also by those who have read
Lorna Doone, for within it lies part of that Ex-
moor Forest in which stalwart John Ridd lived
and wrought his mighty deeds of strength and
love: a land which the Celts kept for long against
both Saxon and Roman, but which Christianity
easily conquered, building Wells Cathedral and
the monastery at Glastonbury. Nowhere else, in
days of travel, could Bagehot find a land of so
great delight save in the northwest corner of Spain,
where a golden light lay upon everything, where
the sea shone with a rare, soft lustre, and where
there was a like varied coast-line to that he knew
and loved at home. He called it " a sort of better
Devonshire: " and Devonshire is Somersetshire, —
only more so! The atmospheric effects of his
county certainly entered the boy Bagehot, and

colored the nature of the man. He had its
glow, its variety, its richness, and its imaginative
depth.

But better than a fair county is a good parentage, and that, too, Bagehot had ; just the parentage
one would wish to have who desired to be a force
in the world's thought. His father, Thomas Wat-
son Bagehot, was for thirty years managing director
and vice-president of Stuckey's Banking Company,
one of the oldest and best of those sturdy joint-stock
companies which have for so many years stood
stoutly up alongside the Bank of England as
managers of the vast English fortune. But he
was something more than a banker. He was a man
of mind, of strong liberal convictions in politics,
and of an abundant knowledge of English history
wherewith to back up his opinions. He was one
of the men who think, and who think in straight
lines ; who see, and see things. His mother
was a Miss Stuckey, a niece of the founder of
the banking company. But it was not her connection with bankers that made her an invaluable
mother. She had, besides beauty, a most lively
and stimulating wit ; such a mind as we most desire to see in a woman, — a mind that stirs without irritating you, that rouses but does not be-
labor, amuses and yet subtly instructs. She could

preside over the young life of her son in such a way
as at once to awaken his curiosity and set him in
the way of satisfying it. She was brilliant company for a boy, and rewarding for a man. She
had suggestive people, besides, among her kinsmen,
into whose companionship she could bring her son.
Bagehot had that for which no university can ever
offer an equivalent, — the constant and intelligent
sympathy of both his parents in his studies, and
their companionship in his tastes. To his father's
strength his mother added vivacity. He would
have been wise, perhaps, without her; but he would
not have been wise so delightfully.

Bagehot got his schooling in Bristol, his university training in London. In Bristol lived Dr.
Prichard, his mother's brother-in-law, and author
of a notable book on the Physical History of Men.
From him Bagehot unquestionably got his bent towards the study of race origins and development.
In London, Cobden and Bright were carrying on
an important part of their great agitation for the
repeal of the corn laws, and were making such
speeches as it stirred and bettered young men to
hear. Bagehot had gone to University Hall, London, rather than to Oxford or Cambridge, because
his father was a Unitarian, and would not have his
son submit to the religious tests then required at

the great universities.   But there can be no doubt
that there was more to be had at University Hall
in that day than at either Oxford or Cambridge.
Oxford and Cambridge were still dragging the very
heavy chains of a hindering tradition ; the faculty
of University Hall contained many thorough and
some eminent scholars ; what was more, University
Hall was in London, and London itself was a
quickening and inspiring teacher for a lad in love
with both books and affairs, as Bagehot was.   He
could ask penetrating questions of his professors,
and he could also ask questions of London, seek
out her secrets of history, and so experience to the
full the charm of her abounding life.   In after
years, though he loved Somersetshire and clung to
it with a strong home-keeping affection, he could
never stay away from London for more than six
weeks at a time.   Eventually he made it his place
of permanent residence.

His university career over, Bagehot did what so
many thousands of young graduates before him
had done, — he studied for the bar ; and then,
having prepared himself to practice law, followed
another large body of young men in deciding to
abandon it.   He joined his father in his business
as ship-owner and banker in Somersetshire, and
in due time took his place among the directors of

Stuckey's Company. For the rest of his life, this man, whom the world knows as a man of letters, was first of all a man of business. In his later years, however, he identified himself with what may be called the literary side of business by becoming editor of that great financial authority, the "London Economist." He had, so to say, married into this position. His wife was the daughter of the Rt. Hon. James Wilson, who was the mind and manager, as well as the founder of the "Economist." Wilson's death seemed to leave the great financial weekly by natural succession to Bagehot; and certainly natural selection never made a better choice. It was under Bagehot that the "Economist" became a sort of financial providence for business men on both sides of the Atlantic. Its sagacious prescience constituted Bagehot himself a sort of supplementary chancellor of the exchequer, the chancellors of both parties resorting to him with equal confidence and solicitude. His constant contact with London, and with the leaders of politics and opinion there, of course materially assisted him also to those penetrating judgments touching the structure and working of English institutions which have made his volume on the English Constitution and his essays on Bolingbroke and Brougham and Peel, on Mr. Gladstone and Sir

George Cornewall Lewis, the admiration and despair of all who read them.

Those who know Bagehot only as the writer of
some of the most delightful and suggestive literary
criticisms in the language wonder that he should
have been an authority on practical politics ; those
who used to regard the " London Economist " as
omniscient, and who knew him only as the editor
of it, marvel that he dabbled in literary criticism,
and incline to ask themselves, when they learn of
his vagaries in that direction, whether he can have
been so safe a guide as they deemed him, after all ;
those who know him through his political writings
alone venture upon the perusal of his miscellaneous
essays with not a little surprise and misgiving that
their master should wander so far afield. And yet
the whole Bagehot is the only Bagehot. Each
part of the man is incomplete, not only, but a trifle
incomprehensible, also, without the other parts.
What delights us most in his literary essays is
their broad practical sagacity, so uniquely married
as it is with pure taste and the style of a rapid
artist in words. What makes his financial and
political writings whole and sound is the scope of
his mind outside finance and politics, the validity
of his observation all around the circle of thought
and affairs. He was the better critic for being a

competent man of business and a trusted financial authority. He was the more sure-footed in his political judgments because of his play of mind in other and supplementary spheres of human activity.

The very appearance of the man was a sort of outer index to the singular variety of capacity that has made him so notable a figure in the literary annals of England. A mass of black, wavy hair; a dark eye, with depths full of slumberous, playful fire; a ruddy skin that bespoke active blood, quick in its rounds; the lithe figure of an excellent horseman; a nostril full, delicate, quivering, like that of a blooded racer, — such were the fitting outward marks of a man in whom life and thought and fancy abounded; the aspect of a man of unflagging vivacity, of wholesome, hearty humor, of a ready intellectual sympathy, of wide and penetrative observation. It is no narrow, logical shrewdness or cold penetration that looks forth at you through that face, even if a bit of mockery does lurk in the privatest corner of the eye. Among the qualities which he seeks out for special praise in Shakespeare is a broad tolerance and sympathy for illogical and common minds. It seems to him an evidence of size in Shakespeare that he was not vexed with smallness, but was patient, nay, sympathetic even, in his portrayal of it. "If every one were logical and literary," he exclaims, " how would there be scavengers, or watchmen, or caulkers, or coopers? A patient sympathy, a kindly fellow-feeling for the narrow intelligence necessarily induced by narrow circumstances, — a narrowness which, in some degrees, seems to be inevitable, and is perhaps more serviceable than most things to the wise conduct of life, — this, though quick and half-bred minds may despise it, seems to be a necessary constituent in the composition of manifold genius. ' How shall the world be served ?' asks the host in Chaucer. We must have cart-horses as well as race-horses, draymen as well as poets. It is no bad thing, after all, to be a slow man and to have one idea a year. You don't make a figure, perhaps, in argumentative society, which requires a quicker species of thought, but is that the worse ? "

One of the things which strike us most in Bagehot himself is his capacity to understand inferior minds ; and there can be no better test of sound genius. He stood in the midst of affairs, and knew the dull duty and humdrum fidelity which make up the equipment of the ordinary mind for business, for the business which keeps the world steady in its grooves and makes it fit for habitation. He perceived quite calmly, though with an odd, sober amusement, that the world is under the dominion, in most things, of the average man, and the average man he knows. He is, he explains, with his characteristic covert humor, " a cool, common person, with a considerate air, with figures in his mind, with his own business to attend to, with a set of ordinary opinions arising from and suited to ordinary life. He can't bear novelty or originalities. He says, ' Sir, I never heard such a thing before in my life ; ' and he thinks this a *reductio ad absurdum*. You may see his taste by the reading of which he approves. Is there a more splendid monument of talent and industry than the 'Times'? No wonder that the average man — that any one — believes in it. . . . But did you ever see anything there you had never seen before? . . . Where are the deep theories, and the wise axioms, and the everlasting sentiments which the writers of the most influential publication in the world have been the first to communicate to an ignorant species? Such writers are far too shrewd. . . . The purchaser desires an article which he can appreciate at sight, which he can lay down and say, ' An excellent article, very excellent ; exactly my own sentiments.' Original theories give trouble ; besides, a grave man on the Coal Exchange does not desire to be an apostle of novelties among the contemporaneous dealers in fuel ; he wants to be provided with remarks he can make on the topics of the day which will not be known not to be his, that are not too profound, which he can fancy the paper only reminded him of. And just in the same way," — thus he proceeds with the sagacious moral, — " precisely as the most popular political paper is not that which is abstractedly the best or most instructive, but that which most exactly takes up the minds of men where it finds them, catches the floating sentiment of society, puts it in such a form as society can fancy would convince another society which did not believe, so the most influential of constitutional statesmen is the one who most felicitously expresses the creed of the moment, who administers it, who embodies it in laws and institutions, who gives it the highest life it is capable of, who induces the average man to think, ' I could not have done it any better if I had had time myself.' "

See how his knowledge of politics proceeds out of his knowledge of men. " You may talk of the tyranny of Nero and Tiberius," he exclaims, " but the real tyranny is the tyranny of your next-door neighbor. What law is so cruel as the law of doing what he does? What yoke is so galling as the necessity of being like him? What espionage of despotism comes to your door so effectually as the eye of the man who lives at your door? Public opinion is a permeating influence, and it exacts obedience to itself; it requires us to think other men's thoughts, to speak other men's words, to follow other men's habits. Of course, if we do not, no formal ban issues, no corporeal pain, the coarse penalty of a barbarous society, is inflicted on the offender, but we are called ' eccentric; ' there is a gentle murmur of ' most unfortunate ideas,' ' singular young man,' ' well intentioned, I dare say, but unsafe, sir, quite unsafe.' The prudent, of course, conform."

There is, no doubt, a touch of mockery in all this, but there is unquestionable insight in it, too, and a sane knowledge also of the fact that dull, common judgments are, after all, the cement of society. It is Bagehot who says somewhere that it is only dull nations, like the Romans and the English, who can become or remain for any length of time self-governing nations, because it is only among them that duty is done through lack of knowledge sufficient or imagination enough to suggest anything else to do : only among them that the stability of slow habit can be had.

It would be superficial criticism to put forward Bagehot's political opinions as themselves the proof of his extraordinary power as a student and analyst

of institutions.   His life, his broad range of study,
his quick versatility, his shrewd appreciation of
common men, his excursions through all the fields
that men traverse in their thought of one another
and in their contact with the world's business, —
these are the soil out of which his political judgments spring, from which they get their sap and
bloom.   In order to know institutions, you must
know men ; you must be able to imagine histories,
to appreciate characters radically unlike your own,
to see into the heart of society and assess its
notions, great and small.   Your average critic, it
must be acknowledged, would be the worst possible
commentator on affairs.   He has all the movements
of intelligence without any of its reality.   But a
man who sees authors with a Chaucerian insight
into them as men, who knows literature as a realm
of vital thought conceived by real men, of actual
motive felt by concrete persons, this is a man whose
opinions you may confidently ask, if not on current
politics, at any rate on all that concerns the permanent relations of men in society.

It is for such reasons that one must first make
known the most masterly of the critics of English
political institutions as a man of catholic tastes and
attainments, shrewdly observant of many kinds of
men and affairs.   Know him once in this way, and

his mastery in political thought is explained. If I were to make choice, therefore, of extracts from his works with a view to recommend him as a politician, I should choose those passages which show him a man of infinite capacity to see and understand men of all kinds, past and present. By showing in his case the equipment of a mind open on all sides to the life and thought of society, and penetrative of human secrets of many sorts, I should authenticate his credentials as a writer upon politics, which is nothing else than the public and organic life of society.

Examples may be taken almost at random. There is the passage on Sydney Smith, in the essay on the First Edinburgh Reviewers. We have all laughed with that great-hearted clerical wit ; but it is questionable whether we have all appreciated him as a man who wrote and wrought wisdom. Indeed, Sydney Smith may be made a very delicate test of sound judgment, the which to apply to friends of whom you are suspicious. There was a man beneath those excellent witticisms, a big, wholesome, thinking man ; but none save men of like wholesome natures can see and value his manhood and his mind at their real worth.

"Sydney Smith was an after-dinner writer. His words have a flow, a vigor, an expression, which is not given to hungry mortals. . . . There is little trace of labor in his composition; it is poured forth like an unceasing torrent, rejoicing daily to run its course. And what courage there is in it! There is as much variety of pluck in writing across a sheet as in riding across a country. Cautious men . . . go tremulously, like a timid rider; they turn hither and thither; they do not go straight across a subject, like a masterly mind. A few sentences are enough for a master of sentences. The writing of Sydney Smith is suited to the broader kind of important questions. For anything requiring fine nicety of speculation, long elaborateness of deduction, evanescent sharpness of distinction, neither his style nor his mind was fit. He had no patience for long argument, no acuteness for delicate precision, no fangs for recondite research. Writers, like teeth, are divided into incisors and grinders. Sydney Smith was a molar. He did not run a long, sharp argument into the interior of a question; he did not, in the common phrase, go deeply into it; but he kept it steadily under the contract of a strong, capable, jawlike understanding, — pressing its surface, effacing its intricacies, grinding it down. Yet this is done without toil. The play of the molar is instinctive and placid; he could not help it; it would seem that he had an enjoyment in it."

One reads this with a feeling that Bagehot both knows and likes Sydney Smith, and heartily appreciates him as an engine of Whig thought; and with the conviction that Bagehot himself, knowing thus and enjoying Smith's freehand method of writing, could have done the like himself, — could himself have made English ring to all the old Whig tunes, like an anvil under the hammer. And yet you have only to turn back a page in the same essay to find quite another Bagehot, — a Bagehot such as Sydney Smith could not have been. He is speaking of that other militant Edinburgh reviewer, Lord Jeffrey, and is recalling, as every one recalls, Jeffrey's review of Wordsworth's " Excursion." The first words of that review, as everybody remembers, were, " This will never do ; " and there followed upon those words, though not a little praise of the poetical beauties of the poem, a thoroughly meant condemnation of the school of poets of which Wordsworth was the greatest representative. Very celebrated in the world of literature is the leading case of Jeffrey *v.* Wordsworth. It is in summing up this case that Bagehot gives us a very different taste of his quality : —

" The world has given judgment. Both Mr. Wordsworth and Lord Jeffrey have received their reward. The one had his own generation, the laughter of men, the applause of drawing-rooms, the concurrence of the crowd ; the other a succeeding age, the fond enthusiasm of secret students, the lonely rapture of lonely minds.   And each has received according to his kind.   If all cultivated men speak differently because of the existence of Wordsworth and Coleridge ; if not a thoughtful English book has appeared for forty years without some trace for good or evil of their influence ; if sermon-writers subsist upon their thoughts ; if ' sacred poets ' thrive by translating their weaker portions into the speech of women ; if, when all this is over, some sufficient part of their writing will ever be found fitting food for wild musing and solitary meditation, surely this is because they possessed the inner nature, — ' an intense and glowing mind,' ' the vision and the faculty divine.'   But if, perchance, in their weaker moments, the great authors of the ' Lyrical Ballads ' did ever imagine that the world was to pause because of their verses, that ' Peter Bell ' would be popular in drawing-rooms, that ' Christabel ' would be perused in the city, that people of fashion would make a handbook of ' The Excursion,' it was well for them to be told at once that this was not so.   Nature ingeniously prepared a shrill artificial voice, which spoke in season and out of season, enough and more than

enough, what will ever be the idea of the cities of
the plain concerning those who live alone among the
mountains, of the frivolous concerning the grave, of
the gregarious concerning the recluse, of those who
laugh concerning those who laugh not, of the common concerning the uncommon, of those who lend
on usury concerning those who lend not ; the notion
of the world of those whom it will not reckon
among the righteous, — it said, ' This won't do! '
And so in all time will the lovers of polished Lib-
eralism speak concerning the intense and lonely
prophet."

This is no longer the Bagehot who could " write
across a sheet " with Sydney Smith. It is now
a Bagehot whose heart is turned away from the
cudgeling Whigs to see such things as are hidden
from the bearers of cudgels, and revealed only to
those who can await in the sanctuary of a quiet
mind the coming of the vision.

Single specimens of such a man's writing do not
suffice, of course, even as specimens. They need
their context to show their appositeness, the full
body of the writing from which they are taken to
show the mass and system of the thought. Even
separated pieces of his matter prepare us, nevertheless, for finding in Bagehot keener, juster esti-
mates of difficult historical and political characters

than it is given the merely exact historian, with
his head full of facts and his heart purged of all
imagination, to speak.   There is his estimate of
the cavalier, for example : " A cavalier is always
young.   The buoyant life arises before us, rich in
hope, strong in vigor, irregular in action : men
young and ardent, ' framed in the prodigality of
nature ; ' open to every enjoyment, alive to every
passion, eager, impulsive ; brave without discipline,
noble without principle ; prizing luxury, despising
danger ; capable of high sentiment, but in each
of whom the

> ' addiction was to courses vain ;
> His companies unlettered, rude, and shallow ;
> His hours filled up with riots, banquets, sports,
> And never noted in him any study,
> Any retirement, any sequestration
> From open haunts and popularity.'

The political sentiment is part of the character ;
the essence of Toryism is enjoyment. . . . The way
to keep up old customs is to enjoy old customs ;
the way to be satisfied with the present state of
things is to enjoy the present state of things.   Over
the cavalier mind this world passes with a thrill of
delight ; there is an exultation in a daily event,
zest in the ' regular thing,' joy at an old feast."

Is it not most natural that the writer of a pas-

sage like that should have been a consummate
critic of politics, seeing institutions through men,
the only natural way? It was as necessary that
he should be able to enjoy Sydney Smith and recognize the seer in Wordsworth as that he should
be able to conceive the cavalier life and point of
view; and in each perception there is the same
power. He is as little at fault in understanding
men of his own day. What would you wish better than his celebrated character of a " constitutional statesman," for example ? " A constitutional
statesman is a man of common opinions and uncommon abilities." Peel is his example. " His
opinions resembled the daily accumulating insensible deposits of a rich alluvial soil. The great
stream of time flows on with all things on its surface; and slowly, grain by grain, a mould of wise
experience is unconsciously left on the still, extended intellect. . . . The stealthy accumulating
words of Peel seem like the quiet leavings of some
outward tendency, which brought these, but might
as well have brought others. There is no peculiar
stamp, either, on the ideas. They might have
been any one's ideas. They belong to the general
diffused stock of observations which are to be
found in the civilized world. . . . He insensibly
takes in and imbibes the ideas of those around him.

If he were left in a vacuum, he would have no ideas."

What strikes one most, perhaps, in all these passages, is the realizing imagination which illuminates them. And it is an imagination with a practical character all its own. It is not a creating, but a conceiving imagination ; not the imagination of the fancy, but the imagination of the understanding. Conceiving imaginations, however, are of two kinds. For the one kind the understanding serves as a lamp of guidance ; upon the other the understanding acts as an electric excitant, a keen irritant. Bagehot's was evidently of the first kind ; Carlyle's, conspicuously of the second. There is something in common between the minds of these two men as they conceive society. Both have a capital grip upon the actual ; both can conceive without confusion the complex phenomena of society ; both send humorous glances of searching insight into the hearts of men. But it is the difference between them that most arrests our attention. Bagehot has the scientific imagination, Carlyle the passionate. Bagehot is the embodiment of witty common sense ; all the movements of his mind illustrate that vivacious sanity which he has himself called "animated moderation." Carlyle, on the other hand, conceives men and their motives too often with a hot intolerance; there is heat in his imagination, — a heat that sometimes scorches and consumes. Life is for him dramatic, full of fierce, imperative forces. Even when the world rings with laughter, it is laughter which, in his ears, is succeeded by an echo of mockery; laughter which is but a defiance of tears. The actual which you touch in Bagehot is the practical, operative actual of a world of workshops and parliaments, — a world of which workshops and parliaments are the natural and desirable products. Carlyle flouts at modern legislative assemblies as "talking shops," and yearns for action such as is commanded by masters of action; preaches the doctrine of work and silence in some thirty volumes octavo. Bagehot points out that prompt, crude action is the instinct and practice of the savage; that talk, the deliberation of assemblies, the slow concert of masses of men, is the cultivated fruit of civilization, nourishing to all the powers of right action in a society which is not simple and primitive, but advanced and complex. He is no more imposed upon by parliamentary debates than Carlyle is. He knows that they are stupid, and, so far as wise utterance goes, in large part futile, too. But he is not irritated, as Carlyle is, for, to say the fact, he sees more than Carlyle sees. He sees the force

and value of the stupidity.   He is wise, along with
Burke, in regarding prejudice as the cement of
society.   He knows that slow thought is the ballast
of a self-governing state.   Stanch, knitted timbers
are as necessary to the ship as sails.   Unless the
hull is conservative in holding stubbornly together
in the face of every argument of sea weather,
there'll be lives and fortunes lost.   Bagehot can
laugh at unreasoning bias.   It brings a merry
twinkle into his eye to undertake the good sport
of dissecting stolid stupidity.   But he would not
for the world abolish bias and stupidity.   He would
much rather have society hold together ; much
rather see it grow than undertake to reconstruct it.
" You remember my joke against you about the
moon," writes Sydney Smith to Jeffrey ; " d—n
the solar system — bad light — planets too distant
— pestered with comets — feeble contrivance ;
could make a better with great ease."   There was
nothing of this in Bagehot.   He was inclined to be
quite tolerant of the solar system.   He understood
that society was more quickly bettered by sympathy than by antagonism.

Bagehot's limitations, though they do not ob-
trude themselves upon your attention as his excel-
lencies do, are in truth as sharp-cut and clear
as his thought itself.   It would not be just the

truth to say that his power is that of critical analysis only, for he can and does construct thought
concerning antique and obscure systems of political
life and social action. But it is true that he does
not construct for the future. You receive stimulation from him and a certain feeling of elation.
There is a fresh air stirring in all his utterances
that is unspeakably refreshing. You open your
mind to the fine influence, and feel younger for having been in such an atmosphere. It is an atmosphere
clarified and bracing almost beyond example elsewhere. But you know what you lack in Bagehot if
you have read Burke. You miss the deep eloquence
which awakens purpose. You are not in contact
with systems of thought or with principles that
dictate action, but only with a perfect explanation.

You would go to Burke, not to Bagehot, for
inspiration in the infinite tasks of self-government;
though you would, if you were wise, go to Bagehot
rather than to Burke if you wished to realize just
what were the practical daily conditions under
which those tasks were to be worked out.

Moreover, there is a deeper lack in Bagehot.
He has no sympathy with the voiceless body of the
people, with the "mass of unknown men." He
conceives the work of government to be a work
which is possible only to the instructed few. He

would have the mass served, and served with devotion, but he would trouble to see them attempt
to serve themselves. He has not the stout fibre
and the unquestioning faith in the right and capacity of inorganic majorities which make the democrat. He has none of the heroic boldness necessary
for faith in wholesale political aptitude and capacity.
He takes democracy in detail in his thought, and
to take it in detail makes it look very awkward
indeed.

And yet surely it would not occur to the veriest
democrat that ever vociferated the " sovereignty of
the people " to take umbrage at anything Bagehot
might chance to say in dissection of democracy.
What he says is seldom provokingly true. There
is something in it all that is better than a " saving
clause," and that is a saving humor. Humor ever
keeps the whole of his matter sound ; it is an excellent salt that keeps sweet the sharpest of his sayings. Indeed, Bagehot's wit is so prominent among
his gifts that I am tempted here to enter a general
plea for wit as fit company for high thoughts and
weighty subjects. Wit does not make a subject
light ; it simply beats it into shape to be handled
readily. For my part, I make free acknowledgment that no man seems to me master of his subject who cannot take liberties with it ; who cannot

slap his propositions on the back and be hail-fellow
well met with them. Suspect a man of shallowness
who always takes himself and all that he thinks
seriously. For light on a dark subject commend
me to a ray of wit. Most of your solemn explanations are mere farthing candles in the great ex-
panse of a difficult question. Wit is not, I admit,
a steady light, but ah! its flashes give you sudden
glimpses of unsuspected things such as you will
never see without it. It is the summer lightning,
which will bring more to your startled eye in an
instant, out of the hiding of the night, than you
will ever be at the pains to observe in the full blaze
of noon.

Wit is movement, is play of mind; and the
mind cannot get play without a sufficient play-
ground. Without movement outside the world of
books, it is impossible a man should see aught but
the very neatly arranged phenomena of that world.
But it is possible for a man's thought to be instructed by the world of affairs without the man
himself becoming a part of it. Indeed, it is exceedingly hard for one who is in and of it to hold
the world of affairs off at arm's length and observe
it. He has no vantage-ground. He had better for
a while seek the distance of books, and get his perspective. The literary politician, let it be distinctly

said, is a very fine, a very superior species of the man thoughtful. He reads books as he would listen to men talk. He stands apart, and looks on, with humorous, sympathetic smile, at the play of policies. He will tell you for the asking what the players are thinking about. He divines at once how the parts are cast. He knows beforehand what each act is to discover. He might readily guess what the dialogue is to contain. Were you short of scene-shifters, he could serve you admirably in an emergency. And he is a better critic of the play than the players.

Had I command of the culture of men, I should wish to raise up for the instruction and stimulation of my nation more than one sane, sagacious, penetrative critic of men and affairs like Walter Bagehot. But that, of course. The proper thesis to draw from his singular genius is this : It is not the constitutional lawyer, nor the student of the mere machinery and legal structure of institutions, nor the politician, a mere handler of that machinery, who is competent to understand and expound government; but the man who finds the materials for his thought far and wide, in everything that reveals character and circumstance and motive. It is necessary to stand with the poets as well as with lawgivers; with the fathers of the race as well as

with your neighbor of to-day; with those who toil
and are sick at heart as well as with those who
prosper and laugh and take their pleasure; with
the merchant and the manufacturer as well as with
the closeted student; with the schoolmaster and
with those whose only school is life; with the
orator and with the men who have wrought always
in silence; in the midst of thought and also in the
midst of affairs, if you would really comprehend
those great wholes of history and of character
which are the vital substance of politics.

V.

THE INTERPRETER OF ENGLISH LIBERTY.

IN the middle of the last century two Irish adventurers crossed over into England in search of their fortunes. Rare fellows they were, bringing treasure with them; but finding it somehow hard to get upon the market: traders with a curious cargo, offering edification in exchange for a living, and concealing the best of English under a rich brogue. They were Edmund Burke and Oliver Goldsmith.

They did not cross over together: 't was no joint venture. They had been fellow students at Trinity College, Dublin; but they had not, so far as we can learn, known each other there. Each went his own way till they became comrades in the reign of Samuel Johnson at the Turk's Head Tavern. Burke stepped very boldly forth into the exposed paths of public life; Goldsmith plunged into the secret ways about Grub Street. The one gave us essays upon public questions incomparable for their reach of view and their splendid power of expres-

sion; the other gave us writings so exquisite for
their delicacy, purity, and finish as to incline us to
love him almost as much as those who knew him
loved him. We could not easily have forgiven
Ireland if she had *not* given us these men. The
one had grave faults of temper ; the other was a
reckless, roystering fellow, with a most irrepressible
Irish disposition ; but how much less we should have
known without Burke, how much less we should
have enjoyed without Goldsmith ! They have conquered places for themselves in English literature
from which we neither can nor would dislodge
them. For their sakes alone we can afford to for-
give Ireland all the trouble she has caused us.

There is no man anywhere to be found in the
annals of Parliament who seems more thoroughly
to belong to England than does Edmund Burke,
indubitable Irishman though he was. His words,
now that they have cast off their brogue, ring out
the authentic voice of the best political thought of
the English race. " If any man ask me," he cries,
" what a free government is, I answer, that, for any
practical purpose, it is what the people think so, —
and that they, and not I, are the natural, lawful,
and competent judges of the matter." " Abstract
liberty, like other mere abstractions, is not to be
found. Liberty adheres in some sensible object ;

and every nation has formed to itself some favorite point, which by way of eminence becomes the criterion of their happiness." These sentences, taken from his writings on American affairs, might serve as a sort of motto of the practical spirit of our race in affairs of government. Look further, and you shall see how his imagination presently illuminates and suffuses his maxims of practical sagacity with a fine blaze of insight, a keen glow of feeling, in which you recognize that other masterful quality of the race, its intense and elevated conviction. "My hold on the colonies," he declares, "is in the close affection which grows from common names, from kindred blood, from similar privileges, and equal protection. These are the ties which, though light as air, are as strong as links of iron. Let the colonies always keep the idea of their civil rights associated with your government, — they will cling and grapple to you, and no force under heaven will be of power to tear them from their allegiance. But let it once be understood that your government may be one thing and their privileges another, that these two things may exist without any mutual relation, — and the cement is gone, the cohesion is loosened, and everything hastens to decay and dissolution. So long as you have the wisdom to keep the sovereign power of this country as the sanctuary of liberty, the sacred temple consecrated to our common faith, wherever the chosen race and sons of England worship freedom, they will turn their faces towards you." " We cannot, I fear," he says proudly of the colonies, " we cannot falsify the pedigree of this fierce people, and persuade them that they are not sprung from a nation in whose veins the blood of freedom circulates. The language in which they would hear you tell them this tale would detect the imposition; your speech would betray you. An Englishman is the unfittest person on earth to argue another Englishman into slavery." Does not your blood stir at these passages? And is it not because, besides loving what is nobly written, you feel that every word strikes towards the heart of the things that have made your blood what it has proved to be in the history of our race?

These passages, it should be remembered, are taken from a speech in Parliament and from a letter written by Burke to his constituents in Bristol. He had no thought to make them permanent sentences of political philosophy. They were meant only to serve an immediate purpose in the advancement of contemporaneous policy. They were framed for the circumstances of the time. They speak out spontaneously amidst matter of the moment: and they could be matched everywhere throughout his pamphlets and public utterances. No other similar productions that I know of have this singular, and as it were inevitable, quality of permanency. They have emerged from the mass of political writings put forth in their time with their freshness untouched, their significance unobscured, their splendid vigor unabated. It is this that we marvel at, that they should remain modern and timely, purged of every element and seed of decay. The man who could do this must needs arrest our attention and challenge our inquiry. We wish to account for him as we should wish to penetrate the secrets of the human spirit and know the springs of genius.

Of the public life of Burke we know all that we could wish. He became so prominent a figure in the great affairs of his day that even the casual observer cannot fail to discern the main facts of his career; while the close student can follow him year by year through every step of his service. But his private life was withdrawn from general scrutiny in an unusual degree. He manifested always a marked reserve about his individual and domestic affairs, deliberately, it would seem, shielding them from impertinent inquiry. He loved the privacy of life in a great city, where one may escape

notice in the crowd and enjoy a grateful " freedom
from remark and petty censure." " Though I
have the honor to represent Bristol," he said to
Boswell, " I should not like to live there; I should
be obliged to be *so much upon my good behavior.*
In London a man may live in splendid society at
one time, and in frugal retirement at another,
without animadversion. There, and there alone, a
man's house is truly his *castle*, in which he can
be in perfect safety from intrusion whenever he
pleases. I never shall forget how well this was
expressed to me one day by Mr. Meynell: 'The
chief advantage of London,' he said, 'is, that a
man is always *so near his burrow.*'" Burke took
to his burrow often enough to pique our curiosity
sorely. This singular, high-minded adventurer had
some queer companions, we know: questionable
fellows, whose life he shared, perhaps with a certain
Bohemian relish, without sharing their morals or
their works. It seems as incongruous that such
wisdom and public spirit as breathe through his
writings should have come to his thought in such
company as that an exquisite idyll like Goldsmith's
" Vicar of Wakefield " should have been conceived
and written in squalid garrets. But neither Burke
nor Goldsmith had been born into such comradeships or such surroundings. Doubtless, as some-

times happens, their minds kept their first freshness, taking no taint from the world that touched them on every hand in their manhood, after their minds had been formed. Goldsmith, as everybody knows, remained an innocent all his life, a naïf and pettish boy amidst sophisticated men; and Burke too, notwithstanding his dignity and commanding intellectual habit, shows sometimes a touch of the same simplicity, a like habit of unguarded self-revelation. 'T was their form, no doubt, of that impulsive and ingenuous quality which we observe in all Irishmen, and which we often mistake for simplicity. 'T was a flavor of their native soil. It was also something more and better than that, however. Not every Irishman displays such hospitality for direct and simple images of truth as these men showed, for that is characteristic only of the open and unsophisticated mind, — the mind that has kept pure and open eyes. Not that Burke always sees the truth; he is even deeply prejudiced often, and there are some things that he cannot see. But the passion that dominates him when he is wrong, as when he is right, is a natural passion, born with him, not acquired from a disingenuous world that mistakes interest for justice. His nature tells in everything. It is stock of his character which he contributes to the subjects his mind handles. He is trading always with the original treasure he brought over with him at the first. He has never impaired his genuineness, or damaged his principles.

Just where Burke got his generous constitution and predisposition to enlightened ways of thinking it is not easy to see. Certainly Richard Burke, his brother, the only other member of the family whose character we discern distinctly, had a quite opposite bent. The father was a steady Dublin attorney, a Protestant, and a man, so far as we know, of solid but not brilliant parts. The mother had been a Miss Nagle, of a Roman Catholic family, which had multiplied exceedingly in County Cork. Of the home and its life we know singularly little. We are told that many children were born to the good attorney, but we hear of only four of them that grew to maturity, Garret, Edmund, Richard, and a sister best known to Edmund's biographers as Mrs. French. Edmund, the second son, was born on the twelfth of January, 1729, in the second year of the reign of George II., Robert Walpole being chief minister of the Crown. How he fared or what sort of lad he was for the first twelve years of his life we have no idea. We only know that in the year 1741, being then twelve years old, he was sent with his brothers Garret and

Richard to the school of one Abraham Shackleton, a most capable and exemplary Quaker, at Ballytore, County Kildare, to get, in some two years' time, what he himself always accounted the best part of his education. The character of the good master at Ballytore told upon the sensitive boy, who all his life through had an eye for such elevation and calm force of quiet rectitude as are to be seen in the best Quakers ; and with Richard Shackleton, the master's son, he formed a friendship from which no vicissitude of his subsequent career ever loosened his heart a whit. All his life long the ardent, imaginative statesman, deeply stirred as he was by the momentous agitation of affairs, — swept away as he was from other friends, — retained his love for the grave, retired, almost austere, but generous and constant man who had been his favorite schoolfellow. It is but another evidence of his un failing regard for whatever was steady, genuine, and open to the day in character and conduct.

At fourteen he left Ballytore and was entered at Trinity College, Dublin. Those were days when youths went to college tender, before they had become too tough to take impressions readily. But Burke, even at that callow age, cannot be said to have been teachable. He learned a vast deal, indeed, but he did not learn much of it from his nominal masters at Trinity. Apparently Master Shackleton, at Ballytore, had enabled him to find his own mind. His four years at college were years of wide and eager reading, but not years of systematic and disciplinary study. With singular, if not exemplary, self-confidence, he took his education into his own hands. He got at the heart of books through their spirit, it would seem, rather than through their grammar. He sought them out for what they could yield him in thought, rather than for what they could yield him in the way of exact scholarship. That this boy should have had such an appetite for the world's literature, old and new, need not surprise us. Other lads before and since have found big libraries all too small for them. What should arrest our attention is, the law of mind disclosed in the habits of such lads : the quick and various curiosity of original minds, and particularly of imaginative minds. They long for matter to expand themselves upon : they will climb any dizzy height from which an exciting prospect is promised : it is their joy by some means to see the world of men and affairs. Burke set out as a boy to see the world that is contained in books ; and in his journeyings he met a man after his own heart in Cicero, the copious orator and versatile man of affairs, — the only man at all like

Burke for richness, expansiveness, and variety of mind in all the ancient world. Cicero he conned as his master and model. And then, having had his fill for the time of discursive study and having completed also his four years of routine, he was graduated, taking his degree in the spring of 1748.

His father had entered him as a student at the Middle Temple in 1747, meaning that he should seek the prizes of his profession in England rather than in the little world at home; but he did not take up his residence in London until 1750, by which time he had attained his majority. What he did with the intervening two years, his biographers do not at all know, and it is idle to speculate, being confident, as we must, that he quite certainly did whatever he pleased. He did the same when he went up to London to live his terms at the Temple. "The law," he declared to Parliament more than twenty years afterwards, "is, in my opinion, one of the first and noblest of human sciences, — a science which does more to quicken and invigorate the understanding than all other kinds of learning put together; but it is not apt, except in persons very happily born, to open and to liberalize the mind exactly in the same proportion;" and, although himself a person "very happily born" in respect of all natural powers, he felt that the life

of a lawyer would inevitably confine his roving
mind within intolerably narrow limits. He learned
the law, as he learned everything else, with an eye
to discovering its points of contact with affairs,
its intimate connections with the structure and
functions of human society ; and, studying it thus,
he made his way to so many of its secrets, won so
firm a mastery of its central principles, as always
to command the respect and even the admiration
of lawyers. But the good attorney in Dublin
was sorely disappointed. This was not what he
had wanted. The son in whom he had centred
his hopes preferred the life of the town to systematic study in his chambers ; wrote for the papers
instead of devoting himself to the special profession
he had been sent to master. " Of his leisure
time," said the " Annual Register " just after his
death, " of his leisure time much was spent in the
company of Mrs. Woffington, a celebrated actress,
whose conversation was not less sought by men of
wit and genius than by men of pleasure."

We know very little about the life of Burke for
the ten years, 1750–60, his first ten years in England, — except that he did *not* diligently apply
himsely to his nominal business, the study of the
law ; and between the years 1752 and 1757 his
biographers can show hardly one authentic trace of

his real life. They know neither his whereabouts nor his employments. Only one scrap of his correspondence remains from those years to give us any hint of the time. Even Richard Shackleton, his invariable confidant and bosom friend, hears never a word from him during that period, and is told afterwards only that his correspondent has been " sometimes in London, sometimes in remote parts of the country, sometimes in France," and will " shortly, please God, be in America." He disappears a poor law student, under suspicion of his father for systematic neglect of duty ; when he reappears he is married to the daughter of a worthy physician and is author of two philosophical works which are attracting a great deal of attention. We have reason to believe that, in the mean time, he did as much writing as they would take for the booksellers ; we know that he frequented the London theatres and several of the innumerable debating clubs with which nether London abounded, whetting his faculties, it is said, upon those of a certain redoubtable baker. He haunted the galleries and lobbies of the House of Commons. His health showed signs of breaking, and Dr. Nugent took him from his lodgings in the Temple to his own house and allowed him to fall in love with his daughter. Partly for the sake of his health, perhaps, but more

particularly, no doubt, for the sake of satisfying an
eager mind and a restless habit, he wandered off to
" remote parts of the country " and to France,
with one William Burke for company, a man either
related to him or not related to him, he did not
himself know which. In 1755, a long-suffering
patience at length exhausted, his father shut the
home treasury against him ; and then, — 't was the
next year, — he published two philosophical works
and married Miss Nugent.

One might say, no doubt, that this is an intelligible enough account of a young fellow's life between twenty and thirty : and that we can fill in
the particulars for ourselves. We have known
other young Irishmen of restless and volatile natures, and need make no mystery of this one.
Goldsmith, too, disappeared, we remember, in that
same decade, making show of studying medicine in
Edinburgh, but not really studying it, and then
wandering off to the Continent, and going it afoot
in light-hearted, happy-go-lucky fashion through
the haunts both of the gay Latin races and the
sad Teutonic, greatly to the delectation, no doubt,
of the natives, — for all the world loves an innocent Irishman, with his heart upon his sleeve.
'T would all be very plain indeed if we found in
Burke that light-hearted vein. But we do not.

The fellow is sober and strenuous from the first, studying the things he was not sent to study with even too intent application, to the damage of his health, and looking through the pleasures of the town to the heart of the nation's affairs. He was a grave youth, evidently, gratifying his mind rather than his senses in the pleasures he sought ; and when he emerges from obscurity it is first to give us a touch of his quality in the matter of intellectual amusement, and then to turn at once to the serious business of the discussion of affairs to which the rest of his life was to be devoted.

The two books which he gave the world in 1756 were "A Vindication of Natural Society," a satirical piece in the manner of Bolingbroke, and "A Philosophical Inquiry into the Origin of Our Ideas of the Sublime and Beautiful," which he had begun when he was nineteen and had since reconsidered and revised. Bolingbroke, not finding revealed religion to his taste, had written a "Vindication of Natural Religion" which his vigorous and elevated style and skillful dialectic had done much to make plausible. Burke put forth his "Vindication of Natural Society" as a posthumous work of the late noble lord, and so skillfully veiled the satirical character of the imitation as wholly to deceive some very grave critics, who thought they

could discern Bolingbroke's flavor upon the tasting.
For the style, too, they took to be unmistakably
Bolingbroke's own. It had all his grandeur and
air of distinction: it had his vocabulary and formal
outline of phrase. The imitation was perfect.
And yet if you will scrutinize it, the style is
not Bolingbroke's, except in a trick or two, but
Burke's. It seems Bolingbroke's rather because
it is cold and without Burke's usual moral fervor
than because it is rich and majestic and various. There is no great formal difference between Burke's style and Bolingbroke's: but there
is a great moral and intellectual difference. When
Burke is not in earnest there is perhaps no important difference at all. And in the " Vindication
of Natural Society " Burke is not in earnest. The
book is not, indeed, a parody, and its satirical
quality is much too covert to make it a successful
satire. Much that Burke urges against civil
society he could urge in good faith, and his mind
works soberly upon it. It is only the main thesis
that he does not seriously mean. The rest he might
have meant as Bolingbroke would have meant it.

The essay on The Sublime and Beautiful, though
much admired by so great a master as Lessing, has
not worn very well as philosophy. It is full, however, of acute and interesting observations, and is

adorned in parts with touches of rich color put on with the authentic strokes of a master. We preserve it, perhaps, only because Burke wrote it; and yet when we read it we feel inclined to pronounce it worth keeping for its own sake.

Both these essays were apprentice work. Burke was trying his hand. They make us the more curious about the conditions of what must have been a notable apprenticeship. Young Burke must have gone to school to the world in a way worth knowing. But we cannot know, and that's the end on't. Probably even William Burke, Edmund's companion, could give us no very satisfactory account of the matter. The explanation lay in what he thought and not in what he did as he knocked about the world.

The company Burke kept was as singular as his talents, though scarcely so eminent. *We* speak of " Burke," but the London of his day spoke of " the Burkes," meaning William, who may or may not have been Edmund's kinsman, Edmund himself, and Richard, Edmund's younger brother, who had followed him to London to become, to say truth, an adventurer emphatically not of the elevated sort. Edmund was destined to become the leader of England's thought in more than one great matter of policy, and has remained a master among all who

think profoundly upon public affairs ; but William
was for long the leader and master of " the Burkes."
He was English born; had been in Westminster
School ; and had probably just come out from
Christ Church, Oxford, when he became the companion of Edmund's wanderings. He was a man
of intellect and literary power enough to be deemed
the possible author of the " Letters of Junius ; " he
was born moreover with an eye for the ways of
the world, and could push his own fortunes with an
unhesitating hand. It was he who first got public
office, and it was he who formed the influential
connections which got Edmund into Parliament.
He himself entered the House at the same time,
and remained there, a useful party member, for
some eight years. He made those from whom he
sought favors dislike him for his audacity in demand-
ing the utmost, and more than the utmost, that he
could possibly hope to get; but he seems to have
made those whom he served love him with a very
earnest attachment. He was self-seeking; but he
was capable of generosity, to the point of self-sac-
rifice even, when he wished to help his friend. He
early formed a partnership with Richard Burke in
immense stock-jobbing speculations in the securities
of the East India Company ; but he also formed a
literary partnership with Edmund in the prepa-

ration of a sketch of the European settlements in America, and made himself respected as a strong party writer in various pamphlets on questions of the day. He could unite the two brothers by speculating with the one and thinking with the other.

Such were "the Burkes." Edmund's home was always the home also of the other two, whenever they wished to make it so; the strongest personal affection, avowed always by Edmund with his characteristic generous warmth, bound the three men together; their purses they had in common. Edmund was not expected, apparently, to take part in the speculations which held William and Richard together; something held him aloof to which they consented, — some natural separateness of mind and character which they evidently accepted and respected. There can hardly be said to have been any aloofness of *disposition* on Edmund's part. There is something in an Irishman, — even in an Irishman who holds himself to the strictest code of upright conduct, — which forbids his acting as moral censor upon others. He can love a man none the less for generous and manly qualities because that man does what he himself would not do. Burke, moreover, had an easy standard all his life about accepting money favors. He seems to have felt somehow that his intense and whole-

hearted devotion to his friends justified gifts and
forgiven loans of money from them. He shared
the prosperity of his kinsmen without compunction,
using what he got most liberally for the assistance
of others ; and when their fortunes came to a sudden ruin, he helped them with what he had. We
ought long ago to have learned that the purest motives and the most elevated standards of conduct
may go along with a singular laxness of moral detail in some men ; and that such characters will
often constrain us to love them to the point of jus-
tifying everything that they ever did. Edmund
Burke's close union with William and Richard
does not present the least obstacle to our admiration for the noble qualities of mind and heart
which he so conspicuously possessed, or make us
for a moment doubt the thorough disinterestedness
of his great career.

Burke's marriage was a very happy one. Mrs.
Burke's thoroughly sweet temperament acted as a
very grateful and potent charm to soothe her husband's mind when shaken by the agitations of public
affairs ; her quiet capacity for domestic management relieved him of many small cares which might
have added to his burdens. Her affection satisfied
his ardent nature. He speaks of her in his will as
" my entirely beloved and incomparable wife," and

every glimpse we get of their home life confirms the estimate. After his marriage the most serious part of his intellectual life begins ; the commanding passion of his mind is disclosed. He turns away from philosophical amusements to public affairs. In 1757 appeared " An Account of the European Settlements in America," which William Burke had doubtless written, but which Edmund had almost certainly radically revised ; and Edmund himself published the first part of " An Abridgment of the History of England " which he never completed. In 1758, he proposed to Dodsley, the publisher, a yearly volume, to be known as the " Annual Register," which should chronicle and discuss the affairs of England and the Continent. It was the period of the Seven Years' War, which meant for England a sharp and glorious contest with France for the possession of America. Burke was willing to write the annals of the critical year 1758 for a hundred pounds; and so, in 1759, the first volume of the " Annual Register " appeared ; and the plan then so wisely conceived has yielded its annual volume to the present day. Burke never acknowledged his connection with this great work, — he never publicly recognized anything he had done upon contract for the publishers, — but it is quite certain that for very many years his was the presiding and plan-

ning mind in the production of the " Register." For
the first few years of its life he probably wrote the
whole of the record of events with his own hand.
It was a more useful apprenticeship than that in
philosophy. It gave him an intimate acquaintance
with affairs which must have served as a direct
preparation for the great contributions he was destined to make to the mind and policy of the Whig
party.

But this, even in addition to other hack work
for the booksellers, did not keep Burke out of pe-
cuniary straits. He sought, but failed to get, an
appointment as consul at Madrid, using the interest
of Dr. Markham, William's master at Westminster
School ; and then he engaged himself as a sort of
private secretary or literary attendant to William
Gerard Hamilton, whom he served, apparently to
the almost entire exclusion of all other employments, for some four years, going with him for a
season to Ireland, where Hamilton for a time held
the appointment of Secretary to the Lord Lieuten-
ant. Hamilton is described by one of Burke's
friends as " a sullen, vain, proud, selfish, cankered-
hearted, envious reptile," and Mr. Morley says that
there is " not a word too many nor too strong in
the description." At any rate, Burke's proud
spirit presently revolted from further service, and

he threw up a pension of three hundred pounds which Hamilton had obtained for him rather than retain any connection with the man, or remain under any sort of obligation to him. In the mean time, however, his relations with Hamilton had put him in the way of meeting many public men of weight and influence, and he had gotten his first direct introduction to the world of affairs.

It was 1764 when he shook himself free from this connection. 1764 is a year to be marked in English literary annals. It was in the spring of that year that that most celebrated of literary clubs was formed at the Turk's Head Tavern, Gerrard Street, Soho, by notable good company : Dr. Johnson, Garrick, Sir Joshua Reynolds, Goldsmith, Sheridan, Gibbon, Dr. Barnard, Beauclerk, Langton, — we know them all ; for has not Boswell given us the freedom of the Club and made us delighted participants in its conversations and diversions ? Into this company Burke was taken at once. His writings had immediately attracted the attention of such men as these, and had promptly procured him an introduction into literary society. His powers told nowhere more brilliantly than in conversation. " It is when you come close to a man in conversation," said Dr. Johnson, " that you discover what his real abilities are. To make a speech in an assembly is a sort of knack. Now I honor Thurlow; Thurlow is a fine fellow, he fairly puts his mind to yours." There can be no disputing the dictum of the greatest master of conversation : and the admirer of Burke must be willing to accept it, at any rate for the nonce, for Johnson admitted that Burke invariably put him on his mettle. " That fellow," he exclaimed, "calls forth all my powers ! " " Burke's talk," he said, " is the ebullition of his mind ; he does not talk from a desire of distinction, but because his mind is full; he is never humdrum, never unwilling to talk, nor in haste to leave off." The redoubtable doctor loved a worthy antagonist in the great game of conversation, and he always gave Burke his ungrudging admiration. When he lay dying, Burke visited his bedside, and, finding Johnson very weak, anxiously expressed the hope that his presence cost him no inconvenience. " I must be in a wretched state indeed," cried the great-hearted old man, "when your company would not be a delight to me." It was short work for Burke to get the admiration of the company at the Turk's Head. But he did much more than that : he won their devoted affection. Goldsmith said that Burke wound his way into a subject like a serpent; but he made his way straight into the hearts of his friends.

His powers are all of a piece: his heart is inextricably mixed up with his mind: his opinions are immediately transmuted into convictions: he does not talk for distinction, because he does not use his mind for the mere intellectual pleasure of it, but because he also deeply feels what he thinks. He speaks without calculation, almost impulsively.

That is the reason why we can be so sure of the essential purity of his nature from the character of his writings. They are not purely intellectual productions: there is no page of abstract reasoning to be found in Burke. His mind works upon concrete objects, and he speaks always with a certain passion, as if his affections were involved. He is irritated by opposition, because opposition in the field of affairs, in which his mind operates, touches some interest that is dear to him. Noble generalizations, it is true, everywhere broaden his matter: there is no more philosophical writer in English in the field of politics than Burke. But look, and you shall see that his generalizations are never derived from abstract premises. The reasoning is upon familiar matter of to-day. He is simply taking questions of the moment to the light, holding them up to be seen where great principles of conduct may shine upon them from the general experience of the race. He is not constructing systems of thought, but simply stripping thought of its accidental features. He is even deeply impatient of abstractions in political reasoning, so passionately is he devoted to what is practicable, and fit for wise men to do. To know such a man is to experience all the warmer forces of the mind, to feel the generous and cheering heat of character; and all noble natures will love such a man, because of kinship of quality. All noble natures that came close to Burke did love him and cherish their knowledge of him. They loaned him money without stint, and then forgave him the loans, as if it were a privilege to help him, and no way unnatural that he should never return what he received, finding his spirit made for fraternal, not for commercial relations.

It is pleasing, as it is also a little touching, to see how his companions thus freely accorded to Burke the immunities and prerogatives of a prince amongst them. No one failed to perceive how large and imperial he was, alike in natural gifts and in the wonderful range of his varied acquirements. Sir James Mackintosh, though he very earnestly combated some of Burke's views, intensely admired his greatness. He declared that Gibbon "might have been taken from a corner of Burke's mind without ever being missed." "A wit said of Gibbon's ' Autobiography ' that he did not know the difference between himself and the Roman Empire. He has narrated his ' progressions from London to Buriton and from Buriton to London ' in the same monotonous, majestic periods that he recorded the fall of states and empires." And we certainly feel a sense of incongruity : the two subjects, we perceive, are hardly commensurable. Perhaps in Burke's case we should have felt differently, — we *do* feel differently. In that extraordinary " Letter to a Noble Lord," in which he defends his pension so proudly against the animadversions of the Duke of Bedford, how magnificently he speaks of his services to the country ; how proud and majestic a piece of autobiography it is! How insignificant does the ancient house of Bedford seem, with all its long generations, as compared with this single and now lonely man, without distinguished ancestry or hope of posterity ! He speaks grandly about himself, as about everything ; and yet I see no disparity between the subject and the manner !

Outside the small circle of those who knew and loved him, his generation did not wholly perceive this. There seemed a touch of pretension in this proud tone taken by a man who had never held high office or exercised great power. He had made great speeches, indeed, no one denied that ; he had

written great party pamphlets, — that everybody
knew; his had been the intellectual force within
the group of Whigs that followed Lord Rockingham, — that, too, the world in general perceived
and acknowledged; and when he died, England
knew the man who had gone to be a great man.
But, for all that, his tone must, in his generation,
have seemed disproportioned to the part he had
played. His great authority is over us rather than
over the men of his own day.

Burke had the thoughts of a great statesman,
and uttered them with unapproachable nobility;
but he never wielded the power of a great statesman. He was kept always in the background in
active politics, in minor posts, and employed upon
subordinate functions. This would be a singular
circumstance, if there were any novelty in it; but
the practice of keeping men of insignificant birth
out of the great offices was a practice which had
" broadened down from precedent to precedent "
until it had become too strong for even Burke to
breast or stem. Perhaps, too, there were faults of
temper which rendered Burke unfit to exercise
authority in directing the details, and determining
the practical measures, of public policy: — but we
shall look into that presently.

In July, 1765, the Marquis of Rockingham

became prime minister of England, and Burke became his private secretary. He owed his intro duction to Lord Rockingham, as usual, to the good offices of William Burke, who seems to have found means of knowing everybody it was to the interest of " the Burkes " to know. A more fortunate con nection could hardly have been made. Lord Rock ingham, though not a man of original powers, was a man of the greatest simplicity and nobleness of character, and, like most upright men, knew how to trust other men. He gave Burke immediate proof of his manly qualities. The scheming old Duke of Newcastle, who ought to have been a connoisseur in low men, mistook Burke for one. Shocked that this obscurely born and unknown fel low should be accorded confidential relations by Lord Rockingham, he hurried to his lordship with an assortment of hastily selected slanders against Burke. His real name, he reported, was O'Bourke; he was an Irish adventurer without character, and a rank Papist to boot; it would ruin the admin istration to have such a man connected with the First Lord of the Treasury. Rockingham, with great good sense and frankness, took the whole matter at once to Burke; was entirely satisfied by Burke's denials; and admitted him immediately to intimate relations of warm personal friendship which only death broke off. William Burke obtained for himself an Undersecretaryship of State and arranged with Lord Verney, at that time his partner in East India speculations, that two of his lordship's parliamentary boroughs should be put at his and Edmund's disposal. Edmund Burke, accordingly, entered Parliament for the borough of Wendover on the 14th of January, 1766, at the age of thirty-seven, and in the first vigor of his powers.

"Now we who know Burke," announced Dr. Johnson, "know that he will be one of the first men in the country." Burke promptly fulfilled the prediction. He made a speech before he had been in the House two weeks ; a speech that made him at once a marked man. His health was now firmly established; he had a commanding physique; his figure was tall and muscular, and his bearing full of a dignity which had a touch almost of haughtiness in it. Although his action was angular and awkward, his extraordinary richness and fluency of utterance drew the attention away from what he was doing to what he was saying. His voice was harsh, and did not harmonize with the melodious measures in which his words poured forth ; but it was of unusual compass, and carried in it a sense of confidence and power. His utterance was too

rapid, his thought bore him too impulsively forward, but the pregnant matter he spoke "filled the
town with wonder." The House was excited by
new sensations. Members were astonished to recognize a broad philosophy of politics running
through this ardent man's speeches. They felt the
refreshment of the wide outlook he gave them, and
were conscious of catching glimpses of excellent
matter for reflection at every turn of his hurrying
thought. They wearied of it, indeed, after a while:
the pace was too hard for most of his hearers, and
they finally gave over following him when the
novelty and first excitement of the exercise had
worn off. He too easily lost sight of his audience
in his search for principles, and they resented his
neglect of them, his indifference to their tastes.
They felt his lofty style of reasoning as a sort of
rebuke, and deemed his discursive wisdom out of
place amidst their own thoughts of imperative personal and party interest. He had, before very
long, to accustom himself, therefore, to speak to an
empty House and subsequent generations. His
opponents never, indeed, managed to feel quite
easy under his attacks: his arrows sought out their
weak places to the quick, and they winced even
when they coughed or seemed indifferent; but they
comforted themselves with the thought that the

orator was also tedious and irritating to his own friends, teasing them too with keen rebukes and vexatious admonitions. The high and wise sort of speaking must always cause uneasiness in a political assembly. The more equal and balanced it is, the more must both parties be threatened with reproof.

I would not be understood as saying that Burke's speeches were impartial. They were not. He had preferences which amounted to prejudices. He was always an intense party man. But then he was a party man with a difference. He believed that the interests of England were bound up with the fortunes of the Rockingham Whigs; but he did not separate the interests of his party and the interests of his country. He cherished party connections because he conceived them to be absolutely necessary for effective public service. " Where men are not acquainted with each other's principles," he said, "nor experienced in each other's talents, nor at all practiced in their mutual habitudes or dispositions by joint efforts in business; no personal confidence, no friendship, no common interest, subsisting among them ; it is evidently impossible that they can act a public part with uniformity, perseverance, or efficacy. In a connection, the most inconsiderable man, by adding to the weight of the whole, has his value, and his use ;

out of it, the greatest talents are wholly unserviceable to the public." " When bad men combine, the good must associate." " It is not enough in a situation of trust in the commonwealth, that a man means well to his country ; it is not enough that in his single person he never did an evil act, but always voted according to his conscience, and even harangued against every design which he apprehended to be prejudicial to the interests of his country. . . . Duty demands and requires, that what is right should not only be made known, but made prevalent ; that what is evil should not only be detected, but defeated. When the public man omits to put himself in a situation of doing his duty with effect, it is an omission that frustrates the purposes of his trust almost as much as if he had formally betrayed it." Burke believed the Rockingham Whigs to be a combination of good men, and he felt that he ought to sacrifice something to keep himself in their connection. He regarded them as men who " believed private honor to be the foundation of public trust ; that friendship was no mean step towards patriotism ; that he who, in the common intercourse of life, showed he regarded somebody besides himself, when he came to act in a public situation, might probably consult some other interest than his own." He admitted

that such confederacies had often " a narrow, big-
oted, and proscriptive spirit; " " but, where duty
renders a critical situation a necessary one," he
said, " it is our business to keep free from the evils
attendant upon it; and not to fly from the situation
itself. If a fortress is seated in an unwholesome
air, an officer of the garrison is obliged to be
attentive to his health, but he must not desert his
station." " A party," he declared, " is a body of
men united for promoting by their joint endeavors
the national interest upon some particular principle
in which they are all agreed." " Men thinking
freely, will," he very well knew, " in particular instances, think differently. But still as the greater
part of the measures which arise in the course of
public business are related to, or dependent on,
some great, *leading, general principles in government*, a man must be peculiarly unfortunate in the
choice of his political company, if he does not agree
with them at least nine times in ten. If he does
not concur in these general principles upon which
the party is founded, and which necessarily draw
on a concurrence in their application, he ought
from the beginning to have chosen some other,
more conformable to his opinions. When the
question is in its nature doubtful, or not very
material, the modesty which becomes an individual,

and that partiality which becomes a well-chosen friendship, will frequently bring on an acquiescence in the general sentiment. Thus the disagreement will naturally be rare; it will be only enough to indulge freedom, without violating concord, or disturbing arrangement."

Certainly there were no party prizes for Burke. During much the greater part of his career the party to which he adhered was in opposition; and even when in office it had only small favors for him. Even his best friends advised against his appointment to any of the great offices of state, deeming him too intemperate and unpractical. And yet the intensity of his devotion to his party never abated a jot. Assuredly there was never a less selfish allegiance. His devotion was for the principles of his party, as he conceived and constructed them. It was a moral and intellectual devotion. He had embarked all his spirit's fortunes in the enterprise. Faults he unquestionably had, which seemed very grave. He was passionate sometimes beyond all bounds: he seriously frightened cautious and practical men by his haste and vehemence in pressing his views for acceptance. He was capable of falling, upon occasion, into a very frenzy of excitement in the midst of debate, when he would often shock moderate men by the

ungoverned license of his language. But his friends
were as much to blame for these outbreaks as he
was. They cut him to the quick by the way in
which they criticised and misunderstood him. His
heart was maddened by the pain of their neglect
of his just claims to their confidence. They seemed
often to use him without trusting him, and their
slights were intolerable to his proud spirit. Practically, and upon a narrow scale of expediency,
they may have been right: perhaps he was *not* circumspect enough to be made a responsible head of
administration. Unquestionably, too, they loved
him and meant him no unkindness. But it was
none the less tragical to treat such a man in such
a fashion. They may possibly have temporarily
served their country by denying to Burke full public acknowledgment of his great services; but they
cruelly wounded a great spirit, and they hardly
served mankind.

They did Burke an injustice, moreover. They
greatly underrated his practical powers. In such
offices as he was permitted to hold he showed in
actual administration the same extraordinary mastery of masses of detail which was the foundation
of his unapproachable mastery of general principles
in his thinking. His thought was always immersed
in matter, and concrete detail did not confuse him

when he touched it any more than it did when he meditated upon it. Immediate contact with affairs always steadied his judgment. He was habitually temperate in the conduct of business. It was only in speech and when debating matters that stirred the depths of his nature that he gave way to uncalculating fervor. He was intemperate in his emotions, but seldom in his actions. He could, and did, write calm state papers in the very midst and heat of parliamentary affairs that subjected him to the fiercest excitements. He was eminently capable of counsel as well as of invective.

He served his party in no servile fashion, for all he adhered to it with such devotion. He sacrificed his intellectual independence as little as his personality in taking intimate part in its counsels. He gave it principles, indeed, quite as often as he accepted principles from it. In the final efforts of his life, when he engaged every faculty of his mind in the contest that he waged with such magnificent wrath against the French revolutionary spirit, he gave tone to all English thought, and direction to many of the graver issues of international policy. Rejected oftentimes by his party, he has at length been accepted by the world.

His habitual identification with opposition rather than with the government gave him a certain advantage. It relaxed party discipline and indulged his independence. It gave leave, too, to the better efforts of his genius: for in opposition it is principles that tell, and Burke was first and last a master of principles. Government is a matter of practical detail, as well as of general measures; but the criticism of government very naturally becomes a matter of the application of general principles, as standards rather than as practical means of policy.

Four questions absorbed the energies of Burke's life and must always be associated with his fame. These were, the American war for independence; administrative reform in the English home government; reform in the government of India; and the profound political agitations which attended the French Revolution. Other questions he studied, deeply pondered, and greatly illuminated, but upon these four he expended the full strength of his magnificent powers. There is in his treatment of these subjects a singular consistency, a very admirable simplicity of standard. It has been said, and it is true, that Burke had no system of political philosophy. He was afraid of abstract system in political thought, for he perceived that questions of government are moral questions, and that questions of morals cannot always be squared with the rules of logic, but run through as many ranges of variety as the circumstances of life itself. "Man acts from adequate motives relative to his interest," he said, "and not on metaphysical speculations. Aristotle, the great master of reasoning, cautions us, and with great weight and propriety, against this species of delusive geometrical accuracy in moral arguments, as the most fallacious of all sophistry." And yet Burke unquestionably had a very definite and determinable system of thought, which was none the less a system for being based upon concrete, and not upon abstract premises. It is said by some writers (even by so eminent a writer as Buckle) that in his later years Burke's mind lost its balance and that he reasoned as if he were insane; and the proof assigned is, that he, a man who loved liberty, violently condemned, not the terrors only, — that of course, — but the very principles of the French Revolution. But to reason thus is to convict one's self of an utter lack of comprehension of Burke's mind and motives: as a very brief examination of his course upon the four great questions I have mentioned will show.

From first to last Burke's thought is conservative. Let his attitude with regard to America serve as an example. He took his stand, as everybody knows, with the colonies, against the mother country; but his object was not revolutionary.

He did not deny the legal right of England to tax the colonies (*we* no longer deny it ourselves), but he wished to preserve the empire, and he saw that to insist upon the right of taxation would be irrevocably to break up the empire, when dealing with such a people as the Americans. He pointed out the strong and increasing numbers of the colonists, their high spirit in enterprise, their jealous love of liberty, and the indulgence England had hitherto accorded them in the matter of self-government, permitting them in effect to become an independent people in respect of all their internal affairs; and he declared the result matter for just pride. " Whilst we follow them among the tumbling mountains of ice, and behold them penetrating into the deepest frozen recesses of Hudson's Bay and Davis's Straits," he exclaimed, in a famous passage of his incomparable speech on Conciliation with America, " whilst we are looking for them beneath the arctic circle, we hear that they have pierced into the opposite region of polar cold, that they are at the antipodes, and engaged under the frozen serpent of the South. Falkland Island, which seemed too remote and romantic an object for the grasp of national ambition, is but a stage and resting place in the progress of their victorious industry. Nor is the equinoctial heat more discouraging to

them than the accumulated winter of both the poles.
We know that whilst some of them draw the line
and strike the harpoon on the coast of Africa,
others run the longitude, and pursue their gigantic
game along the coast of Brazil. No sea but what
is vexed by their fisheries. No climate that is not
witness to their toils. Neither the perseverance of
Holland, nor the activity of France, nor the dex-
terous and firm sagacity of English enterprise,
ever carried this most perilous mode of hardy
industry to the extent to which it has been pushed
by this recent people, — a people who are still, as
it were, but in the gristle, and not yet hardened
into the bone of manhood. When I contemplate
these things, — when I know that the colonies in
general owe little or nothing to any care of ours,
and that they are not squeezed into this happy
form by the constraints of watchful and suspicious
government, but that, through a wise and salutary
neglect, a generous nature has been suffered to
take her own way to perfection, — when I reflect
upon these effects, when I see how profitable they
have been to us, I feel all the pride of power sink,
and all the presumption in the wisdom of human
contrivances melt and die away within me, — my
rigor relents, — I pardon something to the spirit
of liberty."

" I think it necessary," he insisted, " to consider distinctly the true nature and the peculiar circumstances of the object we have before us : because, after all our struggle, whether we will or not, we must govern America according to that nature and those circumstances, and not according to our own imaginations, not according to abstract ideas of right, by no means according to mere general theories of government, the resort to which appears to me, in our present situation, no better than arrant trifling." To attempt to force such a people would be a course of idle folly. Force, he declared, would not only be an odious " but a feeble instrument, for preserving a people so numerous, so active, so growing, so spirited as this, in a profitable and subordinate connection with " England.

" First, Sir," he cried, " permit me to observe, that the use of force alone is but *temporary.* It may subdue for a moment; but it does not remove the necessity of subduing again : and a nation is not governed which is perpetually to be conquered.

" My next objection is its *uncertainty.* Terror is not always the effect of force, and an armament is not a victory. If you do not succeed, you are without resource : for, conciliation failing, force remains; but, force failing, no further hope of reconciliation is left. Power and authority are sometimes bought by kindness ; but they can never be begged as alms by an impoverished and defeated violence.

" A further objection to force is, that you *impair the object* by your very endeavors to preserve it. The thing you fought for is not the thing you recover, but depreciated, sunk, wasted, and consumed in the contest. Nothing less will content me than *whole America*. I do not choose to consume its strength along with our own ; for in all parts it is the British strength I consume. . . . Let me add, that I do not choose wholly to break the American spirit ; because it is the spirit that has made the country.

" Lastly, we have no sort of *experience* in favor of force as an instrument in the rule of our colonies. Their growth and their utility has been owing to methods altogether different. Our ancient indulgence has been said to be pursued to a fault. It may be so ; but we know, if feeling is evidence, that our fault was more tolerable than our attempt to mend it, and our sin far more salutary than our penitence."

" Obedience is what makes government," " freedom, and not servitude, is the cure of anarchy," and you cannot insist upon one rule of obedience for Englishmen in America while you jealously maintain another for Englishmen in England. "For, in order to prove that the Americans have no right to their liberties, we are every day endeavoring to subvert the maxims which preserve the whole spirit of our own. To prove that the Americans ought not to be free, we are obliged to depreciate the value of freedom itself; and we never seem to gain a paltry advantage over them in debate, without attacking some of those principles, or deriding some of those feelings, for which our ancestors have shed their blood." "The question with me is, not whether you have a right to render your people miserable, but whether it is not your interest to make them happy. It is not what a lawyer tells me I *may* do, but what humanity, reason, and justice tell me I *ought* to do. . . . Such is steadfastly my opinion of the absolute necessity of keeping up the concord of this empire by a unity of spirit, though in a diversity of operations, that, if I were sure that the colonists had, at their leaving this country, sealed a regular compact of servitude, that they had solemnly abjured all the rights of citizens, that they had made a vow to renounce all ideas of liberty for them and their posterity to all generations, yet I should hold myself obliged to conform to the temper I found universally prevalent in my own day, and to govern two million of men, impatient of servitude, on the principles of freedom. I am not determining a point of law; I am restoring tranquillity : and the general character and situation of a people must determine what sort of government is fitted for them. That point nothing else can or ought to determine." " All government, indeed every human benefit and enjoyment, every virtue and every prudent act, is founded on compromise and barter. We balance inconveniences ; we give and take; we remit some rights, that we may enjoy others ; and we choose rather to be happy citizens than subtle disputants." " Magnanimity in politics is not seldom the truest wisdom ; and a great empire and little minds go ill together."

Here you have the whole spirit of the man, and in part a view of his eminently practical system of thought. The view is completed when you advance with him to other subjects of policy. He pressed with all his energy for radical reforms in administration, but he earnestly opposed every change that might touch the structure of the constitution itself. He sought to secure the integrity of Parliament, not by changing the system of representation, but by cutting out all roots of corruption. He pressed forward with the most ardent in all plans of just reform, but he held back with the most conserva-

tive from all propositions of radical change. " To
innovate is not to reform," he declared, and there
is " a marked distinction between change and reformation. The former alters the substance of the
objects themselves, and gets rid of all their essential good as well as of all the accidental evil annexed
to them. Change is novelty ; and whether it is to
operate any one of the effects of reformation at all,
or whether it may not contradict the very principle upon which reformation is desired, cannot certainly be known beforehand. Reform is not a
change in the substance or in the primary modification of the object, but a direct application of a
remedy to the grievance complained of. So far as
that is removed, all is sure. It stops there ; and
if it fails, the substance which underwent the operation, at the very worst, is but where it was." This
is the governing motive of his immense labors to
accomplish radical economical reform in the administration of the government. He was not seeking economy merely ; to husband the resources of
the country was no more than a means to an end,
and that end was, to preserve the constitution in its
purity. He believed that Parliament was not truly
representative of the people because so many place-
men found seats in it, and because so many members who might have been independent were bought

by the too abundant favors of the Court. Cleanse Parliament of this corruption, and it would be restored to something like its pristine excellence as an instrument of liberty.

He dreaded to see the franchise extended and the House of Commons radically made over in its constitution. It had never been intended to be merely the people's House. It had been intended to hold all the elements of the state that were not to be found in the House of Lords or the Court. He conceived it to be the essential object of the constitution to establish a balanced and just intercourse between the several forces of an ancient society, and it was well that that balance should be preserved even in the House of Commons, rather than give perilous sweep to a single set of interests. "These opposed and conflicting interests," he said to his French correspondent, "which you considered as so great a blemish in your old and in our present Constitution, interpose a salutary check to all precipitate resolutions. They render deliberation a matter, not of choice, but of necessity; they make all change a subject of *compromise*, which naturally begets moderation; they produce *temperaments*, preventing the sore evil of harsh, crude, unqualified reformations, and rendering all the headlong exertions of arbitrary power, in the few

or in the many, forever impracticable. Through
that diversity of members and interests, general
liberty had as many securities as there are separate
views in the several orders; whilst by pressing
down the whole by the weight of a real monarchy,
the separate parts would have been prevented from
warping and starting from their allotted places."
" *We* wish," he said, " to derive all we possess *as
an inheritance from our forefathers.* Upon that
body and stock of experience we have taken care
not to inoculate any scion alien to the nature of the
original plant." " This idea of a liberal descent
inspires us with a sense of habitual native dignity,
which prevents that upstart insolence almost inevitably adhering to and disgracing those who are
the first acquirers of any .distinction. By this
means our liberty becomes a noble freedom. It
carries an imposing and majestic aspect. It has a
pedigree and illustrating ancestors. It has its
bearings and its ensigns armorial. It has its gallery of portraits, its monumental inscriptions, its
records, evidences, and titles. We procure reverence to our civil institutions on the principle upon
which Nature teaches us to revere individual men :
on account of their age, and on account of those
from whom they are descended."

" When the useful parts of an old establishment

are kept, and what is superadded is to be fitted to
what is retained, a vigorous mind, steady, perse-
vering attention, various powers of comparison
and combination, and the resources of an understanding fruitful in expedients are to be exercised;
they are to be exercised in a continued conflict
with the combined force of opposite vices, with the
obstinacy that rejects all improvement, and the
levity that is fatigued and disgusted with everything of which it is in possession. . . . Political
arrangement, as it is a work for social ends, is to
be only wrought by social means. There mind
must conspire with mind. Time is required to
produce that union of minds which alone can produce all the good we aim at. Our patience will
achieve more than our force. If I might venture
to appeal to what is so much out of fashion in
Paris, — I mean to experience, — I should tell you
that in my course I have known, and, according to
my measure, have coöperated with great men; and
I have never yet seen any plan which has not been
mended by the observations of those who were
much inferior in understanding to the person who
took the lead in the business. By a slow, but well
sustained progress, the effect of each step is
watched; the good or ill success of the first gives
light to us in the second; and so, from light to light,

we are conducted with safety, through the whole series. . . . We are enabled to unite into a consistent whole the various anomalies and contending principles that are found in the minds and affairs of men. From hence arises, not an excellence in simplicity, but one far superior, an excellence in composition. Where the great interests of mankind are concerned through a long succession of generations, that succession ought to be admitted into some share in the counsels which are so deeply to affect them."

It is not possible to escape deep conviction of the wisdom of these reflections. They penetrate to the heart of all practicable methods of reform. Burke was doubtless too timid, and in practical judgment often mistaken. Measures which in reality would operate only as salutary and needed reformations he feared because of the element of change that was in them. He erred when he supposed that progress can in all its stages be made without changes which seem to go even to the substance. But, right or wrong, his philosophy did not come to him of a sudden and only at the end of his life, when he found France desolated and England threatened with madness for love of revolutionary principles of change. It is the key to his thought everywhere, and through all his life.

It is the key (which many of his critics have never found) to his position with regard to the revolution in France. He was roused to that fierce energy of opposition in which so many have thought that they detected madness, not so much because of his deep disgust to see brutal and ignorant men madly despoil an ancient and honorable monarchy, as because he saw the spirit of these men cross the Channel and find lodgment in England, even among statesmen like Fox, who had been his own close friends and companions in thought and policy; not so much because he loved France as because he feared for England. For England he had Shakespeare's love:

> " That fortress built by nature for herself
> *Against infection and the hand of war;*
> That happy breed of men, that little world,
> That precious stone set in the silver sea,
> Which serves it in the office of a wall,
> Or as a moat defensive to a house,
> *Against the envy of less happier lands;*
> That blessed plot, that earth, that realm, that England."

'T was to keep out infection and to preserve such precious stores of manly tradition as had made that little world " the envy of less happier lands " that Burke sounded so effectually that extraordinary alarm against the revolutionary spirit that was racking France from throne to cottage. Let us admit, if you will, that with reference to France herself he was mistaken. Let us say that when he admired the institutions which she was then sweeping away he was yielding to sentiment, and imagining France as perfect as the beauty of the sweet queen he had seen in her radiant youth. Let us concede that he did not understand the condition of France, and therefore did not see how inevitable that terrible revolution was: that in this case, too, the wages of sin was death. He was not defending France, if you look to the bottom of it; he was defending England : — and the things he hated are truly hateful. He hated the French revolutionary philosophy and deemed it unfit for free men. And that philosophy is in fact radically evil and corrupting. No state can ever be conducted on its principles. For it holds that government is a matter of contract and deliberate arrangement, whereas in fact it is an institute of habit, bound together by innumerable threads of association, scarcely one of which has been deliberately placed. It holds that the object of government is liberty, whereas the true object of government is justice; not the advantage of one class, even though that class constitute the majority, but right equity in the adjustment of the interests of all classes. It assumes that government can be made over at will, but assumes it without the slightest historical foundation. For governments have never been successfully and permanently changed except by slow modification operating from generation to generation. It contradicted every principle that had been so laboriously brought to light in the slow stages of the growth of liberty in the only land in which liberty had then grown to great proportions. The history of England is a continuous thesis against revolution; and Burke would have been no true Englishman, had he not roused himself, even fanatically, if there were need, to keep such puerile doctrine out.

If you think his fierceness was madness, look how he conducted the trial against Warren Hastings during those same years: with what patience, with what steadiness in business, with what temper, with what sane and balanced attention to detail, with what statesmanlike purpose! Note, likewise, that his thesis is the same in the one undertaking as in the other. He was applying the same principles to the case of France and to the case of India that he had applied to the case of the colonies. He meant to save the empire, not by changing its constitution, as was the method in France, and so shaking every foundation in order to dislodge an abuse, but by administering it uprightly and in a

liberal spirit. He was persuaded "that government was a practical thing, made for the happiness
of mankind, and not to furnish out a spectacle of
uniformity to gratify the schemes of visionary politicians. Our business," he said, "was to rule, not
to wrangle; and it would be a poor compensation
that we had triumphed in a dispute, whilst we had
lost an empire." The monarchy must be saved
and the constitution vindicated by keeping the
empire pure in all parts, even in the remotest
provinces. Hastings must be crushed in order
that the world might know that no English governor could afford to be unjust. Good government, like all virtue, he deemed to be a practical
habit of conduct, and not a matter of constitutional
structure. It is a great ideal, a thoroughly English
ideal; and it constitutes the leading thought of all
Burke's career.

In short, as I began by saying, this man, an
Irishman, speaks the best English thought upon the
essential questions of politics. He is thoroughly,
characteristically, and to the bottom English in all
his thinking. He is more liberal than Englishmen
in his treatment of Irish questions, of course; for
he understands them, as no Englishman of his
generation did. But for all that he remains the
chief spokesman for England in the utterance of

the fundamental ideals which have governed the action of Englishmen in politics. " All the ancient, honest, juridical principles and institutions of England," such was his idea, "are so many clogs to check and retard the headlong course of violence and oppression. They were invented for this one good purpose, that what was not *just* should not be *convenient.*" This is fundamental English doctrine. English liberty has consisted in making it unpleasant for those who were unjust, and thus getting them in the habit of being just for the sake of a *modus vivendi.* Burke is the apostle of the great English gospel of Expediency.

The politics of English-speaking peoples has never been speculative ; it has always been profoundly practical and utilitarian. Speculative politics treats men and situations as they are supposed to be ; practical politics treats them (upon no general plan, but in detail) as they are found to be at the moment of actual contact. With reference to America Burke argues: No matter what your legal right in the case, it is not *expedient* to treat America as you propose : a numerous and spirited people like the colonists will not submit ; and your experiment will cost you your colonies. In the case of administrative reform, again, it is the higher sort of expediency he urges : If you wish to keep your government from revolution, keep it from corruption, and by making it pure render it permanent. To the French he says, It is not *expedient* to destroy thus recklessly these ancient parts of your constitution. How will you replace them? How will you conduct affairs at all after you shall have deprived yourselves of all balance and of all old counsel? It is both better and easier to reform than to tear down and reconstruct.

This is unquestionably the message of Englishmen to the world, and Burke utters it with incomparable eloquence. A man of sensitive imagination and elevated moral sense, of a wide knowledge and capacity for affairs, he stood in the midst of the English nation speaking its moral judgments upon affairs, its character in political action, its purposes of freedom, equity, wide and equal progress. It is the immortal charm of his speech and manner that gives permanence to his works. Though his life was devoted to affairs with a constant and unalterable passion, the radical features of Burke's mind were literary. He was a man of books, without being under the dominance of what others had written. He got knowledge out of books and the abundance of matter his mind craved to work its constructive and imaginative effects upon. It is singular how devoid of all direct references to books his writings are. The materials of his thought never reappear in the same form in which he obtained them. They have been smelted and recoined. They have come under the drill and inspiration of a great constructive mind, have caught life and taken structure from it. Burke is not literary because he takes from books, but because he makes books, transmuting what he writes upon into literature. It is this inevitable literary quality, this sure mastery of style, that mark the man, as much as his thought itself. He is a master in the use of the great style. Every sentence, too, is steeped in the colors of an extraordinary imagination. The movement takes your breath and quickens your pulses. The glow and power of the matter rejuvenate your faculties.

And yet the thought, too, is quite as imperishable as its incomparable vehicle.

> "The deepest, plainest, highest, clearest pen,
> The voice most echoed by consenting men;
> The soul which answered best to all well said
> By others, and which most requital made;
> Tuned to the highest key of ancient Rome,
> Returning all her music with his own;
> In whom, with nature, study claimed a part,
> And yet who to himself owed all his art."

VI.

THE TRUTH OF THE MATTER.

"GIVE us the facts, and nothing but the facts," is the sharp injunction of our age to its historians. Upon the face of it, an eminently reasonable requirement. To tell the truth simply, openly, without reservation, is the unimpeachable first principle of all right dealing; and historians have no license to be quit of it. Unquestionably they must tell us the truth, or else get themselves enrolled among a very undesirable class of persons, not often frankly named in polite society. But the thing is by no means so easy as it looks. The truth of history is a very complex and very occult matter. It consists of things which are invisible as well as of things which are visible. It is full of secret motives, and of a chance interplay of trivial and yet determining circumstances; it is shot through with transient passions, and broken athwart here and there by what seem cruel accidents; it cannot all be reduced to statistics or newspaper items or official recorded statements. And so it turns out, when the actual test of experiment is made, that the historian must

have something more than a good conscience, must
be something more than a good man.   He must
have an eye to see the truth; and nothing but a
very catholic imagination will serve to illuminate
his matter for him: nothing less than keen and
steady insight will make even illumination yield
him the truth of what he looks upon.   Even when
he has seen the truth, only half his work is done,
and that not the more difficult half.   He must
then make others see it just as he does: only when
he has done that has he told the truth.   What an
art of penetrative phrase and just selection must
he have to take others into the light in which he
stands!   Their dullness, their ignorance, their prepossessions, are to be overcome and driven in, like
a routed troop, upon the truth.   The thing is infinitely difficult.   The skill and strategy of it cannot
be taught.   And so historians take another way,
which is easier: they tell part of the truth, — the
part most to their taste, or most suitable to their
talents, — and obtain readers to their liking among
those of similar tastes and talents to their own.

We have our individual preferences in history,
as in every other sort of literature.   And there are
histories to every taste: histories full of the piquant
details of personal biography, histories that blaze
with the splendors of courts and resound with

drum and trumpet, and histories that run upon the
humbler but greater levels of the life of the people;
colorless histories, so passionless and so lacking in
distinctive mark or motive that they might have
been set up out of a dictionary without the intervention of an author, and partisan histories, so
warped and violent in every judgment that no
reader not of the historian's own party can stomach
them; histories of economic development, and histories that speak only of politics; those that tell
nothing but what it is pleasant and interesting to
know, and those that tell nothing at all that one
cares to remember. One must be of a new and
unheard-of taste not to be suited among them all.

The trouble is, after all, that men do not invariably find the truth to their taste, and will often
deny it when they hear it; and the historian has to
do much more than keep his own eyes clear: he
has also to catch and hold the eye of his reader.
'T is a nice art, as much intellectual as moral.
How shall he take the palate of his reader at un-
awares, and get the unpalatable facts down his
throat along with the palatable? Is there no way
in which all the truth may be made to hold together
in a narrative so strongly knit and so harmoniously
colored that no reader will have either the wish or
the skill to tear its patterns asunder, and men will

take it all, unmarred and as it stands, rather than miss the zest of it?

It is evident the thing cannot be done by the " dispassionate " annalist. The old chroniclers, whom we relish, were not dispassionate. We love some of them for their sweet quaintness, some for their childlike credulity, some for their delicious inconsequentiality. But our modern chroniclers are not so. They are, above all things else, knowing, thoroughly informed, subtly sophisticated. They would not for the world contribute any spice of their own to the narrative; and they are much too watchful, circumspect, and dutiful in their care to keep their method pure and untouched by any thought of theirs to let us catch so much as a glimpse of the chronicler underneath the chronicle. Their purpose is to give simply the facts, eschewing art, and substituting a sort of monumental index and table of the world's events.

The trouble is that men refuse to be made any wiser by such means. Though they will readily enough let their eyes linger upon a monument of art, they will heedlessly pass by a mere monument of industry. It suggests nothing to them. The materials may be suitable enough, but the handling of them leaves them dead and commonplace. An interesting circumstance thus comes to light. It is nothing less than this, that the facts do not of themselves constitute the truth. The truth is abstract, not concrete. It is the just idea, the right revelation of what things mean. It is evoked only by such arrangements and orderings of facts as suggest interpretations. The chronological arrangement of events, for example, may or may not be the arrangement which most surely brings the truth of the narrative to light ; and the best arrangement is always that which displays, not the facts themselves, but the subtle and else invisible forces that lurk in the events and in the minds of men, — forces for which events serve only as lasting and dramatic words of utterance. Take an instance. How are you to enable men to know the truth with regard to a period of revolution ? Will you give them simply a calm statement of recorded events, simply a quiet, unaccentuated narrative of what actually happened, written in a monotone, and verified by quotations from authentic documents of the time ? You may save yourself the trouble. As well make a pencil sketch in outline of a raging conflagration ; write upon one portion of it "flame," upon another "smoke;" here "town hall, where the fire started," and there "spot where fireman was killed." It is a chart, not a picture. Even if you made a veritable picture of it, you

could give only part of the truth so long as you
confined yourself to black and white. Where
would be all the wild and terrible colors of the
scene: the red and tawny flame; the masses of
smoke, carrying the dull glare of the fire to the
very skies, like a great signal banner thrown to the
winds; the hot and frightened faces of the crowd;
the crimsoned gables down the street, with the
faint light of a lamp here and there gleaming
white from some hastily opened casement? Without the colors your picture is not true. No inventory of items will even represent the truth: the
fuller and more minute you make your inventory,
the more will the truth be obscured. The little
details will take up as much space in the statement
as the great totals into which they are summed up;
and, the proportions being false, the whole is false.
Truth, fortunately, takes its own revenge. No one
is deceived. The reader of the chronicle lays it
aside. It lacks verisimilitude. He cannot realize
how any of the things spoken of can have happened. He goes elsewhere to find, if he may, a
real picture of the time, and perhaps finds one that
is wholly fictitious. No wonder the grave and
monk-like chronicler sighs. He of course wrote to
be read, and not merely for the manual exercise of
it; and when he sees readers turn away his heart

misgives him for his fellow-men. Is it as it always was, that they do not wish to know the truth? Alas! good eremite, men do not seek the truth as they should; but do you know what the truth is? It is a thing ideal, displayed by the just proportion of events, revealed in form and color, dumb till facts be set in syllables, articulated into words, put together into sentences, swung with proper tone and cadence. It is not revolutions only that have color. Nothing in human life is without it. In a monochrome you can depict nothing but a single incident; in a monotone you cannot often carry truth beyond a single sentence. Only by art in all its variety can you depict as it is the various face of life.

Yes; but what sort of art? There is here a wide field of choice. Shall we go back to the art of which Macaulay was so great a master? We could do worse. It must be a great art that can make men lay aside the novel and take up the history, to find there, in very fact, the movement and drama of life. What Macaulay does well he does incomparably. Who else can mass the details as he does, and yet not mar or obscure, but only heighten, the effect of the picture as a whole? Who else can bring so amazing a profusion of knowledge within the strait limits of a simple plan,

nowhere encumbered, everywhere free and obvious
in its movement ?   How sure the strokes, and how
bold and vivid the result !   Yet when we have laid
the book aside, when the charm and the excitement
of the telling narrative have worn off, when we
have lost step with the swinging gait at which the
style goes, when the details have faded from our
recollection, and we sit removed and thoughtful,
with only the greater outlines of the story sharp
upon our minds, a deep misgiving and dissatisfaction take possession of us.   We are no longer
young, and we are chagrined that we should have
been so pleased and taken with the glitter and
color and mere life of the picture.   Let boys be
cajoled by rhetoric, we cry; men must look deeper.
What of the judgment of this facile and eloquent
man ?   Can we agree with him, when he is not
talking and the charm is gone ?   What shall we
say of his assessment of men and measures ?   Is
he just ?   Is he himself in possession of the whole
truth ?   Does he open the matter to us as it was ?
Does he not, rather, rule us like an advocate, and
make himself master of our judgments ?

Then it is that we become aware that there were
two Macaulays : Macaulay the artist, with an exquisite gift for telling a story, filling his pages with
little vignettes it is impossible to forget, fixing

these with an inimitable art upon the surface of
a narrative that did not need the ornament they
gave it, so strong and large and adequate was it;
and Macaulay the Whig, subtly turning narrative
into argument, and making history the vindication
of a party. The mighty narrative is a great engine
of proof. It is not told for its own sake. It is
evidence summed up in order to justify a judgment. We detect the tone of the advocate, and
though if we are just we must deem him honest,
we cannot deem him safe. The great story-teller
is discredited; and, willingly or unwillingly, we
reject the guide who takes it upon himself to determine for us what we shall see. That, we feel
sure, cannot be true which makes of so complex a
history so simple a thesis for the judgment. There
is art here; but it is the art of special pleading,
misleading even to the pleader.

If not Macaulay, what master shall we follow?
Shall our historian not have his convictions, and
enforce them? Shall he not be our guide, and
speak, if he can, to our spirits as well as to our
understandings? Readers are a poor jury. They
need enlightenment as well as information; the
matter must be interpreted to them as well as related. There are moral facts as well as material,
and the one sort must be as plainly told as the

other. Of what service is it that the historian should have insight if we are not to know how the matter stands in his view? If he refrain from judgment, he may deceive us as much as he would were his judgment wrong; for we must have enlightenment, — that is his function. We would not set him up merely to tell us tales, but also to display to us characters, to open to us the moral and intent of the matter. Were the men sincere? Was the policy righteous? We have but just now seen that the " facts " lie deeper than the mere visible things that took place, that they involve the moral and motive of the play. Shall not these, too, be brought to light?

Unquestionably every sentence of true history must hold a judgment in solution. All cannot be told. If it were possible to tell all, it would take as long to write history as to enact it, and we should have to postpone the reading of it to the leisure of the next world. A few facts must be selected for the narrative, the great majority left unnoted. But the selection — for what purpose it is to be made? For the purpose of conveying *an impression* of the truth. Where shall you find a more radical process of judgment? The "essential" facts taken, the " unessential " left out! Why, you may make the picture what you will, and in any case it must

be the express image of the historian's fundamental
judgments. It is his purpose, or should be, to give
a true impression of his theme as a whole, — to
show it, not lying upon his page in an open and
dispersed analysis, but set close in intimate syn-
thesis, every line, every stroke, every bulk even,
omitted which does not enter of very necessity into
a single and unified image of the truth.

It is in this that the writing of history differs,
and differs very radically, from the statement of
the results of original research. The writing of
history must be based upon original research and
authentic record, but it can no more be directly
constructed by the piecing together of bits of
original research than by the mere reprinting together of state documents. Individual research
furnishes us, as it were, with the private documents
and intimate records without which the public
archives are incomplete and unintelligible. But
by themselves these are wholly out of perspective.
It is the consolation of those who produce them to
make them so. They would lose heart were they
forbidden to regard all facts as of equal importance.
It is facts they are after, and only facts, — facts
for their own sake, and without regard to their
several importance. These are their ore, — very
precious ore, — which they are concerned to get

out, not to refine. They have no direct concern
with what may afterwards be done at the mint or
in the goldsmith's shop. They will even boast that
they care not for the beauty of the ore, and are
indifferent how, or in what shape, it may become
an article of commerce. Much of it is thrown
away in the nice processes of manufacture, and you
shall not distinguish the product of the several
mines in the coin, or the cup, or the salver.

The historian must, indeed, himself be an investigator. He must know good ore from bad ; must
distinguish fineness, quality, genuineness ; must stop
to get out of the records for himself what he lacks
for the perfection of his work. But for all that,
he must know and stand ready to do every part of
his task like a master workman, recognizing and
testing every bit of stuff he uses. Standing sure,
a man of science as well as an artist, he must take
and use all of his equipment for the sake of his
art, — not to display his materials, but to subordinate and transform them in his effort to make, by
every touch and cunning of hand and tool, the perfect image of what he sees, the very truth of his
seer's vision of the world. The true historian
works always for the whole impression, the truth
with unmarred proportions, unexaggerated parts,
undistorted visage. He has no favorite parts of

the story which he boasts are bits of his own, but loves only the whole of it, the full and unspoiled image of the day of which he writes, the crowded and yet consistent details which carry, without obtrusion of themselves, the large features of the time. Any exaggeration of the parts makes all the picture false, and the work is to do over. " Test every bit of material," runs the artist's rule, " and then forget the material ; " forget its origin and the dross from which it has been freed, and think only and always of the great thing you would make of it, the pattern and form in which you would lose and merge it. That is its only high use.

'T is a pity to see how even the greatest minds will often lack the broad and catholic vision with which the just historian must look upon men and affairs. There is Carlyle, with his shrewd and seeing eye, his unmatched capacity to assess strong men and set the scenery for tragedy or intrigue, his breathless ardor for great events, his amazing flashes of insight, and his unlooked-for steady light of occasional narrative. The whole matter of what he writes is too dramatic. Surely history was not all enacted so hotly, or with so passionate a rush of men upon the stage. Its quiet scenes must have been longer, not mere pauses and interludes while

the tragic parts were being made up. There is not
often ordinary sunlight upon the page. The lights
burn now wan, now lurid. Men are seen disquieted
and turbulent, and may be heard in husky cries or
rude, untimely jests. We do not recognize our
own world, but seem to see another such as ours
might become if peopled by like uneasy Titans.
Incomparable to tell of days of storm and revolution, speaking like an oracle and familiar of destiny and fate, searching the hearts of statesmen
and conquerors with an easy insight in every day of
action, this peasant seer cannot give us the note of
piping times of peace, or catch the tone of slow
industry ; watches ships come and go at the docks,
hears freight-vans thunder along the iron highways
of the modern world, and loaded trucks lumber
heavily through the crowded city streets, with a
hot disdain of commerce, prices current, the hag-
gling of the market, the smug ease of material
comfort bred in a trading age. There is here no
broad and catholic vision, no wise tolerance, no
various power to know, to sympathize, to interpret.
The great seeing imagination of the man lacks that
pure radiance in which things are seen steadily and
seen whole.

It is not easy, to say truth, to find actual examples when you are constructing the ideal historian,

the man with the vision and the faculty divine to see affairs justly and tell of them completely. If you are not satisfied with this passionate and intolerant seer of Chelsea, whom will you choose? Shall it be Gibbon, whom all praise, but so few read? He, at any rate, is passionless, it would appear. But who could write epochal history with passion? All hot humors of the mind must, assuredly, cool when spread at large upon so vast a surface. One must feel like a sort of minor providence in traversing that great tract of world history, and catch in spite of one's self the gait and manner of a god. This stately procession of generations moves on remote from the ordinary levels of our human sympathy. 'T is a wide view of nations and peoples and dynasties, and a world shaken by the travail of new births. There is here no scale by which to measure the historian of the sort we must look to see handle the ordinary matter of national history. The "Decline and Fall" stands impersonal, like a monument. We shall reverence it, but we shall not imitate it.

If we look away from Gibbon, exclude Carlyle, and question Macaulay; if we put the investigators on one side as not yet historians, and the deliberately picturesque and entertaining *raconteurs* as not yet investigators, we naturally turn, I suppose, to such a man as John Richard Green, at once the patient scholar, — who shall adequately say how nobly patient? — and the rare artist, working so like a master in the difficult stuffs of a long national history. The very life of the man is as beautiful as the moving sentences he wrote with so subtle a music in the cadence. We know whence the fine moral elevation of tone came that sounds through all the text of his great narrative. True, not everybody is satisfied with our *doctor angelicus.* Some doubt he is too ornate. Others are troubled that he should sometimes be inaccurate. Some are willing to use his history as a manual; while others cannot deem him satisfactory for didactic uses, hesitate how they shall characterize him, and quit the matter vaguely with saying that what he wrote is "at any rate literature." Can there be something lacking in Green, too, notwithstanding he was impartial, and looked with purged and open eyes upon the whole unbroken life of his people, — notwithstanding he saw the truth and had the art and mastery to make others see it as he did, in all its breadth and multiplicity?

Perhaps even this great master of narrative lacks variety — as who does not? His method, whatever the topic, is ever the same. His sentences, his paragraphs, his chapters are pitched one and all in the same key. It is a very fine and moving key. Many an elevated strain and rich harmony commend it alike to the ear and to the imagination. It is employed with an easy mastery, and is made to serve to admiration a wide range of themes. But it is always the same key, and some themes it will not serve. An infinite variety plays through all history. Every scene has its own air and singularity. Incidents cannot all be rightly set in the narrative if all be set alike. As the scene shifts, the tone of the narrative must change : the narrator's choice of incident and his choice of words ; the speed and method of his sentence ; his own thought, even, and point of view. Surely his battle pages must resound with the tramp of armies and the fearful din and rush of war. In peace he must catch by turns the hum of industry, the bustle of the street, the calm of the country-side, the tone of parliamentary debate, the fancy, the ardor, the argument of poets and seers and quiet students. Snatches of song run along with sober purpose and strenuous endeavor through every nation's story. Coarse men and refined, mobs and ordered assemblies, science and mad impulse, storm and calm, are all alike ingredients of the various life. It is not all epic. There is rough comedy and brutal violence. The drama can scarce be given any strict, unbroken harmony of incident, any close logical sequence of act or nice unity of scene. To pitch it all in one key, therefore, is to mistake the significance of the infinite play of varied circumstance that makes up the yearly movement of a people's life.

It would be less than just to say that Green's pages do not reveal the variety of English life the centuries through. It is his glory, indeed, as all the world knows, to have broadened and diversified the whole scale of English history. Nowhere else within the compass of a single book can one find so many sides of the great English story displayed with so deep and just an appreciation of them all, or of the part of each in making up the whole. Green is the one man among English historians who has restored the great fabric of the nation's history where its architecture was obscure, and its details were likely to be lost or forgotten. Once more, because of him, the vast Gothic structure stands complete, its majesty and firm grace enhanced at every point by the fine tracery of its restored details.

Where so much is done, it is no doubt unreasonable to ask for more. But the very architectural symmetry of this great book imposes a limitation upon it. It is full of a certain sort of variety; but

it is only the variety of a great plan's detail, not
the variety of English life. The noble structure
obeys its own laws rather than the laws of a people's fortunes. It is a monument conceived and
reared by a consummate artist, and it wears upon
its every line some part of the image it was meant
to bear, of a great, complex, aspiring national existence. But, though it symbolizes, it does not contain that life. It has none of the irregularity of
the actual experiences of men and communities.
It explains, but it does not contain, their variety.
The history of every nation has certainly a plan
which the historian must see and reproduce; but
he must reconstruct the people's life, not merely
expound it. The scope of his method must be as
great as the variety of his subject; it must change
with each change of mood, respond to each varying
impulse in the great process of events. No rigor
of a stately style must be suffered to exclude the
lively touches of humor or the rude sallies of
strength that mark it everywhere. The plan of
the telling must answer to the plan of the fact, —
must be as elastic as the topics are mobile. The
matter should rule the plan, not the plan the matter.

The ideal is infinitely difficult, if, indeed, it be
possible to any man not Shakespearean; but the

difficulty of attaining it is often unnecessarily enhanced. Ordinarily the historian's preparation for
his task is such as to make it unlikely he will
perform it naturally. He goes first, with infinite
and admirable labor, through all the labyrinth of
document and detail that lies up and down his
subject; collects masses of matter great and small,
for substance, verification, illustration; piles his
notes volumes high; reads far and wide upon the
tracks of his matter, and makes page upon page
of references; and then, thoroughly stuffed and
sophisticated, turns back and begins his narrative.
'T is impossible then that he should begin naturally.
He sees the end from the beginning, and all the in-
termediate way from beginning to end; he has made
up his mind about too many things; uses his details
with a too free and familiar mastery, not like one
who tells a story so much as like one who dissects a
cadaver. Having swept his details together beforehand, like so much scientific material, he discourses
upon them like a demonstrator, — thinks too little
in subjection to them. They no longer make a
fresh impression upon him. They are his tools,
not his objects of vision.

It is not by such a process that a narrative is
made vital and true. It does not do to lose the
point of view of the first listener to the tale, or to

rearrange the matter too much out of the order of nature. You must instruct your reader as the events themselves would have instructed him, had he been able to note them as they passed. The historian must not lose his own fresh view of the scene as it passed and changed more and more from year to year and from age to age. He must keep with the generation of which he writes, not be too quick to be wiser than they were or look back upon them in his narrative with head over shoulder. He must write of them always in the atmosphere they themselves breathed, not hastening to judge them, but striving only to realize them at every turn of the story, to make their thoughts his own, and call their lives back again, rebuilding the very stage upon which they played their parts. Bring the end of your story to mind while you set about telling its beginning, and it seems to have no parts: beginning, middle, end, are all as one, — are merely like parts of a pattern which you see as a single thing stamped upon the stuff under your hand.

Try the method with the history of our own land and people. How will you begin? Will you start with a modern map and a careful topographical description of the continent? And then, having made your nineteenth-century framework for the

narrative, will you ask your reader to turn back
and see the seventeenth century, and those lonely
ships coming in at the capes of the Chesapeake?
He will never see them so long as you compel him
to stand here at the end of the nineteenth century
and look at them as if through a long retrospect.
The attention both of the narrator and of the
reader, if history is to be seen aright, must look
forward, not backward. It must see with a contemporaneous eye. Let the historian, if he be
wise, know no more of the history as he writes
than might have been known in the age and day
of which he is writing. A trifle too much knowledge will undo him. It will break the spell for
his imagination. It will spoil the magic by which
he may raise again the image of days that are
gone. He must of course know the large lines of
his story; it must lie as a whole in his mind. His
very art demands that, in order that he may know
and keep its proportions. But the details, the
passing incidents of day and year, must come fresh
into his mind, unreasoned upon as yet, untouched
by theory, with their first look upon them. It is
here that original documents and fresh research
will serve him. He must look far and wide upon
every detail of the time, see it at first hand, and
paint as he looks; selecting, as the artist must, but

selecting while the vision is fresh, and not from old sketches laid away in his notes, — selecting from the life itself.

Let him remember that his task is radically different from the task of the investigator. The investigator must display his materials, but the historian must convey his impressions. He must stand in the presence of life, and reproduce it in his narrative; must recover a past age; make dead generations live again and breathe their own air; show them native and at home upon his page. To do this, his own impressions must be as fresh as those of an unlearned reader, his own curiosity as keen and young at every stage. It may easily be so as his reading thickens, and the atmosphere of the age comes stealthily into his thought, if only he take care to push forward the actual writing of his narrative at an equal pace with his reading, painting thus always direct from the image itself. His knowledge of the great outlines and bulks of the picture will be his sufficient guide and restraint the while, will give proportion to the individual strokes of his work. But it will not check his zest, or sophisticate his fresh recovery of the life that is in the crowding colors of the canvas.

A nineteenth-century plan laid like a standard and measure upon a seventeenth-century narrative will infallibly twist it and make it false. Lay a modern map before the first settlers at Jamestown and Plymouth, and then bid them discover and occupy the continent. With how superior a nineteenth-century wonder and pity will you see them grope, and stumble, and falter! How like children they will seem to you, and how simple their age, and ignorant! As stalwart men as you they were in fact; mayhap wiser and braver too; as fit to occupy a continent as you are to draw it upon paper. If you would know them, go back to their age; breed yourself a pioneer and woodsman; look to find the South Sea up the nearest northwest branch of the spreading river at your feet; discover and occupy the wilderness with them; dream what may be beyond the near hills, and long all day to see a sail upon the silent sea; go back to them and see them in their habit as they lived.

The picturesque writers of history have all along been right in theory: they have been wrong only in practice. It *is* a picture of the past we want — its express image and feature; but we want the true picture and not simply the theatrical matter, — the manner of Rembrandt rather than of Rubens. All life may be pictured, but not all of life is picturesque. No great, no true historian would put false or adventitious colors into his narrative, or let a glamour rest where in fact it never was. The writers who select an incident merely because it is striking or dramatic are shallow fellows. They see only with the eye's retina, not with that deep vision whose images lie where thought and reason sit. The real drama of life is disclosed only with the whole picture ; and that only the deep and fervid student will see, whose mind goes daily fresh to the details, whose narrative runs always in the authentic colors of nature, whose art it is to see, and to paint what he sees.

It is thus and only thus we shall have the truth of the matter : by art, — by the most difficult of all arts ; by fresh study and first-hand vision ; at the mouths of men who stand in the midst of old letters and dusty documents and neglected records, not like antiquarians, but like those who see a distant country and a far-away people before their very eyes, as real, as full of life and hope and incident, as the day in which they themselves live. Let us have done with humbug and come to plain speech. The historian needs an imagination quite as much as he needs scholarship, and consummate literary art as much as candor and common honesty. Histories are written in order that the bulk of men may read and realize ; and it is as bad to bungle the telling of the story as to lie, as fatal to lack a

vocabulary as to lack knowledge. In no case can
you do more than convey an impression, so various
and complex is the matter. If you convey a false
impression, what difference does it make how you
convey it ? In the whole process there is a nice
adjustment of means to ends which only the artist
can manage. There is an art of lying ; — there is
equally an art, — an infinitely more difficult art,
— of telling the truth.

VII.

A CALENDAR OF GREAT AMERICANS.

BEFORE a calendar of great Americans can be made out, a valid canon of Americanism must first be established. Not every great man born and bred in America was a great " American." Some of the notable men born among us were simply great Englishmen; others had in all the habits of their thought and life the strong flavor of a peculiar region, and were great New Englanders or great Southerners; others, masters in the fields of science or of pure thought, showed nothing either distinctively national or characteristically provincial, and were simply great men; while a few displayed odd cross-strains of blood or breeding. The great Englishmen bred in America, like Hamilton and Madison; the great provincials, like John Adams and Calhoun; the authors of such thought as might have been native to any clime, like Asa Gray and Emerson; and the men of mixed breed, like Jefferson and Benton, — must be excluded from our present list. We must pick out men who have created or exemplified a distinctively American standard and type of greatness.

To make such a selection is not to create an artificial standard of greatness, or to claim that greatness is in any case hallowed or exalted merely because it is American. It is simply to recognize a peculiar stamp of character, a special make-up of mind and faculties, as the specific product of our national life, not displacing or eclipsing talents of a different kind, but supplementing them, and so adding to the world's variety. There is an American type of man, and those who have exhibited this type with a certain unmistakable distinction and perfection have been great "Americans." It has required the utmost variety of character and energy to establish a great nation, with a polity at once free and firm, upon this continent, and no sound type of manliness could have been dispensed with in the effort. We could no more have done without our great Englishmen, to keep the past steadily in mind and make every change conservative of principle, than we could have done without the men whose whole impulse was forward, whose whole genius was for origination, natural masters of the art of subduing a wilderness.

Certainly one of the greatest figures in our history is the figure of Alexander Hamilton. Ameri-

can historians, though compelled always to admire
him, often in spite of themselves, have been inclined, like the mass of men in his own day, to look
at him askance. They hint, when they do not
plainly say, that he was not "American." He rejected, if he did not despise, democratic principles ;
advocated a government as strong, almost, as a
monarchy ; and defended the government which
was actually set up, like the skilled advocate he
was, only because it was the strongest that could
be had under the circumstances. He believed in
authority, and he had no faith in the aggregate
wisdom of masses of men. He had, it is true, that
deep and passionate love of liberty, and that steadfast purpose in the maintenance of it, that mark
the best Englishmen everywhere ; but his ideas of
government stuck fast in the old-world politics, and
his statesmanship was of Europe rather than of
America. And yet the genius and the steadfast
spirit of this man were absolutely indispensable to
us. No one less masterful, no one less resolute
than he to drill the minority, if necessary, to have
their way against the majority, could have done the
great work of organization by which he established
the national credit, and with the national credit the
national government itself. A pliant, popular,
optimistic man would have failed utterly in the

task. A great radical mind in his place would have brought disaster upon us : only a great conservative genius could have succeeded. It is safe to say that, without men of Hamilton's cast of mind, building the past into the future with a deep passion for order and old wisdom, our national life would have miscarried at the very first. This tried English talent for conservation gave to our fibre at the very outset the stiffness of maturity.

James Madison, too, we may be said to have inherited. His invaluable gifts of counsel were of the sort so happily imparted to us with our English blood at the first planting of the States which formed the Union. A grave and prudent man, and yet brave withal when new counsel was to be taken, he stands at the beginning of our national history, even in his young manhood, as he faced and led the constitutional convention, a type of the slow and thoughtful English genius for affairs. He held old and tested convictions of the uses of liberty; he was competently read in the history of government; processes of revolution were in his thought no more than processes of adaptation : exigencies were to be met by modification, not by experiment. His reasonable spirit runs through all the proceedings of the great convention that gave us the Constitution, and that noble instrument

seems the product of character like his. For all it
is so American in its content, it is in its method a
thoroughly English production, so full is it of old
principles, so conservative of experience, so carefully compounded of compromises, of concessions
made and accepted. Such men are of a stock so
fine as to need no titles to make it noble, and yet
so old and so distinguished as actually to bear the
chief titles of English liberty. Madison came of
the long line of English constitutional statesmen.

There is a type of genius which closely approaches this in character, but which is, nevertheless, distinctively American. It is to be seen in
John Marshall and in Daniel Webster. In these
men a new set of ideas find expression, ideas which
all the world has received as American. Webster
was not an English but an American constitutional
statesman. For the English statesman constitutional issues are issues of policy rather than issues
of law. He constantly handles questions of change:
his constitution is always a-making. He must at
every turn construct, and he is deemed conservative
if only his rule be consistency and continuity with
the past. He will search diligently for precedent,
but he is content if the precedent contain only a
germ of the policy he proposes. His standards are
set him, not by law, but by opinion: his constitu-

tion is an ideal of cautious and orderly change. Its fixed element is the conception of political liberty: a conception which, though steeped in history, must ever be added to and altered by social change. The American constitutional statesman, on the contrary, constructs policies like a lawyer. The standard with which he must square his conduct is set him by a document upon whose definite sentences the whole structure of the government directly rests. That document, moreover, is the concrete embodiment of a peculiar theory of government. That theory is, that definitive laws, selected by a power outside the government, are the structural iron of the entire fabric of politics, and that nothing which cannot be constructed upon this stiff framework is a safe or legitimate part of policy. Law is, in his conception, creative of states, and they live only by such permissions as they can extract from it. The functions of the judge and the functions of the man of affairs have, therefore, been very closely related in our history, and John Marshall, scarcely less than Daniel Webster, was a constitutional statesman. With all Madison's conservative temper and wide-eyed prudence in counsel, the subject-matter of thought for both of these men was not English liberty or the experience of men everywhere in self-govern-

ment, but the meaning stored up in the explicit
sentences of a written fundamental law. They
taught men the new — the American — art of
extracting life out of the letter, not of statutes
merely (that art was not new), but of statute-built
institutions and documented governments : the art
of saturating politics with law without grossly dis-
coloring law with politics. Other nations have
had written constitutions, but no other nation has
ever filled a written constitution with this singularly
compounded content, of a sound legal conscience
and a strong national purpose. It would have
been easy to deal with our Constitution like subtle
dialecticians ; but Webster and Marshall did much
more and much better than that. They viewed
the fundamental law as a great organic product, a
vehicle of life as well as a charter of authority ; in
disclosing its life they did not damage its tissue ;
and in thus expanding the law without impairing
its structure or authority they made great contributions alike to statesmanship and to jurisprudence.
Our notable literature of decision and commentary
in the field of constitutional law is America's
distinctive gift to the history and the science of
law. John Marshall wrought out much of its substance ; Webster diffused its great body of principles throughout national policy, mediating between

the law and affairs. The figures of the two men must hold the eye of the world as the figures of two great national representatives, as the figures of two great Americans.

The representative national greatness and function of these men appear more clearly still when they are contrasted with men like John Adams and John C. Calhoun, whose greatness was not national. John Adams represented one element of our national character, and represented it nobly, with a singular force and greatness. He was an eminent Puritan statesman, and the Puritan ingredient has colored all our national life. We have got strength and persistency and some part of our steady moral purpose from it. But in the quick growth and exuberant expansion of the nation it has been only one element among many. The Puritan blood has mixed with many another strain. The stiff Puritan character has been mellowed by many a transfusion of gentler and more hopeful elements. So soon as the Adams fashion of man became more narrow, intense, acidulous, intractable, according to the tendencies of its nature, in the person of John Quincy Adams, it lost the sympathy, lost even the tolerance, of the country, and the national choice took its reckless leap from a Puritan President to Andrew Jackson, a man cast in the rough original pattern of American life at the heart of the continent. John Adams had not himself been a very acceptable President. He had none of the national optimism, and could not understand those who did have it. He had none of the characteristic adaptability of the delocalized American, and was just a bit ridiculous in his stiffness at the Court of St. James, for all he was so honorable and so imposing. His type, — be it said without disrespect, — was provincial. Unmistakably a great man, his greatness was of the commonwealth, not of the empire.

Calhoun, too, was a great provincial. Although a giant, he had no heart to use his great strength for national purposes. In his youth, it is true, he did catch some of the generous ardor for national enterprise which filled the air in his day; and all his life through, with a truly pathetic earnestness, he retained his affection for his first ideal. But when the rights and interests of his section were made to appear incompatible with a liberal and boldly constructive interpretation of the Constitution, he fell out of national counsels and devoted all the strength of his extraordinary mind to holding the nation's thought and power back within the strait limits of a literal construction of the law. In powers of reasoning his mind deserves to rank with Webster's and Marshall's : he handled questions of law like a master, as they did. He had, moreover, a keen insight into the essential principles and character of liberty. His thought moved eloquently along some of the oldest and safest lines of English thought in the field of government. He made substantive contributions to the permanent philosophy of politics. His reasoning has been discredited, not so much because it was not theoretically sound within its limits, as because its practical outcome was a negation which embarrassed the whole movement of national affairs. He would have held the nation still, in an old equipoise, at one time normal enough, but impossible to maintain. Webster and Marshall gave leave to the energy of change inherent in all the national life, making law a rule, but not an interdict ; a living guide, but not a blind and rigid discipline. Calhoun sought to fix law as a barrier across the path of policy, commanding the life of the nation to stand still. The strength displayed in the effort, the intellectual power and address, abundantly entitle him to be called great ; but his purpose was not national. It regarded only a section of the country, and marked him, — again be it said with all respect, — a great provincial.

Jefferson was not a thorough American because

of the strain of French philosophy that permeated and weakened all his thought. Benton was altogether American so far as the natural strain of his blood was concerned, but he had encumbered his natural parts and inclinations with a mass of undigested and shapeless learning. Bred in the West, where everything was new, he had filled his head with the thought of books (evidently very poor books) which exhibited the ideals of communities in which everything was old. He thought of the Roman Senate when he sat in the Senate of the United States. He paraded classical figures whenever he spoke, upon a stage where both their costume and their action seemed grotesque. A pedantic frontiersman, he was a living and a pompous antinomy. Meant by nature to be an American, he spoiled the plan by applying a most unsuitable gloss of shallow and irrelevant learning. Jefferson was of course an almost immeasurably greater man than Benton, but he was un-American in somewhat the same way. He brought a foreign product of thought to a market where no natural or wholesome demand for it could exist. There were not two incompatible parts in him, as in Benton's case : he was a philosophical radical by nature as well as by acquirement ; his reading and his temperament went suitably together. The man is homogeneous throughout. The American shows in him very plainly, too, notwithstanding the strong and inherent dash of what was foreign in his make-up. He was a natural leader and manager of men, not because he was imperative or masterful, but because of a native shrewdness, tact, and sagacity, an inborn art and aptness for combination, such as no Frenchman ever displayed in the management of common men. Jefferson had just a touch of rusticity about him, besides; and it was not pretense on his part or merely a love of power that made him democratic. His indiscriminate hospitality, his almost passionate love for the simple equality of country life, his steady devotion to what he deemed to be the cause of the people, all mark him a genuine democrat, a nature native to America. It is his speculative philosophy that is exotic, and that runs like a false and artificial note through all his thought. It was un-American in being abstract, sentimental, rationalistic, rather than practical. That he held it sincerely need not be doubted; but the more sincerely he accepted it so much the more thoroughly was he un-American. His writings lack hard and practical sense. Liberty, among us, is not a sentiment, but a product of experience; its derivation is not rationalistic, but practical. It is a hard-headed spirit of independence, not the conclusion of a syllogism. The very aërated quality of Jefferson's principles gives them an air of insincerity, which attaches to them rather because they do not suit the climate of the country and the practical aspect of affairs than because they do not suit the character of Jefferson's mind and the atmosphere of abstract philosophy. It is because both they and the philosophical system of which they form a part do seem suitable to his mind and character, that we must pronounce him, though a great man, not a great American.

It is by the frank consideration of such concrete cases that we may construct, both negatively and affirmatively, our canons of Americanism. The American spirit is something more than the old, the immemorial Saxon spirit of liberty from which it sprung. It has been bred by the conditions attending the great task which we have all the century been carrying forward : the task, at once material and ideal, of subduing a wilderness and covering all the wide stretches of a vast continent with a single free and stable polity. It is, accordingly, above all things, a hopeful and confident spirit. It is progressive, optimistically progressive, and ambitious of objects of national scope and advantage. It is unpedantic, unprovincial, unspeculative, unfastidious; regardful of law, but as using it, not as being used by it or dominated by any formalism whatever ; in a sense unrefined, because full of rude force ; but prompted by large and generous motives, and often as tolerant as it is resolute. No one man, unless it be Lincoln, has ever proved big or various enough to embody this active and full-hearted spirit in all its qualities ; and the men who have been too narrow or too speculative or too pedantic to represent it have, nevertheless, added to the strong and stirring variety of our national life, making it fuller and richer in motive and energy ; but its several aspects are none the less noteworthy as they separately appear in different men.

One of the first men to exhibit this American spirit with an unmistakable touch of greatness and distinction was Benjamin Franklin. It was characteristic of America that this self-made man should become a philosopher, a founder of philosophical societies, an authoritative man of science ; that his philosophy of life should be so homely and so practical in its maxims, and uttered with so shrewd a wit ; that one region should be his birthplace and another his home ; that he should favor effective political union among the colonies from the first, and should play a sage and active part in the establishment of national independence and the

planning of a national organization ; and that he
should represent his countrymen in diplomacy
abroad. They could have had no spokesman who
represented more sides of their character. Franklin
was a sort of multiple American. He was versatile
without lacking solidity; he was a practical statesman without ceasing to be a sagacious philosopher.
He came of the people, and was democratic; but
he had raised himself out of the general mass of
unnamed men, and so stood for the democratic law,
not of equality, but of self-selection in endeavor.
One can feel sure that Franklin would have succeeded in any part of the national life that it might
have fallen to his lot to take part in. He will
stand the final and characteristic test of Americanism : he would unquestionably have made a successful frontiersman, capable at once of wielding the
axe and of administering justice from the fallen
trunk.

Washington hardly seems an American, as most
of his biographers depict him. He is too colorless,
too cold, too prudent. He seems more like a wise
and dispassionate Mr. Alworthy, advising a nation
as he would a parish, than like a man building
states and marshaling a nation in a wilderness.
But the real Washington was as thoroughly an
American as Jackson or Lincoln. What we take

for lack of passion in him was but the reserve and self-mastery natural to a man of his class and breeding in Virginia. He was no parlor politician, either. He had seen the frontier, and far beyond it where the French forts lay. He knew the rough life of the country as few other men could. His thoughts did not live at Mount Vernon. He knew difficulty as intimately and faced it always with as quiet a mastery as William the Silent. This calm, straightforward, high-spirited man, making charts of the western country, noting the natural land and water routes into the heart of the continent, marking how the French power lay, conceiving the policy which should dispossess it, and the engineering achievements which should make the utmost resources of the land our own; counseling Braddock how to enter the forest, but not deserting him because he would not take advice; planning step by step, by patient correspondence with influential men everywhere, the meetings, conferences, common resolves which were finally to bring the great constitutional convention together; planning, too, always for the country as well as for Virginia; and presiding at last over the establishment and organization of the government of the Union: he certainly — the most suitable instrument of the national life at every moment of crisis — is a great American.

Those noble words which he uttered amidst the first doubtings of the constitutional convention might serve as a motto for the best efforts of liberty wherever free men strive: "Let us raise a standard to which the wise and honest can repair; the event is in the hand of God."

In Henry Clay we have an American of a most authentic pattern. There was no man of his generation who represented more of America than he did. The singular, almost irresistible attraction he had for men of every class and every temperament came, not from the arts of the politician, but from the instant sympathy established between him and every fellow-countryman of his. He does not seem to have exercised the same fascination upon foreigners. They felt toward him as some New Englanders did: he seemed to them plausible merely, too indiscriminately open and cordial to be sincere, — a bit of a charlatan. No man who really takes the trouble to understand Henry Clay, or who has quick enough parts to sympathize with him, can deem him false. It is the odd combination of two different elements in him that makes him seem irregular and inconstant. His nature was of the West, blown through with quick winds of ardor and aggression, a bit reckless and defiant; but his art was of the East, ready with soft and placating phrases, reminiscent of old and reverenced ideals, thoughtful of compromise and accommodation. He had all the address of the trained and sophisticated politician, bred in an old and sensitive society; but his purposes ran free of cautious restraints, and his real ideals were those of the somewhat bumptious Americanism which was pushing the frontier forward in the West, which believed itself capable of doing anything it might put its hand to, despised conventional restraints, and followed a vague but resplendent " manifest destiny " with lusty hurrahs. His purposes were sincere, even if often crude and uninstructed; it was only because the subtle arts of politics seemed inconsistent with the direct dash and bold spirit of the man that they sat upon him like an insincerity. He thoroughly, and by mere unconscious sympathy, represented the double America of his day, made up of a West which hurried and gave bold strokes, and of an East which held back, fearing the pace, thoughtful and mindful of the instructive past. The one part had to be served without offending the other: and that was Clay's mediatorial function.

Andrew Jackson was altogether of the West. Of his sincerity nobody has ever had any real doubt; and his Americanism is now at any rate equally unimpeachable. He was like Clay with the social imagination of the orator and the art and sophistication of the Eastern politician left out. He came into our national politics like a cyclone from off the Western prairies. Americans of the present day perceptibly shudder at the very recollection of Jackson. He seems to them a great Vandal, playing fast and loose alike with institutions and with tested and established policy, debauching politics like a modern spoilsman. But whether we would accept him as a type of ourselves or not, the men of his own day accepted him with enthusiasm. He did not need to be explained to them. They crowded to his standard like men free at last, after long and tedious restraint, to make their own choice, follow their own man. There can be no mistaking the spontaneity of the thoroughgoing support he received. His was the new type of energy and self-confidence bred by life outside the States that had been colonies. It was a terrible energy, threatening sheer destruction to many a carefully wrought arrangement handed on to us from the past; it was a perilous self-confidence, founded in sheer strength rather than in wisdom. The government did not pass through the throes of that signal awakening of the new national spirit without serious rack and damage.

But it was no disease. It was only an incautious, abounding, madcap strength which proved so dangerous in its readiness for every rash endeavor. It was necessary that the West should be let into the play: it was even necessary that she should assert her right to the leading rôle. It was done without good taste, but that does not condemn it. We have no doubt refined and schooled the hoyden influences of that crude time, and they are vastly safer now than then, when they first came bounding in; but they mightily stirred and enriched our blood from the first. Now that we have thoroughly suffered this Jackson change and it is over, we are ready to recognize it as quite as radically American as anything in all our history.

Lincoln, nevertheless, rather than Jackson, was the supreme American of our history. In Clay, East and West were mixed without being fused or harmonized: he seems like two men. In Jackson there was not even a mixture; he was all of a piece, and altogether unacceptable to some parts of the country, — a frontier statesman. But in Lincoln the elements were combined and harmonized. The most singular thing about the wonderful career of the man is the way in which he steadily grew into a national stature. He began an amorphous, unlicked cub, bred in the rudest of human lairs;

but, as he grew, everything formed, informed,
transformed him. The process was slow but unbroken. He was not fit to be President until he
actually became President. He was fit then
because, learning everything as he went, he had
found out how much there was to learn, and had
still an infinite capacity for learning. The quiet
voices of sentiment and murmurs of resolution
that went whispering through the land, his ear
always caught, when others could hear nothing but
their own words. He never ceased to be a common
man : that was his source of strength. But he
was a common man with genius, a genius for things
American, for insight into the common thought,
for mastery of the fundamental things of politics
that inhere in human nature and cast hardly more
than their shadows on constitutions ; for the practical niceties of affairs ; for judging men and assessing
arguments. Jackson had no social imagination :
no unfamiliar community made any impression on
him. His whole fibre stiffened young, and nothing
afterward could modify or even deeply affect it.
But Lincoln was always a-making ; he would have
died unfinished if the terrible storms of the war
had not stung him to learn in those four years
what no other twenty could have taught him.
And, as he stands there in his complete manhood,

at the most perilous helm in Christendom, what a marvelous composite figure he is! The whole country is summed up in him : the rude Western strength, tempered with shrewdness and a broad and humane wit ; the Eastern conservatism, regardful of law and devoted to fixed standards of duty. He even understood the South, as no other Northern man of his generation did. He respected, because he comprehended, though he could not hold, its view of the Constitution ; he appreciated the inexorable compulsions of its past in respect of slavery ; he would have secured it once more, and speedily if possible, in its right to self-government, when the fight was fought out. To the Eastern politicians he seemed like an accident ; but to history he must seem like a providence.

Grant was Lincoln's suitable instrument, a great American general, the appropriate product of West Point. A Western man, he had no thought of commonwealths politically separate, and was instinctively for the Union ; a man of the common people, he deemed himself always an instrument, never a master, and did his work, though ruthlessly, without malice ; a sturdy, hard-willed, taciturn man, a sort of Lincoln the Silent in thought and spirit. He does not appeal to the imagination very deeply ; there is a sort of common greatness about him, great gifts combined singularly with a great mediocrity ; but such peculiarities seem to make him all the more American, — national in spirit, thoroughgoing in method, masterful in purpose.

And yet it is no contradiction to say that Robert E. Lee also was a great American. He fought on the opposite side, but he fought in the same spirit, and for a principle which is in a sense scarcely less American than the principle of Union. He represented the idea of the inherent — the essential — separateness of self-government. This was not the principle of secession : that principle involved the separate right of the several self-governing units of the federal system to judge of national questions independently, and as a check upon the federal government, — to adjudge the very objects of the Union. Lee did not believe in secession, but he did believe in the local rootage of all government. This is at the bottom, no doubt, an English idea ; but it has had a characteristic American development. It is the reverse side of the shield which bears upon its obverse the devices of the Union, a side too much overlooked and obscured since the war. It conceives the individual State a community united by the most intimate associations, the first home and foster-mother of every man born into the citizenship of the nation. Lee considered himself a member of one of these great families ; he could not conceive of the nation apart from the State : above all, he could not live in the nation divorced from his neighbors. His own community should decide his political destiny and duty.

This was also the spirit of Patrick Henry and of Sam Houston, — men much alike in the cardinal principle of their natures. Patrick Henry resisted the formation of the Union only because he feared to disturb the local rootage of self-government, to disperse power so widely that neighbors could not control it. It was not a disloyal or a separatist spirit, but only a jealous spirit of liberty. Sam Houston, too, deemed the character a community should give itself so great a matter that the community, once made, ought itself to judge of the national associations most conducive to its liberty and progress. Without liberty of this intensive character there could have been no vital national liberty ; and Sam Houston, Patrick Henry, and Robert E. Lee are none the less great Americans because they represented only one cardinal principle of the national life. Self-government has its intrinsic antinomies as well as its harmonies.

Among men of letters Lowell is doubtless most

typically American, though Curtis must find an eligible place in the list. Lowell was self-conscious, though the truest greatness is not; he was a trifle too " smart," besides, and there is no " smartness " in great literature. But both the self-consciousness and the smartness must be admitted to be American; and Lowell was so versatile, so urbane, of so large a spirit, and so admirable in the scope of his sympathies, that he must certainly go on the calendar.

There need be no fear that we shall be obliged to stop with Lowell in literature, or with any of the men who have been named in the field of achievement. We shall not in the future have to take one type of Americanism at a time. The frontier is gone: it has reached the Pacific. The country grows rapidly homogeneous. With the same pace it grows various, and multiform in all its life. The man of the simple or local type cannot any longer deal in the great manner with any national problem. The great men of our future must be of the composite type of greatness: sound-hearted, hopeful, confident of the validity of liberty, tenacious of the deeper principles of American institutions, but with the old rashness schooled and sobered, and instinct tempered by instruction. They must be wise with an adult, not with an adolescent wisdom. Some day we shall be of one mind, our ideals fixed, our purposes harmonized, our nationality complete and consentaneous: then will come our great literature and our greatest men.

VIII.

THE COURSE OF AMERICAN HISTORY.[1]

IN the field of history, learning should be deemed to stand among the people and in the midst of life. Its function there is not one of pride merely: to make complaisant record of deeds honorably done and plans nobly executed in the past. It has also a function of guidance: to build high places whereon to plant the clear and flaming lights of experience, that they may shine alike upon the roads already traveled and upon the paths not yet attempted. The historian is also a sort of prophet. Our memories direct us. They give us knowledge of our character, alike in its strength and in its weakness: and it is so we get our standards for endeavor, — our warnings and our gleams of hope. It is thus we learn what manner of nation we are of, and divine what manner of people we should be.

And this is not in national records merely. Local history is the ultimate substance of national history. There could be no epics were pastorals

[1] An address delivered before the New Jersey Historical Society.

not also true, — no patriotism, were there no homes,
no neighbors, no quiet round of civic duty; and I,
for my part, do not wonder that scholarly men
have been found not a few who, though they might
have shone upon a larger field, where all eyes
would have seen them win their fame, yet chose
to pore all their lives long upon the blurred and
scattered records of a country-side, where there was
nothing but an old church or an ancient village.
The history of a nation is only the history of its
villages written large. I only marvel that these
local historians have not seen more in the stories
they have sought to tell. Surely here, in these old
hamlets that antedate the cities, in these little
communities that stand apart and yet give their
young life to the nation, is to be found the very
authentic stuff of romance for the mere looking.
There is love and courtship and eager life and
high devotion up and down all the lines of every
genealogy. What strength, too, and bold endeavor
in the cutting down of forests to make the clear-
ings; what breath of hope and discovery in scaling
for the first time the nearest mountains; what
longings ended or begun upon the coming in of
ships into the harbor; what pride of earth in the
rivalries of the village; what thoughts of heaven
in the quiet of the rural church! What forces of

slow and steadfast endeavor there were in the building of a great city upon the foundations of a hamlet : and how the plot broadens and thickens and grows dramatic as communities widen into states! Here, surely, sunk deep in the very fibre of the stuff, are the colors of the great story of men, — the lively touches of reality and the striking images of life.

It must be admitted, I know, that local history can be made deadly dull in the telling. The men who reconstruct it seem usually to build with kiln-dried stuff, — as if with a purpose it should last. But that is not the fault of the subject. National history may be written almost as ill, if due pains be taken to dry it out. It is a trifle more difficult : because merely to speak of national affairs is to give hint of great forces and of movements blown upon by all the airs of the wide continent. The mere largeness of the scale lends to the narrative a certain dignity and spirit. But some men will manage to be dull though they should speak of creation. In writing of local history the thing is fatally easy. For there is some neighborhood history that lacks any large significance, which is without horizon or outlook. There are details in the history of every community which it concerns no man to know again when once they are past and decently buried in the records : and these are the very details, no doubt, which it is easiest to find upon a casual search. It is easier to make out a list of county clerks than to extract the social history of the county from the records they have kept, — though it is not so important: and it is easier to make a catalogue of anything than to say what of life and purpose the catalogue stands for. This is called collecting facts " for the sake of the facts themselves; " but if I wished to do aught for the sake of the facts themselves I think I should serve them better by giving their true biographies than by merely displaying their faces.

The right and vital sort of local history is the sort which may be written with lifted eyes, — the sort which has an horizon and an outlook upon the world. Sometimes it may happen, indeed, that the annals of a neighborhood disclose some singular adventure which had its beginning and its ending there: some unwonted bit of fortune which stands unique and lonely amidst the myriad trans- actions of the world of affairs, and deserves to be told singly and for its own sake. But usually the significance of local history is, that it is part of a greater whole. A spot of local history is like an inn upon a highway: it is a stage upon a far journey: it is a place the national history has passed through. There mankind has stopped and lodged by the way. Local history is thus less than national history only as the part is less than the whole. The whole could not dispense with the part, would not exist without it, could not be understood unless the part also were understood. Local history is subordinate to national only in the sense in which each leaf of a book is subordinate to the volume itself. Upon no single page will the whole theme of the book be found ; but each page holds a part of the theme. Even were the history of each locality exactly like the history of every other (which it cannot be), it would deserve to be written, — if only to corroborate the history of the rest, and verify it as an authentic part of the record of the race and nation. The common elements of a nation's life are the great elements of its life, the warp and woof of the fabric. They cannot be too much or too substantially verified and explicated. It is so that history is made solid and fit for use and wear.

Our national history, of course, has its own great and spreading pattern, which can be seen in its full form and completeness only when the stuff of our national life is laid before us in broad surfaces and upon an ample scale. But the detail of the pattern, the individual threads of the great fabric, are to be found only in local history. There is all the intricate weaving, all the delicate shading, all the nice refinement of the pattern, — gold thread mixed with fustian, fine thread laid upon coarse, shade combined with shade. Assuredly it is this that gives to local history its life and importance. The idea, moreover, furnishes a nice criterion of interest. The life of some localities is, obviously, more completely and intimately a part of the national pattern than the life of other localities, which are more separate and, as it were, put upon the border of the fabric. To come at once and very candidly to examples, the local history of the Middle States, — New York, New Jersey, and Pennsylvania, — is much more structurally a part of the characteristic life of the nation as a whole than is the history of the New England communities or of the several States and regions of the South. I know that such a heresy will sound very rank in the ears of some: for I am speaking against accepted doctrine. But acceptance, be it never so general, does not make a doctrine true.

Our national history has been written for the most part by New England men. All honor to them! Their scholarship and their characters alike have given them an honorable enrollment amongst the great names of our literary history; and no

just man would say aught to detract, were it never
so little, from their well-earned fame. They have
written our history, nevertheless, from but a single
point of view. From where they sit, the whole of
the great development looks like an Expansion of
New England. Other elements but play along the
sides of the great process by which the Puritan has
worked out the development of nation and polity.
It is he who has gone out and possessed the land:
the man of destiny, the type and impersonation of
a chosen people. To the Southern writer, too, the
story looks much the same, if it be but followed to
its culmination, — to its final storm and stress and
tragedy in the great war. It is the history of the
Suppression of the South. Spite of all her splendid contributions to the steadfast accomplishment
of the great task of building the nation ; spite of
the long leadership of her statesmen in the national
counsels ; spite of her joint achievements in the
conquest and occupation of the West, the South
was at last turned upon on every hand, rebuked,
proscribed, defeated. The history of the United
States, we have learned, was, from the settlement
at Jamestown to the surrender at Appomattox, a
long-drawn contest for mastery between New England and the South, — and the end of the contest
we know. All along the parallels of latitude ran

the rivalry, in those heroical days of toil and adventure during which population crossed the continent, like an army advancing its encampments.
Up and down the great river of the continent, too,
and beyond, up the slow incline of the vast steppes
that lift themselves toward the crowning towers of
the Rockies, — beyond that, again, in the gold-
fields and upon the green plains of California, the
race for ascendency struggled on, — till at length
there was a final coming face to face, and the masterful folk who had come from the loins of New
England won their consummate victory.

It is a very dramatic form for the story. One
almost wishes it were true. How fine a unity it
would give our epic ! But perhaps, after all, the
real truth is more interesting. The life of the
nation cannot be reduced to these so simple terms.
These two great forces, of the North and of the
South, unquestionably existed, — were unquestionably projected in their operation out upon the
great plane of the continent, there to combine or
repel, as circumstances might determine. But the
people that went out from the North were not an
unmixed people ; they came from the great Middle
States as well as from New England. Their
transplantation into the West was no more a
reproduction of New England or New York or

Pennsylvania or New Jersey than Massachusetts
was a reproduction of old England, or New Nether-
land a reproduction of Holland. The Southern
people, too, whom they met by the western rivers
and upon the open prairies, were transformed, as
they themselves were, by the rough fortunes of the
frontier. A mixture of peoples, a modification of
mind and habit, a new round of experiment and
adjustment amidst the novel life of the baked and
untilled plain, and the far valleys with the virgin
forests still thick upon them: a new temper, a new
spirit of adventure, a new impatience of restraint,
a new license of life, — these are the characteristic
notes and measures of the time when the nation
spread itself at large upon the continent, and was
transformed from a group of colonies into a family
of States.

The passes of these eastern mountains were the
arteries of the nation's life. The real breath of
our growth and manhood came into our nostrils
when first, like Governor Spotswood and that gal-
lant company of Virginian gentlemen that rode
with him in the far year 1716, the Knights of the
Order of the Golden Horseshoe, our pioneers stood
upon the ridges of the eastern hills and looked
down upon those reaches of the continent where
lay the untrodden paths of the westward migration.

There, upon the courses of the distant rivers that gleamed before them in the sun, down the farther slopes of the hills beyond, out upon the broad fields that lay upon the fertile banks of the " Father of Waters," up the long tilt of the continent to the vast hills that looked out upon the Pacific — there were the regions in which, joining with people from every race and clime under the sun, they were to make the great compounded nation whose liberty and mighty works of peace were to cause all the world to stand at gaze. Thither were to come Frenchmen, Scandinavians, Celts, Dutch, Slavs, — men of the Latin races and of the races of the Orient, as well as men, a great host, of the first stock of the settlements: English, Scots, Scots-Irish, — like New England men, but touched with the salt of humor, hard, and yet neighborly too. For this great process of growth by grafting, of modification no less than of expansion, the colonies, — the original thirteen States, — were only preliminary studies and first experiments. But the experiments that most resembled the great methods by which we peopled the continent from side to side and knit a single polity across all its length and breadth, were surely the experiments made from the very first in the Middle States of our Atlantic seaboard.

Here from the first were mixture of population, variety of element, combination of type, as if of the nation itself in small. Here was never a simple body, a people of but a single blood and extraction, a polity and a practice brought straight from one motherland. The life of these States was from the beginning like the life of the country: they have always shown the national pattern. In New England and the South it was very different. There some of the great elements of the national life were long in preparation: but separately and with an individual distinction ; without mixture, — for long almost without movement. That the elements thus separately prepared were of the greatest importance, and run everywhere like chief threads of the pattern through all our subsequent life, who can doubt? They give color and tone to every part of the figure. The very fact that they are so distinct and separately evident throughout, the very emphasis of individuality they carry with them, but proves their distinct origin. The other elements of our life, various though they be, and of the very fibre, giving toughness and consistency to the fabric, are merged in its texture, united, confused, almost indistinguishable, so thoroughly are they mixed, intertwined, interwoven, like the essential strands of the stuff itself: but these of the Puritan and the Southerner, though they run everywhere with the rest and seem upon a superficial view themselves the body of the cloth, in fact modify rather than make it.

What in fact has been the course of American history? How is it to be distinguished from European history? What features has it of its own, which give it its distinctive plan and movement? We have suffered, it is to be feared, a very serious limitation of view until recent years by having all our history written in the East. It has smacked strongly of a local flavor. It has concerned itself too exclusively with the origins and Old-World derivations of our story. Our historians have made their march from the sea with their heads over shoulder, their gaze always backward upon the landing-places and homes of the first settlers. In spite of the steady immigration, with its persistent tide of foreign blood, they have chosen to speak often and to think always of our people as sprung after all from a common stock, bearing a family likeness in every branch, and following all the while old, familiar, family ways. The view is the more misleading because it is so large a part of the truth without being all of it. The common British stock did first make the country, and has always set the pace. There were common institutions up and down the coast; and these had formed and hardened for a persistent growth before the great westward migration began which was to re-shape and modify every element of our life. The national government itself was set up and made strong by success while yet we lingered for the most part upon the eastern coast and feared a too distant frontier.

But, the beginnings once safely made, change set in apace. Not only so: there had been slow change from the first. We have no frontier now, we are told, — except a broken fragment, it may be, here and there in some barren corner of the western lands, where some inhospitable mountain still shoulders us out, or where men are still lacking to break the baked surface of the plains and occupy them in the very teeth of hostile nature. But at first it was all frontier, — a mere strip of settlements stretched precariously upon the sea-edge of the wilds: an untouched continent in front of them, and behind them an unfrequented sea that almost never showed so much as the momentary gleam of a sail. Every step in the slow process of settlement was but a step of the same kind as the first, an advance to a new frontier like the old. For long we lacked, it is true, that new breed of frontiersmen born in after years beyond the mountains. Those first frontiersmen had still a touch of the timidity of the Old World in their blood: they lacked the frontier heart. They were " Pilgrims " in very fact, — exiled, not at home. Fine courage they had : and a steadfastness in their bold design which it does a faint-hearted age good to look back upon. There was no thought of drawing back. Steadily, almost calmly, they extended their seats. They built homes, and deemed it certain their children would live there after them. But they did not love the rough, uneasy life for its own sake. How long did they keep, if they could, within sight of the sea! The wilderness was their refuge ; but how long before it became their joy and hope ! Here was their destiny cast ; but their hearts lingered and held back. It was only as generations passed and the work widened about them that their thought also changed, and a new thrill sped along their blood. Their life had been new and strange from their first landing in the wilderness. Their houses, their food, their clothing, their neighborhood dealings were all such as only the frontier brings. Insensibly they were themselves changed. The strange life became familiar ; their adjustment to it was at length unconscious and without effort; they had no plans which were not inseparably a part and a product of it. But, until they had turned their backs once for all upon the sea; until they saw their western borders cleared of the French; until the mountain passes had grown familiar, and the lands beyond the central and constant theme of their hope, the goal and dream of their young men, they did not become an American people.

When they did, the great determining movement of our history began. The very visages of the people changed. That alert movement of the eye, that openness to every thought of enterprise or adventure, that nomadic habit which knows no fixed home and has plans ready to be carried any whither, — all the marks of the authentic type of the " American " as we know him came into our life. The crack of the whip and the song of the teamster, the heaving chorus of boatmen poling their heavy rafts upon the rivers, the laughter of the camp, the sound of bodies of men in the still forests, became the characteristic notes in our air. A roughened race, embrowned in the sun, hardened in manner by a coarse life of change and danger, loving the rude woods and the crack of the rifle, living to begin something new every day, striking with the broad and open hand, delicate in nothing but the touch of the trigger, leaving cities in its track as if by accident rather than design, settling again to the steady ways of a fixed life only when it must : such was the American people whose achievement it was to be to take possession of their continent from end to end ere their national government was a single century old. The picture is a very singular one ! Settled life and wild side by side : civilization frayed at the edges, — taken forward in rough and ready fashion, with a song and a swagger, — not by statesmen, but by woodsmen and drovers, with axes and whips and rifles in their hands, clad in buckskin, like huntsmen.

It has been said that we have here repeated some of the first processes of history ; that the life and methods of our frontiersmen take us back to the fortunes and hopes of the men who crossed Europe when her forests, too, were still thick upon her. But the difference is really very fundamental, and much more worthy of remark than the likeness. Those shadowy masses of men whom we see moving upon the face of the earth in the faraway, questionable days when states were forming : even those stalwart figures we see so well as they emerge from the deep forests of Germany, to displace the Roman in all his western provinces and set up the states we know and marvel upon at this day, show us men working their new work at their own level. They do not turn back a long cycle of years from the old and settled states, the ordered

cities, the tilled fields, and the elaborated governments of an ancient civilization, to begin as it were
once more at the beginning. They carry alike
their homes and their states with them in the camp
and upon the ordered march of the host. They
are men of the forest, or else men hardened always
to take the sea in open boats. They live no more
roughly in the new lands than in the old. The
world has been frontier for them from the first.
They may go forward with their life in these new
seats from where they left off in the old. How
different the circumstances of our first settlement
and the building of new states on this side the
sea! Englishmen, bred in law and ordered government ever since the Norman lawyers were followed
a long five hundred years ago across the narrow
seas by those masterful administrators of the strong
Plantagenet race, leave an ancient realm and come
into a wilderness where states have never been ;
leave a land of art and letters, which saw but yes-
terday "the spacious times of great Elizabeth,"
where Shakespeare still lives in the gracious leisure
of his closing days at Stratford, where cities teem
with trade and men go bravely dight in cloth of
gold, and turn back six centuries, — nay, a thousand
years and more, — to the first work of building
states in a wilderness ! They bring the steadied

habits and sobered thoughts of an ancient realm into the wild air of an untouched continent. The weary stretches of a vast sea lie, like a full thousand years of time, between them and the life in which till now all their thought was bred. Here they stand, as it were, with all their tools left behind, centuries struck out of their reckoning, driven back upon the long dormant instincts and forgotten craft of their race, not used this long age. Look how singular a thing: the work of a primitive race, the thought of a civilized! Hence the strange, almost grotesque groupings of thought and affairs in that first day of our history. Subtle politicians speak the phrases and practice the arts of intricate diplomacy from council chambers placed within log huts within a clearing. Men in ruffs and lace and polished shoe-buckles thread the lonely glades of primeval forests. The microscopical distinctions of the schools, the thin notes of a metaphysical theology are woven in and out through the labyrinths of grave sermons that run hours long upon the still air of the wilderness. Belief in dim refinements of dogma is made the test for man or woman who seeks admission to a company of pioneers. When went there by an age since the great flood when so singular a thing was seen as this: thousands of civilized men suddenly rusticated and

bade do the work of primitive peoples, — Europe
frontiered !

Of course there was a deep change wrought, if
not in these men, at any rate in their children ;
and every generation saw the change deepen. It
must seem to every thoughtful man a notable thing
how, while the change was wrought, the simples
of things complex were revealed in the clear air of
the New World : how all accidentals seemed to
fall away from the structure of government, and
the simple first principles were laid bare that abide
always ; how social distinctions were stripped off,
shown to be the mere cloaks and masks they were,
and every man brought once again to a clear realization of his actual relations to his fellows ! It
was as if trained and sophisticated men had been
rid of a sudden of their sophistication and of all
the theory of their life, and left with nothing but
their discipline of faculty, a schooled and sobered
instinct. And the fact that we kept always, for
close upon three hundred years, a like element in
our life, a frontier people always in our van, is, so
far, the central and determining fact of our national
history. " East " and " West," an ever-changing
line, but an unvarying experience and a constant
leaven of change working always within the body
of our folk. Our political, our economic, our social

life has felt this potent influence from the wild border all our history through. The "West" is the great word of our history. The "Westerner" has been the type and master of our American life. Now at length, as I have said, we have lost our frontier: our front lies almost unbroken along all the great coast line of the western sea. The Westerner, in some day soon to come, will pass out of our life, as he so long ago passed out of the life of the Old World. Then a new epoch will open for us. Perhaps it has opened already. Slowly we shall grow old, compact our people, study the delicate adjustments of an intricate society, and ponder the niceties, as we have hitherto pondered the bulks and structural framework, of government. Have we not, indeed, already come to these things? But the past we know. We can "see it steady and see it whole;" and its central movement and motive are gross and obvious to the eye.

Till the first century of the Constitution is rounded out we stand all the while in the presence of that stupendous westward movement which has filled the continent: so vast, so various, at times so tragical, so swept by passion. Through all the long time there has been a line of rude settlements along our front wherein the same tests of power and of institutions were still being made that were

made first upon the sloping banks of the rivers of
old Virginia and within the long sweep of the Bay
of Massachusetts. The new life of the West has
reacted all the while — who shall say how power-
fully? — upon the older life of the East; and yet
the East has moulded the West as if she sent forward to it through every decade of the long process
the chosen impulses and suggestions of history.
The West has taken strength, thought, training,
selected aptitudes out of the old treasures of the
East, — as if out of a new Orient; while the East
has itself been kept fresh, vital, alert, originative
by the West, her blood quickened all the while, her
youth through every age renewed. Who can say in
a word, in a sentence, in a volume, what destinies
have been variously wrought, with what new examples of growth and energy, while, upon this unex-
ampled scale, community has passed beyond community across the vast reaches of this great continent!

The great process is the more significant because
it has been distinctively a national process. Until
the Union was formed and we had consciously set
out upon a separate national career, we moved but
timidly across the nearer hills. Our most remote
settlements lay upon the rivers and in the open
glades of Tennessee and Kentucky. It was in the

years that immediately succeeded the war of 1812
that the movement into the West began to be a
mighty migration. Till then our eyes had been
more often in the East than in the West. Not
only were foreign questions to be settled and our
standing among the nations to be made good, but
we still remained acutely conscious and deliberately
conservative of our Old-World connections. For
all we were so new a people and lived so simple and
separate a life, we had still the sobriety and the
circumspect fashions of action that belong to an old
society. We were, in government and manners,
but a disconnected part of the world beyond the
seas. Its thought and habit still set us our standards of speech and action. And this, not because
of imitation, but because of actual and long abiding
political and social connection with the mother
country. Our statesmen, — strike but the names
of Samuel Adams and Patrick Henry from the list,
together with all like untutored spirits, who stood
for the new, unreverencing ardor of a young democracy, — our statesmen were such men as might
have taken their places in the House of Commons
or in the Cabinet at home as naturally and with as
easy an adjustment to their place and task as in
the Continental Congress or in the immortal Constitutional Convention. Think of the stately ways

and the grand air and the authoritative social understandings of the generation that set the new government afoot, — the generation of Washington and John Adams. Think, too, of the conservative tradition that guided all the early history of that government : that early line of gentlemen Presidents: that steady " cabinet succession to the Presidency " which came at length to seem almost like an oligarchy to the impatient men who were shut out from it. The line ended, with a sort of chill, in stiff John Quincy Adams, too cold a man to be a people's prince after the old order of Presidents ; and the year 1829, which saw Jackson come in, saw the old order go out.

The date is significant. Since the war of 1812, undertaken as if to set us free to move westward, seven States had been admitted to the Union : and the whole number of States was advanced to twenty-four. Eleven new States had come into partnership with the old thirteen. The voice of the West rang through all our counsels ; and, in Jackson, the new partners took possession of the Government. It is worth while to remember how men stood amazed at the change : how startled, chagrined, dismayed the conservative States of the East were at the revolution they saw effected, the riot of change they saw set in ; and no man who

has once read the singular story can forget how
the eight years Jackson reigned saw the Government, and politics themselves, transformed. For
long, — the story being written in the regions
where the shock and surprise of the change was
greatest, — the period of this momentous revolution was spoken of amongst us as a period of
degeneration, the birth-time of a deep and permanent demoralization in our politics. But we see it
differently now. Whether we have any taste or
stomach for that rough age or not, however much
we may wish that the old order might have stood,
the generation of Madison and Adams have been
prolonged, and the good tradition of the early days
handed on unbroken and unsullied, we now know
that what the nation underwent in that day of
change was not degeneration, great and perilous as
were the errors of the time, but regeneration.
The old order was changed, once and for all. A
new nation stepped, with a touch of swagger, upon
the stage, — a nation which had broken alike with
the traditions and with the wisely wrought experience of the Old World, and which, with all the
haste and rashness of youth, was minded to work
out a separate policy and destiny of its own. It
was a day of hazards, but there was nothing sinister
at the heart of the new plan. It was a wasteful

experiment, to fling out, without wise guides, upon untried ways; but an abounding continent afforded enough and to spare even for the wasteful. It was sure to be so with a nation that came out of the secluded vales of a virgin continent. It was the bold frontier voice of the West sounding in affairs. The timid shivered, but the robust waxed strong and rejoiced, in the tonic air of the new day.

It was then we swung out into the main paths of our history. The new voices that called us were first silvery, like the voice of Henry Clay, and spoke old familiar words of eloquence. The first spokesmen of the West even tried to con the classics, and spoke incongruously in the phrases of politics long dead and gone to dust, as Benton did. But presently the tone changed, and it was the truculent and masterful accents of the real frontiersman that rang dominant above the rest, harsh, impatient, and with an evident dash of temper. The East slowly accustomed itself to the change; caught the movement, though it grumbled and even trembled at the pace; and managed most of the time to keep in the running. But it was always henceforth to be the West that set the pace. There is no mistaking the questions that have ruled our spirits as a nation during the present century. The public land question, the tariff

question, and the question of slavery,— these dominate from first to last. It was the West that
made each one of these the question that it was.
Without the free lands to which every man who
chose might go, there would not have been that
easy prosperity of life and that high standard of
abundance which seemed to render it necessary
that, if we were to have manufactures and a diversified industry at all, we should foster new under-
takings by a system of protection which would
make the profits of the factory as certain and as
abundant as the profits of the farm. It was the
constant movement of the population, the constant
march of wagon trains into the West, that made it
so cardinal a matter of policy whether the great
national domain should *be* free land or not : and
that was the land question. It was the settlement
of the West that transformed slavery from an
accepted institution into passionate matter of controversy.

Slavery within the States of the Union stood
sufficiently protected by every solemn sanction the
Constitution could afford. No man could touch it
there, think, or hope, or purpose what he might.
But where new States were to be made it was not
so. There at every step choice must be made :
slavery or no slavery ?— a new choice for every

new State: a fresh act of origination to go with
every fresh act of organization. Had there been
no Territories, there could have been no slavery
question, except by revolution and contempt of
fundamental law. But with a continent to be peopled, the choice thrust itself insistently forward at
every step and upon every hand. This was the
slavery question : not what should be done to reverse the past, but what should be done to redeem
the future. It was so men of that day saw it, —
and so also must historians see it. We must not
mistake the programme of the Anti-Slavery Society for the platform of the Republican party,
or forget that the very war itself was begun ere
any purpose of abolition took shape amongst those
who were statesmen and in authority. It was a
question, not of freeing men, but of preserving a
Free Soil. Kansas showed us what the problem
was, not South Carolina : and it was the Supreme
Court, not the slave-owners, who formulated the
matter for our thought and purpose.

And so, upon every hand and throughout every
national question, was the commerce between East
and West made up: that commerce and exchange
of ideas, inclinations, purposes, and principles which
has constituted the moving force of our life as a
nation. Men illustrate the operation of these sin-

gular forces better than questions can : and no man illustrates it better than Abraham Lincoln.

> "Great captains with their guns and drums
> Disturb our judgment for the hour;
> But at last silence comes :
> These all are gone, and, standing like a tower,
> Our children shall behold his fame,
> The kindly-earnest, brave, foreseeing man,
> Sagacious, patient, dreading praise not blame,
> New birth of our new soil, the first American."

It is a poet's verdict; but it rings in the authentic tone of the seer. It must be also the verdict of history. He would be a rash man who should say he understood Abraham Lincoln. No doubt natures deep as his, and various almost to the point of self-contradiction, can be sounded only by the judgment of men of a like sort, — if any such there be. But some things we all may see and judge concerning him. You have in him the type and flower of our growth. It is as if Nature had made a typical American, and then had added with liberal hand the royal quality of genius, to show us what the type could be. Lincoln owed nothing to his birth, everything to his growth: had no training save what he gave himself ; no nurture, but only a wild and native strength. His life was his schooling, and every day of it gave to his character a new touch of development. His manhood not only, but his perception also, expanded with his life. His eyes, as they looked more and more abroad, beheld the national life, and comprehended it : and the lad who had been so rough-cut a provincial became, when grown to manhood, the one leader in all the nation who held the whole people singly in his heart : — held even the Southern people there, and would have won them back. And so we have in him what we must call the perfect development of native strength, the rounding out and nationalization of the provincial. Andrew Jackson was a type, not of the nation, but of the West. For all the tenderness there was in the stormy heart of the masterful man, and staunch and simple loyalty to all who loved him, he learned nothing in the East; kept always the flavor of the rough school in which he had been bred ; was never more than a frontier soldier and gentleman. Lincoln differed from Jackson by all the length of his unmatched capacity to learn. Jackson could understand only men of his own kind; Lincoln could understand men of all sorts and from every region of the land : seemed himself, indeed, to be all men by turns, as mood succeeded mood in his strange nature. He never ceased to stand, in his bony angles, the express image of the ungainly frontiersman. His mind never lost the vein of coarseness that had marked him grossly when a youth. And yet how he grew and strengthened in the real stuff of dignity and greatness: how nobly he could bear himself without the aid of grace! He kept always the shrewd and seeing eye of the woodsman and the hunter, and the flavor of wild life never left him: and yet how easily his view widened to great affairs; how surely he perceived the value and the significance of whatever touched him and made him neighbor to itself!

Lincoln's marvelous capacity to extend his comprehension to the measure of what he had in hand is the one distinguishing mark of the man: and to study the development of that capacity in him is little less than to study, where it is as it were perfectly registered, the national life itself. This boy lived his youth in Illinois when it was a frontier State. The youth of the State was coincident with his own: and man and State kept equal pace in their striding advance to maturity. The frontier population was an intensely political population. It felt to the quick the throb of the nation's life, — for the nation's life ran through it, going its eager way to the westward. The West was not separate from the East. Its communities were every day receiving fresh members from the East, and the fresh impulse of direct suggestion. Their

blood flowed to them straight from the warmest
veins of the older communities. More than that,
elements which were separated in the East were
mingled in the West: which displayed to the eye
as it were a sort of epitome of the most active and
permanent forces of the national life. In such
communities as these Lincoln mixed daily from the
first with men of every sort and from every quarter
of the country. With them he discussed neighborhood politics, the politics of the State, the politics
of the nation, — and his mind became traveled as
he talked. How plainly amongst such neighbors,
there in Illinois, must it have become evident that
national questions were centring more and more in
the West as the years went by: coming as it were
to meet them. Lincoln went twice down the
Mississippi, upon the slow rafts that carried wares
to its mouth, and saw with his own eyes, so used
to look directly and point-blank upon men and
affairs, characteristic regions of the South. He
worked his way slowly and sagaciously, with that
larger sort of sagacity which so marked him all his
life, into the active business of state politics; sat
twice in the state legislature, and then for a term
in Congress, — his sensitive and seeing mind open
all the while to every turn of fortune and every
touch of nature in the moving affairs he looked

upon. All the while, too, he continued to canvass, piece by piece, every item of politics, as of old, with his neighbors, familiarly around the stove, or upon the corners of the street, or more formally upon the stump; and kept always in direct contact with the ordinary views of ordinary men. Meanwhile he read, as nobody else around him read, and sought to gain a complete mastery over speech, with the conscious purpose to prevail in its use; derived zest from the curious study of mathematical proof, and amusement as well as strength from the practice of clean and naked statements of truth. It was all irregularly done, but strenuously, with the same instinct throughout, and with a steady access of facility and power. There was no sudden leap for this man, any more than for other men, from crudeness to finished power, from an understanding of the people of Illinois to an understanding of the people of the United States. And thus he came at last, with infinite pains and a wonder of endurance, to his great national task with a self-trained capacity which no man could match, and made upon a scale as liberal as the life of the people. You could not then set this athlete a pace in learning or in perceiving that was too hard for him. He knew the people and their life as no other man did or could: and now stands in

his place singular in all the annals of mankind, the
" brave, sagacious, foreseeing, patient man " of the
people, " new birth of our new soil, the first
American."

We have here a national man presiding over
sectional men. Lincoln understood the East better
than the East understood him or the people from
whom he sprung : and this is every way a very
noteworthy circumstance. For my part, I read a
lesson in the singular career of this great man. Is
it possible the East remains sectional while the
West broadens to a wider view ?

" Be strong-backed, brown-handed, upright as your pines ;
By the scale of a hemisphere shape your designs,"

is an inspiring programme for the woodsman and
the pioneer ; but how are you to be brown-handed
in a city office ? What if you never see the upright
pines ? How are you to have so big a purpose on
so small a part of the hemisphere ? As it has
grown old, unquestionably, the East has grown
sectional. There is no suggestion of the prairie in
its city streets, or of the embrowned ranchman and
farmer in its well-dressed men. Its ports teem with
shipping from Europe and the Indies. Its newspapers run upon the themes of an Old World. It
hears of the great plains of the continent as of foreign parts, which it may never think to see except

from a car window. Its life is self-centred and selfish. The West, save where special interests centre (as in those pockets of silver where men's eyes catch as it were an eager gleam from the very ore itself) : the West is in less danger of sectionalization. Who shall say in that wide country where one region ends and another begins, or, in that free and changing society, where one class ends and another begins ?

This, surely, is the moral of our history. The East has spent and been spent for the West : has given forth her energy, her young men and her substance, for the new regions that have been a-making all the century through. But has she learned as much as she has taught, or taken as much as she has given ? Look what it is that has now at last taken place. The westward march has stopped, upon the final slopes of the Pacific ; and now the plot thickens. Populations turn upon their old paths; fill in the spaces they passed by neglected in their first journey in search of a land of promise ; settle to a life such as the East knows as well as the West, — nay, much better. With the change, the pause, the settlement, our people draw into closer groups, stand face to face, to know each other and be known : and the time has come for the East to learn in her turn ; to broaden her understanding of political and economic conditions to the scale of a hemisphere, as her own poet bade. Let us be sure that we get the national temperament ; send our minds abroad upon the continent, become neighbors to all the people that live upon it, and lovers of them all, as Lincoln was.

Read but your history aright, and you shall not find the task too hard. Your own local history, look but deep enough, tells the tale you must take to heart. Here upon our own seaboard, as truly as ever in the West, was once a national frontier, with an elder East beyond the seas. Here, too, various peoples combined, and elements separated elsewhere effected a tolerant and wholesome mixture. Here, too, the national stream flowed full and strong, bearing a thousand things upon its currents. Let us resume and keep the vision of that time; know ourselves, our neighbors, our destiny, with lifted and open eyes ; see our history truly, in its great proportions ; be ourselves liberal as the great principles we profess ; and so be the people who might have again the heroic adventures and do again the heroic work of the past. 'T is thus we shall renew our youth and secure our age against decay.

WHEN A MAN COMES
TO HIMSELF
BY
WOODROW WILSON

WHEN A MAN COMES TO HIMSELF

I

It is a very wholesome and regenerating change which a man undergoes when he "comes to himself." It is not only after periods of recklessness or infatuation, when he has played the spendthrift or the fool, that a man comes to himself. He comes to himself after experiences of which he alone may be aware: when he has left off being wholly preoccupied with his own powers and interests and with every petty plan that centers in himself; when he has cleared his eyes to see the world as it is, and his own true place and function in it.

It is a process of disillusionment. The scales have fallen away. He sees himself soberly, and knows under what conditions his powers must act, as well as what his powers are. He has got rid of earlier prepossessions about the world of men and affairs, both those which were too favorable and those which were too unfavorable—both those of the nursery and those of a young man's reading.

He has learned his own paces, or, at any rate, is in a fair way to learn them; has found his footing and the true nature of the "going" he must look for in the world; over what sorts of roads he must expect to make his running, and at what expenditure of effort; whither his goal lies, and what cheer he may expect by the way. It is a process of disillusionment, but it disheartens no soundly made man. It brings him into a light which guides instead of deceiving him; a light which does not make the way look cold to any man whose eyes are fit for use in the open, but which shines wholesomely, rather upon the obvious path, like the honest rays of the frank sun, and makes traveling both safe and cheerful.

II

There is no fixed time in a man's life at which he comes to himself, and some men never come to themselves at all. It is a change reserved for the thoroughly sane and healthy, and for those who can detach themselves from tasks and drudgery long and often enough to get, at any rate once and again, a view of the proportions of life and of the stage and plot of its action. We speak often with amusement, sometimes with distaste and uneasiness, of men who "have no sense of humor," who take themselves too seriously, who are intense, self-absorbed, over-confident in matters of opinion, or else go plumed with conceit, proud of we cannot tell what, enjoying, appreciating, thinking of nothing so much as themselves. These are men who have not suffered that wholesome change. They have not come to themselves. If they be serious men, and real forces in the world, we may conclude that they have been too much and too long absorbed; that their tasks and responsibilities long ago rose about them like a flood, and have kept them swimming with sturdy stroke the years through, their eyes level with the troubled surface —no horizon in sight, no passing fleets, no comrades but those who struggled in the flood like themselves. If they be frivolous, light-headed, men without purpose or achievement, we may conjecture, if we do not know, that they were born so, or spoiled by fortune, or befuddled by self-indulgence. It is no great matter what we think of them.

It is enough to know that there are some laws which govern a man's awakening to know himself and the right part to play. A man *is* the part he plays among his fellows. He is not isolated; he cannot be. His life is made up of the relations he bears to others—is made or marred by those relations, guided by them, judged by them, expressed in them. There is nothing else upon which he can

spend his spirit—nothing else that we can see. It
is by these he gets his spiritual growth; it is by
these we see his character revealed, his purpose,
and his gifts. Some play with a certain natural
passion, an unstudied directness, without grace,
without modulation, with no study of the masters
or consciousness of the pervading spirit of the
plot; others give all their thought to their costume
and think only of the audience; a few act as those
who have mastered the secrets of a serious art, with
deliberate subordination of themselves to the great
end and motive of the play, spending themselves
like good servants, indulging in no wilfulness, ob-
truding no eccentricity, lending heart and tone and
gesture to the perfect progress of the action. These
have "found themselves," and have all the ease of
a perfect adjustment.

Adjustment is exactly what a man gains when he
comes to himself. Some men gain it late, some
early; some get it all at once, as if by one distinct
act of deliberate accommodation; others get it by
degrees and quite imperceptibly. No doubt to most
men it comes by the slow processes of experience
—at each stage of life a little. A college man
feels the first shock of it at graduation, when the
boy's life has been lived out and the man's life
suddenly begins. He has measured himself with
boys; he knows their code and feels the spur of

their ideals of achievement. But what the world expects of him he has yet to find out, and it works, when he has discovered it, a veritable revolution in his ways both of thought and of action. He finds a new sort of fitness demanded of him, executive, thorough-going, careful of details, full of drudgery and obedience to orders. Everybody is ahead of him. Just now he was a senior, at the top of a world he knew and reigned in, a finished product and pattern of good form. Of a sudden he is a novice again, as green as in his first school year, studying a thing that seems to have no rules—at sea amid crosswinds, and a bit seasick withal. Presently, if he be made of stuff that will shake into shape and fitness, he settles to his tasks and is comfortable. He has come to himself: understands what capacity is, and what it is meant for; sees that his training was not for ornament or personal gratification, but to teach him how to use himself and develop faculties worth using. Henceforth there is a zest in action, and he loves to see his strokes tell.

The same thing happens to the lad come from the farm into the city, a big and novel field, where crowds rush and jostle, and a rustic boy must stand puzzled for a little how to use his placid and unjaded strength. It happens, too, though in a deeper and more subtle way, to the man who marries for love, if the love be true and fit for foul weather. Mr. Bagehot used to say that a bachelor was "an amateur in life," and wit and wisdom are married in the jest. A man who lives only for himself has not begun to live—has yet to learn his use, and his real pleasure, too, in the world. It is not necessary he should marry to find himself out, but it is necessary he should love. Men have come to themselves serving their mothers with an unselfish devotion, or their sisters, or a cause for whose sake they forsook ease and left off thinking of themselves. It is unselfish action, growing slowly into the high habit of devotion, and at last, it may be, into a sort of consecration, that teaches a man the wide meaning of his life, and makes of him a steady professional in living, if the motive be not necessity, but love. Necessity may make a mere drudge of a man, and no mere drudge ever made a professional of himself; that demands a higher spirit and a finer incentive than his.

III

Surely a man has come to himself only when he has found the best that is in him, and has satisfied his heart with the highest achievement he is fit for. It is only then that he knows of what he is capable and what his heart demands. And, assuredly, no thoughtful man ever came to the end

of his life, and had time and a little space of calm
from which to look back upon it, who did not
know and acknowledge that it was what he had
done unselfishly and for others, and nothing else,
that satisfied him in the retrospect, and made him
feel that he had played the man. That alone seems
to him the real measure of himself, the real standard of his manhood. And so men grow by having
responsibility laid upon them, the burden of other
people's business. Their powers are put out at
interest, and they get usury in kind. They are like
men multiplied. Each counts manifold. Men who
live with an eye only upon what is their own are
dwarfed beside them—seem fractions while they
are integers. The trustworthiness of men trusted
seems often to grow with the trust.

It is for this reason that men are in love with
power and greatness: it affords them so pleasur-
able an expansion of faculty, so large a run for
their minds, an exercise of spirit so various and
refreshing; they have the freedom of so wide a
tract of the world of affairs. But if they use power
only for their own ends, if there be no unselfish
service in it, if its object be only their personal
aggrandizement, their love to see other men tools
in their hands, they go out of the world small, disquieted, beggared, no enlargement of soul vouchsafed them, no usury of satisfaction. They have

added nothing to themselves. Mental and physical
powers alike grow by use, as every one knows; but
labor for oneself alone is like exercise in a gym-
nasium. No healthy man can remain satisfied
with it, or regard it as anything but a preparation
for tasks in the open, amid the affairs of the world
—not sport, but business—where there is no orderly apparatus, and every man must devise the
means by which he is to make the most of himself.
To make the most of himself means the multipli-
cation of his activities, and he must turn away
from himself for that. He looks about him, studies
the face of business or of affairs, catches some intimation of their larger objects, is guided by the
intimation, and presently finds himself part of the
motive force of communities or of nations. It
makes no difference how small a part, how insignificant, how unnoticed. When his powers begin
to play outward, and he loves the task at hand, not
because it gains him a livelihood, but because it
makes him a life, he has come to himself.

Necessity is no mother to enthusiasm. Necessity
carries a whip. Its method is compulsion, not love.
It has no thought to make itself attractive; it is
content to drive. Enthusiasm comes with the revelation of true and satisfying objects of devotion;
and it is enthusiasm that sets the powers free. It
is a sort of enlightenment. It shines straight upon

ideals, and for those who see it the race and struggle are henceforth toward these. An instance will point the meaning. One of the most distinguished and most justly honored of our great philanthropists spent the major part of his life absolutely absorbed in the making of money—so it seemed to those who did not know him. In fact, he had very early passed the stage at which he looked upon his business as a means of support or of material comfort. Business had become for him an intellectual pursuit, a study in enterprise and increment. The field of commerce lay before him like a chessboard; the moves interested him like the manoeuvers of a game. More money was more power, a greater advantage in the game, the means of shaping men and events and markets to his own ends and uses. It was his will that set fleets afloat and determined the havens they were bound for; it was his foresight that brought goods to market at the right time; it was his suggestion that made the industry of unthinking men efficacious; his sagacity saw itself justified at home not only, but at the ends of the earth. And as the money poured in, his government and mastery increased, and his mind was the more satisfied. It is so that men make little kingdoms for themselves, and an international power undarkened by diplomacy, undirected by parliaments.

IV

It is a mistake to suppose that the great captains of industry, the great organizers and directors of manufacture and commerce and monetary exchange, are engrossed in a vulgar pursuit of wealth. Too often they suffer the vulgarity of wealth to display itself in the idleness and ostentation of their wives and children, who "devote themselves," it may be, "to expense regardless of pleasure"; but we ought not to misunderstand even that, or condemn it unjustly. The masters of industry are often too busy with their own sober and momentous calling to have time or spare thought enough to govern their own households. A king may be too faithful a statesman to be a watchful father. These men are not fascinated by the glitter of gold: the appetite for power has got hold upon them. They are in love with the exercise of their faculties upon a great scale; they are organizing and overseeing a great part of the life of the world. No wonder they are captivated. Business is more interesting than pleasure, as Mr. Bagehot said, and when once the mind has caught its zest, there's no disengaging it. The world has reason to be grateful for the fact.

It was this fascination that had got hold upon the faculties of the man whom the world was afterward to know, not as a prince among merchants

—for the world forgets merchant princes—but as a prince among benefactors; for beneficence breeds gratitude, gratitude admiration, admiration fame, and the world remembers its benefactors. Business, and business alone, interested him, or seemed to him worth while. The first time he was asked to subscribe money for a benevolent object he declined. Why *should* he subscribe? What affair would be set forward, what increase of efficiency would the money buy, what return would it bring in? Was good money to be simply given away, like water poured on a barren soil, to be sucked up and yield nothing? It was not until men who understood benevolence on its sensible, systematic, practical, and really helpful side explained it to him as an investment that his mind took hold of it and turned to it for satisfaction. He began to see that education was a thing of infinite usury; that money devoted to it would yield a singular increase to which there was no calculable end, an increase in perpetuity—increase of knowledge, and therefore of intelligence and efficiency, touching generation after generation with new impulses, adding to the sum total of the world's fitness for affairs—an invisible but intensely real spiritual usury beyond reckoning, because compounded in an unknown ratio from age to age. Henceforward beneficence was as interesting to him as business—

was, indeed, a sort of sublimated business in which money moved new forces in a commerce which no man could bind or limit.

He had come to himself—to the full realization of his powers, the true and clear perception of what it was his mind demanded for its satisfaction. His faculties were consciously stretched to their right measure, were at last exercised at their best. He felt the keen zest, not of success merely, but also of honor, and was raised to a sort of majesty among his fellow-men, who attended him in death like a dead sovereign. He had died dwarfed had he not broken the bonds of mere money-getting; would never have known himself had he not learned how to spend it; and ambition itself could not have shown him a straighter road to fame.

This is the positive side of a man's discovery of the way in which his faculties are to be made to fit into the world's affairs, and released for effort in a way that will bring real satisfaction. There is a negative side also. Men come to themselves by discovering their limitations no less than by dis- covering their deeper endowments and the mastery that will make them happy. It is the discovery of what they can *not* do, and ought not to attempt, that transforms reformers into statesmen; and great should be the joy of the world over every re- former who comes to himself. The spectacle is not

rare; the method is not hidden. The practicability
of every reform is determined absolutely and always
by "the circumstances of the case," and only those
who put themselves into the midst of affairs, either
by action or by observation, can know what those
circumstances are or perceive what they signify.
No statesman dreams of doing whatever he pleases;
he knows that it does not follow that because a
point of morals or of policy is obvious to him it
will be obvious to the nation, or even to his own
friends; and it is the strength of a democratic polity
that there are so many minds to be consulted and
brought to agreement, and that nothing can be
wisely done for which the thought, and good deal
more than the thought, of the country, its sentiment
and its purpose, have not been prepared. Social
reform is a matter of cooperation, and, if it be of a
novel kind, requires an infinite deal of converting
to bring the efficient majority to believe in it and
support it. Without their agreement and support it
is impossible.

V

It is this that the more imaginative and impatient reformers find out when they come to themselves, if that calming change ever comes to them.
Oftentimes the most immediate and drastic means
of bringing them to themselves is to elect them to

legislative or executive office. That will reduce
over-sanguine persons to their simplest terms. Not
because they find their fellow-legislators or officials incapable of high purpose or indifferent to the
betterment of the communities which they represent. Only cynics hold that to be the chief reason
why we approach the millennium so slowly, and
cynics are usually very ill-informed persons. Nor
is it because under our modern democratic arrangements we so subdivide power and balance
parts in government that no one man can tell for
much or turn affairs to his will. One of the most
instructive studies a politician could undertake
would be a study of the infinite limitations laid upon
the power of the Russian Czar, notwithstanding
the despotic theory of the Russian constitution—
limitations of social habit, of official prejudice, of
race jealousies, of religious predilections, of administrative machinery even, and the inconvenience
of being himself only one man, caught amidst a
rush of duties and responsibilities which never halt
or pause. He can do only what can be done with
the Russian people. He cannot change them at
will. ‹ He is himself of their own stuff, and immersed in the life which forms them, as it forms
him. He is simply the leader of the Russians.

An English or American statesman is better off.
He leads a thinking nation, not a race of peasants

topped by a class of revolutionists and a caste of
nobles and officials. He can explain new things
to men able to understand, persuade men willing
and accustomed to make independent and intelligent
choices of their own. An English statesman has an
even better opportunity to lead than an American
statesman, because in England executive power and
legislative initiative are both intrusted to the same
grand committee, the ministry of the day. The ministers both propose what shall be made law and determine how it shall be enforced when enacted. And
yet English reformers, like American, have found
office a veritable cold-water bath for their ardor for
change. Many a man who has made his place in affairs as the spokesman of those who see abuses and
demand their reformation has passed from denunci-
ation to calm and moderate advice when he got
into Parliament, and has turned veritable conservative when made a minister of the crown. Mr.
Bright was a notable example. Slow and careful
men had looked upon him as little better than a
revolutionist so long as his voice rang free and
imperious from the platforms of public meetings.
They greatly feared the influence he should exercise in Parliament, and would have deemed the
constitution itself unsafe could they have foreseen
that he would some day be invited to take office and
a hand of direction in affairs. But it turned out

that there was nothing to fear. Mr. Bright lived to see almost every reform he had urged accepted and embodied in legislation; but he assisted at the process of their realization with greater and greater temperateness and wise deliberation as his part in affairs became more and more prominent and responsible, and was at the last as little like an agitator as any man that served the queen.

It is not that such men lose courage when they find themselves charged with the actual direction of the affairs concerning which they have held and uttered such strong, unhesitating, drastic opinions. They have only learned discretion. For the first time they see in its entirety what it was that they were attempting. They are at last at close quarters with the world. Men of every interest and variety crowd about them; new impressions throng them; in the midst of affairs the former special objects of their zeal fall into new environments, a better and truer perspective; seem no longer so susceptible to separate and radical change. The real nature of the complex stuff of life they were seeking to work in is revealed to them—its intricate and delicate fiber, and the subtle, secret interrelationship of its parts—and they work circumspectly, lest they should mar more than they mend. Moral enthusiasm is not, uninstructed and of itself, a suitable guide to practicable and lasting reformation; and if the reform sought be the reformation of others as well as of himslf, the reformer should look to it that he knows the true relation of his will to the wills of those he would change and guide. When hc has discovered that relation, he has come to himself: has discovered his real use and planning part in the general world of men; has come to the full command and satisfying employment of his faculties. Otherwise he is doomed to live for ever in a fool's paradise, and can be said to have come to himself only on the supposition that he is a fool.

VI

Every man—if I may adopt and paraphrase a passage from Dr. South—every man hath both an absolute and a relative capacity: an absolute in that he hath been endued with such a nature and such parts and faculties; and a relative in that he is part of the universal community of men, and so stands in such a relation to the whole. When we say that a man has come to himself, it is not of his absolute capacity that we are thinking, but of his relative. He has begun to realize that he is part of a whole, and to know *what* part, suitable for what service and achievement.

It was once fashionable—and that not a very long time ago—to speak of political society with a certain distaste, as a necessary evil, an irritating but inevitable restriction upon the "natural" sovereignty and entire self-government of the individual. That was the dream of the egotist. It was a theory in which men were seen to strut in the proud consciousness of their several and "absolute" capacities. It would be as instructive as it would be difficult to count the errors it has bred in political thinking. As a matter of fact, men have never dreamed of wishing to do without the "trammels" of organized society, for the very good reason that those trammels are in reality no trammels at all, but indispensable aids and spurs to the attainment of the highest and most enjoyable things man is capable of. Political society, the life of men in states, is an abiding natural relationship. It is neither a mere convenience nor a mere necessity. It is not a mere voluntary association, not a mere corporation. It is nothing deliberate or artificial, devised for a special purpose. It is in real truth the eternal and natural expression and embodiment of a form of life higher than that of the individual—that common life of mutual helpfulness, stimulation, and contest which gives leave and opportunity to the individual life, makes it possible, makes it full and complete.

It is in such a scene that man looks about to discover his own place and force. In the midst of men organized, infinitely cross-related, bound by ties of interest, hope, affection, subject to authorities, to opinion, to passion, to visions and desires which no man can reckon, he casts eagerly about to find where he may enter in with the rest and be a man among his fellows. In making his place he finds, if he seek intelligently and with eyes that see, more than ease of spirit and scope for his mind. He finds himself—as if mists had cleared away about him and he knew at last his neighborhood among men and tasks.

What every man seeks is satisfaction. He deceives himself so long as he imagines it to lie in self-indulgence, so long as he deems himself the center and object of effort. His mind is spent in vain upon itself. Not in action itself, not in "pleasure," shall it find its desires satisfied, but in consciousness of right, of powers greatly and nobly spent. It comes to know itself in the motives which satisfy it, in the zest and power of rectitude. Christianity has liberated the world, not as a system of ethics, not as a philosophy of altruism, but by its revelation of the power of pure and unselfish love. Its vital principle is not its code, but its motive. Love, clear-sighted, loyal, personal, is its breath and immortality. Christ came, not to save Himself, assuredly, but to save the world. His motive, His example, are every man's key to his own gifts and happiness. The ethical code he taught may no doubt be matched, here a piece and there a piece, out of other religions, other teachings and philosophies. Every thoughtful man born with a conscience must know a code of right and of pity to which he ought to conform; but without the motive of Christianity, without love, he may be the purest altruist and yet be as sad and as unsatisfied as Marcus Aurelius.

Christianity gave us, in the fullness of time, the perfect image of right living, the secret of social and of individual well-being; for the two are not separable, and the man who receives and verifies that secret in his own living has discovered not only the best and only way to serve the world, but also the one happy way to satisfy himself. Then, indeed, has he come to himself. Henceforth he knows what his powers mean, what spiritual air they breathe, what ardors of service clear them of lethargy, relieve them of all sense of effort, put them at their best. After this fretfulness passes away, experience mellows and strengthens and makes more fit, and old age brings, not senility, not satiety, not regret, but higher hope and see maturity.

THE END